Symmes M Jelley

The Voice of Labor

Containing Special Contributions by Leading Workingmen....

Symmes M Jelley

The Voice of Labor
Containing Special Contributions by Leading Workingmen....

ISBN/EAN: 9783337205218

Printed in Europe, USA, Canada, Australia, Japan

Cover: Foto ©ninafisch / pixelio.de

More available books at **www.hansebooks.com**

T. V. POWDERLY.

THE VOICE OF LABOR

CONTAINING

Special Contributions by Leading Workingmen throughout the United States, with Opinions of Statesmen and Legislators upon the Great Issues of the Day.

PLAIN TALK BY MEN OF INTELLECT

ON

LABOR'S RIGHTS, WRONGS, REMEDIES

AND PROSPECTS.

History of the Knights of Labor, their Aims, Usefulness, Etc.

The Political Future of the Workingman.

THE QUESTIONS OF LAND, LABOR, CAPITAL, TRANSPORTATION, REFORM, PROGRESS AND SOCIAL CONDITION OF THE WORKINGMAN THOROUGHLY INVESTIGATED.

HISTORY OF THE FARMERS' ALLIANCE.

REVISED AND ENLARGED.

By S. M. JELLEY.

Illustrated with Fine Portraits and Engravings.

H. J. SMITH & CO.:

PHILADELPHIA.   CHICAGO.   KANSAS CITY

SAN FRANCISCO.

1888.

PUBLISHERS' PREFACE.

It has been said that the literature of an age is but the reflex of the times, and THE VOICE OF LABOR is not an exception. The labor movement has been a great theme for both the people and the press during the last few years, and in consequence there has risen a demand for literature upon the subject.

The workingman of to-day seeks to understand the economics which govern his financial condition, yet beyond the speeches of the men at the head of his organizations, the labor press and a few so-called labor books, the sources of knowledge in this direction tending to his benefit, are comparatively limited.

In order to present the various phases of the great problem, as viewed by reformers, we have secured from those prominently identified with the labor movement, from statesmen, editors, writers and workingmen, much of the material made use of by the author.

A candid exposition of facts concerning the welfare of the wealth-producing classes, and of the methods by which they can remedy the wrongs that prevent them from bettering their condition, cannot prove to be other than a valuable source of benefit and instruction.

AUTHOR'S PREFACE.

The readers who will best appreciate the contents of this book are those who are not biased by false ideas, and those who have given social science and the labor question some thought. For an exhaustive work upon each phase of the question the pages of a score of volumes would be required, therefore, I have dealt only with the greater causes and remedies of the problem.

The request of the publishers for the opinions of those interested in the labor movement met with response of such a heterogeneous character, in which so many diverse views were expressed, that to determine on the best selection seemed well-nigh a hopeless task.

Careful consideration, however, with the broad principle of justice to all as a guide, enabled me to choose such matter as will be approved by all unprejudiced minds. My aim has been to avoid the propaganda of anarchists and communists, and to present only the economics of trustworthy authors and those who have the elevation and improvement of the workingman sincerely at heart.

In the preparation of the following pages I am especially indebted to many contributors, among whom are:

Hon. Jesse Harper, Danville, Ill.
Alfred Taylor, Ed. Sentinel, Birmingham, Ala.
W. D. Vincent, Clay Center, Kan.
Prof. J. W. Gaul, Monmouth, Ill.
J. R. Sovereign, Atlantic, Ia.
Hon. William Baker, Newark, O.
John Davis, Junction City, Kan.
Henry Schaidt, Ed. Lonaconing Review, Md.
Col. D. S. Curtiss, Washington, D. C.
Albert Owen, Boston, Mass., Author of Integral Co-Operation.
J. J. Woodall, Hartselle, Ala.
Hon. A. J. Streeter, New Windsor, Ill.
R. F. Rowell, Orrington, Me.
Hon. John Seitz, Tiffin, O.
S. M. Baldwin, Washington, D. C.
Hon. O. W. Barnard, Manteno, Ill.
N. M. Lovin, Muskogee, Ind.
C. T. Parker, Douglasville, Ga.
G. W. Phillippo, Geneseo, Ill.
Dr. H. J. Parker, Clayton, Ill.
O. J. Sutton, Akron, O.
W. H. Robb, Creston, Ia.

G. R. Williams, Milan, Mich.
W. W. Jones, Camargo, Ill.
W. H. Davidson, Calera, Ala.
Charles Sears, Williamsburg, Kan.
R. C. McBeath, Bradsfordsville, Ky.
D. W. Smith, Lewiston, Me.
N. B. Stack, Birmingham, Ala.
James Mitchell, Ed. Fort Wayne Dispatch, Ind.
A. A. Beaton, Rockland, Me.
David Ross, Oglesby, Ill.
Hon. J. W. Breidenthal, Chetopa, Kan.
Hon. Henry Smith, Milwaukee, Wis.
F. P. Sargeant, Terre Haute, Ind.
G. W. Johnson, Ed. Advance, Fond du Lac, Wis.

And a number of others, whose valuable material has been unavailable because of limited space.

S. M. J.

CONTENTS.

CHAPTER I.—A GLANCE AT THE PAST.

THE FIRST APPEARANCE OF THE WORKINGMAN IN ENGLISH HISTORY—HIS POSITION—PHYSICAL CONDITION—THE "BLACK DEATH"—THE PEASANTS' WAR IN 1381—THE STRUGGLES OF SERFDOM—THE WORKINGMAN IN AMERICAN COLONIES—THE SPIRIT OF LIBERTY—PROGRESS OF LABOR AFTER THE REVOLUTIONARY WAR—YEARS OF PEACE AND PLENTY—THE GREAT REBELLION—THE DEVELOPMENT OF MANUFACTURING—TABLE OF WAGES FROM 1752 TO 1886—THE UPRISING OF THE FARMERS—THE GRANGE—RAPID INCREASE OF THE POWER OF CAPITAL—THE EVENTS OF 1886—LABOR A POWERFUL SOCIAL FACTOR......15

CHAPTER II.—LAND AND TAXES.

LAND MONOPOLY THE BANE OF THE WORLD—ITS EFFECT IN THE PAST—EGYPT'S DOWNFALL—GOLDEN BABYLON CRUSHED BY LAND-OWNERS—THEY RUIN THE ROMAN EMPIRE—IMPROPER MANAGEMENT OF OUR PUBLIC DOMAIN—VAST TRACTS OF VALUABLE LAND GIVEN TO CORPORATIONS—TWENTY MILLIONS OF ACRES HELD BY

FOREIGNERS—POWDERLY ON BONANZA FARMS—HENRY GEORGE'S THEORIES—HIS BOOK, "PROGRESS AND POVERTY"—HIS POSITION DEFINED—THE UTOPIAN IDEA OF CONFISCATION—PROF. W. T. HARRIS ON GEORGEISM—GROUND RENT—STATISTICS—CAPITAL'S GRIP AT THE THROAT OF LAND PROPERTY—TAX THE RICH AS WELL AS THE POOR—HOW JUST ASSESSMENTS MAY BE MADE. 26

CHAPTER III.—THE GREAT QUESTION OF MONEY AND LABOR.

THE PROBLEM WHICH ALL NATIONS ARE CONSIDERING—WEALTH RIGHTFULLY BELONGS TO THE PRODUCER—ECONOMISTS AND THE PRECIOUS METALS—CHARACTERISTICS OF MONEY—MONETARY STANDARDS OF DIFFERENT NATIONS—THE GOLD STANDARD—THE SILVER STANDARD—THE DOUBLE STANDARD—HISTORY OF BANKING—RISE OF THE NATIONAL BANKS—OPINIONS OF STATESMEN—LABOR AND CAPITAL—THE WAGE FUND PRINCIPLE—PROFITS AND WAGES—THE ATTITUDE OF LABOR—INFLATION OF CURRENCY—HON. ALFRED TAYLOR'S REMARKS—DANIEL WEBSTER ON LABOR—MONEY THE GREAT HUMAN BLESSING—VOLUME OF MONEY—LINCOLN'S IDEAS—HORACE GREELY—BURKE—THE NEW ISSUES OF TO-DAY. . . 45

CHAPTER IV.—GOVERNMENT LOANS TO THE PEOPLE.

MAN SHALL EARN HIS BREAD BY THE SWEAT OF HIS BROW—INTEREST AND USURY—THE MOSAIC LAW—THE POWER OF INTEREST—ILLUSTRATIONS—LOANS TO

THE PEOPLE A FEASIBLE PROJECT—THE GOVERNMENT LOANS TO THE BANKERS—LOANS TO THE PEOPLE AT A LOW RATE WOULD BE A BLESSING—HOW THE FARMERS WOULD SECURE PROSPERITY—MILLIONAIRES AND PAUPERS ARE INCREASING—REGULATION OF THE VOLUME OF MONEY—GARFIELD'S THEORY—TOTAL NATIONAL DEBT—HYPOCRITICAL POLITICIANS—USURY NOTHING MORE THAN ROBBERY. 64

CHAPTER V.—THE NATIONAL BANKING SYSTEM.

THE MONETARY CHANGE DEMANDED BY WORKINGMEN—AIM OF THE KNIGHTS OF LABOR—SOULLESS CORPORATIONS HAVE NO PITY—ATTITUDE OF BANKING CORPORATIONS—"SPECIE BASIS"—"INTRINSIC VALUE"—"HONEST MONEY"—MONEY IN ANCIENT AGES—IRON, BRASS, TIN, CLOTH, LEATHER AND WOODEN MONEY—GREAT FINANCIERS ON METALIC MONEY—HOW THE NATIONAL BANKS ABSORB THE NATION'S WEALTH—DEBT THEIR FOUNDATION—HOW THE BANKERS SECURE DOUBLE INTEREST—ENORMOUS SUMS OF MONEY WITHDRAWN FROM JUST TAXATION—THE IMMENSE EARNINGS OF THE INDIANAPOLIS NATIONAL BANK—WHAT WORKINGMEN SHOULD HAVE....... 86

CHAPTER VI.—TRANSPORTATION.

GOVERNMENT PREROGATIVES DANGEROUS IN THE HANDS OF CORPORATIONS—NO ONE CLASS INDEPENDENT—CORPORATIONS NOT ENTITLED TO DISCRIMINATION—THE COUNTRY SUFFERING FROM RAILROAD EXTOR-

TIONS—WHAT THE BALLOT SHOULD ACCOMPLISH—
THE TELEGRAPHS—TELEPHONES—RAILROADS—THE
GOVERNMENT'S SUCCESS WITH THE POSTAL SYSTEM—
THE POWER OF SYNDICATES AND CORPORATIONS—
THEIR IMMENSE WEALTH—DANIEL WEBSTER'S GREAT
WARNING................................... 101

CHAPTER VII.—"OVERPRODUCTION."

THERE CAN BE NO OVERPRODUCTION WHEN MONEY IS
PLENTY—SCARCITY OF MONEY PRODUCES STRIKES AND
RIOTS—WHY MONEY IS WITHDRAWN FROM CIRCULA-
TION—LINCOLN'S WARNING IN 1861—OVERPRODUCT-
ION DOES NOT STARVE CHILDREN—INTEREST ON BONDS
A GREAT VAMPIRE TO THE NATION—BONDS TAXED IN
ENGLAND AND FRANCE—GEN. WEAVER ON TAXATION
—THE INTER-STATE COMMERCE LAW—REPORT OF THE
SILVER COMMISSIONERS — PLAIN FACTS — SHOWING
MADE BY UNITED STATES TREASURER IN 1887 OF THE
NATION'S MONEY—IDLE CAPITAL MAKES IDLE MA-
CHINERY AND THE WORKINGMAN SUFFERS...... 115

CHAPTER VIII.—HARD TIMES.

THE KNIGHTS OF LABOR AT RICHMOND—A COMMITTEE
ON HARD TIMES—THEIR REPORT—THE INTRICACIES
OF DISTRIBUTION OF WEALTH—AN ANALYSIS OF THE
SUBJECT—SENATOR SHERMAN'S IDEAS IN 1869—JOHN
A. LOGAN'S THEORY—THE UNITED STATES TREASURER
IN 1820—JOHN STUART MILL, THE GREAT ENGLISH
ECONOMIST — SIR ARCHIBALD WILSON — SECRETARY
M'CULLOCH — BOUTWELL — THE BURNING OF $100,-

000,000—PETER COOPER ON INDUSTRIAL DEPRESSION—THE FLUCTUATION OF FINANCES THE CAUSE OF HARD TIMES—A STEADY STANDARD A FIRM FOUNDATION.................................131

CHAPTER IX.—HARD TIMES—Continued.

THE DIFFERENT CLASSES OF SOCIETY—MONEY EARNERS AND MONEY USERS—THE PREDATORY STRATUM—LAWS FOR THE CONTRACTION OF MONEY VOLUME—7 YEARS OF SHRINKAGE IN THE UNITED STATES—THE PRACTICAL QUESTIONS OF TO-DAY, LAND, LABOR, FINANCE AND TRANSPORTATION—THE DECISION OF JUDGE GRESHAM IN THE WABASH RAILROAD CASE—THE KNIGHTS OF LABOR AN ORDER OF PEACE AND EDUCATION.............................148

CHAPTER X.—WAGES.

WAGES A SUBJECT OF VAST IMPORTANCE—GREAT NATIONS ARE NOW DEALING WITH IT—THE ECONOMICS OF WAGES—INDUSTRIAL CONDITIONS INCESSANTLY CHANGE—A TABLE OF STATISTICS—THE PROGRESS OF WAGES—ECONOMY DOES NOT DEMAND LOW WAGES—WHAT HIGH WAGES WILL DO—HON. WILLIAM WALSH ON WAGES—INCREASE OF CAPITAL DEMANDS INCREASE OF LABOR—TO PROTECT LABOR A SACRED DUTY—DR. PARKER ON REGULATION OF WAGES—CO-OPERATION THE ULTIMATUM OF PRODUCTIVE INDUSTRY...................................157

CHAPTER XI.—ORIGIN AND PROGRESS
OF TRADES UNIONS.

THE DISCLOSURE OF HISTORY—ANTIQUITY OF COMBINATIONS BY WORKINGMEN—THE OLD GUILDS OF EUROPE—THE FIRST AUTHENTIC ORGANIZATIONS—THE POWER OF ORGANIZATIONS SIX HUNDRED YEARS AGO—THE CRUELTIES PRACTICED IN ENGLAND—THE SECRET OF THEIR STRENGTH—UNIONS HAVE ELEVATED WAGES—WORKINGMEN CANNOT BE TOO WELL PAID—UNION MEN THE BEST WORKMEN—LITERATURE FOR LABOR—UNIONS ARE EDUCATING WORKINGMEN—THEIR GREAT FUTURE.............................. 173

CHAPTER XII.—AMERICAN LABOR UNIONS

THE FIRST AMERICAN TRADE UNION — JOURNEYMEN SHIPWRIGHTS—NEW YORK TYPOGRAPHICAL SOCIETY—FIRST LABOR PARTY—FRANKLIN SOCIETY OF PRINTERS—NATIONAL TYPOGRAPHICAL UNION—THE INTERNATIONAL—HAT FINISHERS—IRON MOULDERS—MECHANICAL ENGINEERS OF AMERICA—BROTHERHOOD LOCOMOTIVE ENGINEERS—LOCOMOTIVE FIREMEN—CIGAR MAKERS—BRICKLAYERS AND STONEMASONS—PATRONS OF HUSBANDRY—GRANGE—RAILWAY CONDUCTORS—BOOT AND SHOEMAKERS — GERMAN-AMERICAN TYPOGRAPHICAL—HORSE-SHOERS—IRON AND STEEL HEATERS—GRANITE CUTTERS—LAKE SEAMEN—BOILER MAKERS—CARPENTERS AND JOINERS—HAT MAKERS—MINERS AND MINE LABORERS—BAKERS—SWITCHMEN—TAILORS—TELEGRAPH MEN—FURNITURE—COOPERS—ETC.—ETC................... 184

CHAPTER XIII.—THE KNIGHTS OF LABOR.

THE CAUSE OF THEIR ORGANIZATION—THE GREAT POWER OF THE ORDER—URIAH STEVENS, THE FOUNDER—EARLY HISTORY—STRUGGLES—ATTACKED BY PULPIT AND PRESS—ITS GROWTH—CHARACTER OF ITS MEMBERS—WHO THEY ARE—PRESENT NUMBER—A SEMI-SECRET ORDER—THEIR PREAMBLE AND PLATFORM OF PRINCIPLES—MANNER OF JOINING—WHO ARE ELIGIBLE—LAWS AND REGULATIONS OF THE KNIGHTS—LOCAL, DISTRICT AND GENERAL ASSEMBLIES—PASS-WORDS, SIGNS AND GRIPS—WOMEN AS MEMBERS—INTERESTING INFORMATION—BIOGRAPHY OF MR. POWDERLY—THE OFFICERS—THE EXECUTIVE COMMITTEE—A DESCRIPTION OF THE MANAGEMENT. . 193

CHAPTER XIV.—STRIKES AND LOCKOUTS.

A CAUSE OF RECENT STRIKES—WHY WORKINGMEN STRIKE—STATISTICS OF STRIKES IN 1880—SUCCESSES AND FAILURES—COMPLETE REVIEW OF THEIR EFFECT—AMOUNT OF LOSS INCURRED—AGGREGATE LOSSES IN APRIL AND MAY, 1886—PUBLIC SYMPATHY FOR STRIKERS—POWDERLY ON STRIKES—GREAT THOUGHTS—THE POWER OF WEALTH GIVING WAY TO JUSTICE AND RIGHT—A NEW POWER DAWNING UPON THE WORLD—A BRIGHT FUTURE AT HAND—IDEAS FOR WORKINGMEN TO THINK AND ACT UPON. 210

CHAPTER XV.—EIGHT HOURS.

EFFECT OF THE EIGHT HOUR AGITATION—NUMBER OF MEN IN THE MOVEMENT IN 1886 — THE BENEFITS CLAIMED—LABOR NOT A COMMODITY—A BIRDS-EYE VIEW OF THE WORKING WORLD — THE AGENTS OF CORPORATIONS—EXACTIONS ARE FETTERS—APPEALS AND MUTTERED DISCONTENT—A GREAT PLEA—THIRST FOR KNOWLEDGE SHOULD BE GRATIFIED—ROBERT G. INGERSOLL'S ELOQUENT WORDS ON THE SUBJECT—HOURS OF LABOR SHOULD BE SHORTENED.......228

CHAPTER XVI.—ARBITRATION.

ARBITRATION NOT AN EXPERIMENT—THE JUSTINIAN LAW—ENGLISH AND ROMAN LAW—JUDICIAL BOARDS OF ARBITRATION—PRESIDENT CLEVELAND'S MESSAGE ON THE QUESTION — RICHARD GRIFFITHS, G. W. F., ON ARBITRATION—GEORGE RODGERS — FRENCH COURTS OF ARBITRATION — HOW THE GREAT BRICKLAYERS' STRIKE IN CHICAGO WAS SETTLED—JUDGE TULEY'S DECISION—ARBITRATION JUST FOR EMPLOYER AND WORKINGMEN—THE SCALES OF JUSTICE A TRUE BALANCE..................238

CHAPTER XVII.—CO-OPERATION.

ALL GREAT ENTERPRISES DEPEND ON CO-OPERATION—A COMMON OBJECT IS A COMMON ADVANTAGE—ORGANIZATION AND CO-OPERATION A GREAT POWER—

WAGE SYSTEM OPPOSED TO CO-OPERATION—CO-OPERATION A SUCCESS—LECLAIRE'S GREAT ORGANIZATION—RAILROAD CO-OPERATION IN FRANCE—INDUSTRIAL PARTNERSHIP IN ENGLAND—ALFRED TAYLOR ON THE SUBJECT—D. S. CURTISS—DEVELOPMENT AND EXTENT OF CO-OPERATION IN THE UNITED STATES—COMPLETE REVIEW OF WHAT HAS BEEN DONE............253

CHAPTER XVIII.—HOME THE PALLADIUM OF SOCIETY.

MAN WITHOUT A HOME AN OUTCAST—THE STATE IS BUT THE INDIVIDUAL, THE INDIVIDUAL A MINIATURE STATE—HOME THE BULWARK OF VIRTUE—CICERO'S MAXIM—DEFECTS OF OUR SOCIAL SYSTEM—THE BURDEN OF INDIRECT TAXATION—HANDWRITING ON THE WALL—CO-OPERATION A BLESSING FOR THE PEOPLE—SUCCESS OF CORPORATIONS—"SWEET HOME" CAN BE MADE A REALITY—WISDOM FOR THE HOMELESS......274

CHAPTER XIX.—PRISON LABOR.

A GREAT QUESTION—HOW CONVICTS ARE EMPLOYED—OCCUPATIONS IN VARIOUS PRISONS—WORKING FOR THE STATE—THE CONTRACT SYSTEM—THE LEASE PLAN—E. C. WINES ON THE CONTRACT SYSTEM—ITS EFFECT—ABUSES—SHOULD BE ABOLISHED—LEASES AND FAULTS THEREOF—57,500 CONVICT WORKMEN PITTED AGAINST HONEST LABOR—DR. SEAMAN'S VIEWS—DEMANDS OF THE PUBLIC—CARROLL D. WRIGHT'S REPORT—PRISON LABOR MUST NOT CONFLICT WITH INTERESTS OF THE WORKINGMAN...290

CHAPTER XX.—LIQUOR AND THE WORKINGMAN.

THE ENORMOUS AMOUNT OF MONEY EXPENDED FOR LIQUOR—MR. POWDERLY ARRAIGNS THE DRUNKARD—HIS POWERFUL SPEECH AT LYNN, MASS.—HOW LIQUOR PRODUCES POVERTY—FIFTEEN MILLION PEOPLE SPEND SEVEN HUNDRED MILLION DOLLARS ANNUALLY FOR LIQUOR—LIQUOR COSTS THE PEOPLE THREE TIMES AS MUCH AS CLOTHING—INTEMPERANCE A CURSE TO THE WORKINGMAN............................ 302

CHAPTER XXI.—THE FARMER AND HIS INTERESTS.

CAPITAL DRIFTING AWAY FROM AGRICULTURE — THE LABOR QUESTION LINKED WITH THE FARMER — HON. W. F. SADLER BEFORE THE GRANGE — AN ABLE DISCOURSE — A STARTLING ARRAY OF FACTS AND FIGURES—THE AVARICE OF CAPITAL—MR. JOHN NORRIS ON RAILROAD MONOPOLY — CHARLES SEARS' MEASURES—A BALEFUL WARNING—MR. CHARLES SEARS' EXPOSITION OF TRUTHS — PUBLIC CARRIERS AND MONEY LOANERS ARE ABSORBING CAPITAL—A PEACEFUL MODE OF ADJUSTMENT—MEASURES AND REMEDIES—UNITED EFFORT BY REFORM PARTIES NECESSARY TO SUCCESS—LABOR ASCENDING THE THRONE OF POLITICS............................ 313

CHAPTER XXII.—FOREIGNERS AND FOREIGNERS.

The immigration of to-day a great evil—500,000 immigrants in 1887—Official figures—Over 8,000,000 aliens in this country—A flood of paupers and criminals tainting the nation—H. H. Boyesen on unrestricted immigration—The evil of anarchy and communism one of the curses of the foul stream—Summary legislation a just demand of workingmen — American labor menaced by foreign immigration — Hostile sentiment throughout the land—A question of the day.................................327

CHAPTER XXIII.—THOUGHTS OF TO-DAY.

Hon. John Seitz—Labor entitled to first consideration—Opinions of R. F. Rowell—Hon. George L. Wellington—Hon. Jesse Harper — Hon. O. W. Barnard —H. E. Baldwin—Hon. Alf. Taylor—N. M. Lovin— C. B. Fenton—C. T. Parker—Rev. Dr. Thomas — G. W. Phillippo — O. J. Sutton—W. H. Robb—J. D. Hardy—W. W. Jones—Com. Miners and Mine Laborers—W. H. Davidson—R. C. McBeath—D. W. Smith—N. B. Stack—Hon. William Baker—James Mitchell—Hon. A. J. Streeter—The notorious Hazard Circular — A. A. Beaton................................339

CHAPTER XXIV.—SIGNS OF THE TIMES.

Views of David Ross—The magnitude of the labor problem—Out of agitation come many benefits

—EDUCATION IS REQUIRED FOR ADVANCEMENT—THE MASSES ARE THINKING—REFORM PARTIES—UNION LABOR PARTY IN THE VAN—ORGANIZATION THE WATCHWORD—HON. J. W. BREIDENTHAL—BRIGHT PROSPECTS WEST, NORTH, SOUTH AND EAST—LABOR IN POLITICS—WITH ORGANIZATION AND COMMON PURPOSE SUCCESS IS CERTAIN—A PLATFORM BROAD ENOUGH FOR ALL IS NEEDED—HON. HENRY SMITH—FUTURE OF THE WORKINGMAN—CONCLUSION....358

CHAPTER XXV.—THE FARMERS' ALLIANCE.

EARLY STRUGGLES OF THE FARMERS' ALLIANCE—ITS RULES—ITS PROGRESS—ADVANTAGES OF CO-OPERATION—THE TEXAS CHARTER—THE NATIONAL ALLIANCE—PREAMBLE—EDUCATION FUNDAMENTAL TO GOOD GOVERNMENT—BUSINESS MATTERS—POLITICAL MATTERS—GENERAL REMARKS—WOMEN OF THE ALLIANCE........................375

ILLUSTRATIONS.

T. V. Powderly,	Frontispiece.
Richard Griffiths,	37
Frederick Turner,	65
Charles H. Litchman,	79
Hon. W. D. Vincent,	93
Hon. Henry Smith,	107
J. R. Sovereign,	121
Hon. William Baker,	135
A Miner's Cottage,	149
Happy Toilers,	165
Coal Under Different Aspects,	179
Honest Tom Makes a Speech,	187
Uriah Stephens,	205
Between Strike and Family,	221
Locomotive Works,	231
Bricklaying,	245
Knife, Fork and Spoon Workers,	257
A Happy Home,	269

Midnight Fires—Blast Furnaces,	281
Hay Making in the Olden Times,	295
Bottle Blowers,	307
Hon. John Seitz,	321
Bessemer Steel Manufactory,	333
Mining in Colorado,	343

THE VOICE OF LABOR.

CHAPTER I.

A GLANCE AT THE PAST.

THE FIRST APPEARANCE OF THE WORKINGMAN IN ENGLISH HISTORY—HIS POSITION—PHYSICAL CONDITION—THE "BLACK DEATH"—THE PEASANTS' WAR IN 1381—THE STRUGGLES OF SERFDOM—THE WORKINGMAN IN AMERICAN COLONIES—THE SPIRIT OF LIBERTY—PROGRESS OF LABOR AFTER THE REVOLUTIONARY WAR—YEARS OF PEACE AND PLENTY—THE GREAT REBELLION—THE DEVELOPMENT OF MANUFACTURING—TABLE OF WAGES FROM 1752 TO 1886—THE UPRISING OF THE FARMERS—THE GRANGE—RAPID INCREASE OF THE POWER OF CAPITAL—THE EVENTS OF 1886—LABOR A POWERFUL SOCIAL FACTOR.

The workingman first appears in English history in the character of a serf, or slave. He owned neither land, cattle, nor goods, but was wholly dependent upon his lord, who furnished him with shelter, food and clothing, and in return was entitled to his services and was responsible for his conduct.

He belonged to the estate, and if the land changed ownership, he followed it and served under the new lord. He had no civil rights, neither for or against any one, save through the lord of the manor. His physical condition was one of comparative ease and plenty, as he was well fed and housed. When not working for his lord he was at liberty to cultivate his garden, gather fuel from the manor forest and devote his time to his family.

This condition was not absolute, for he might accumulate a little money, purchase a piece of land and thus free himself. If he was able to master a trade, as a mechanic he received higher pay than a serf, but in other respects he stood on the same footing. In towns and cities he had no civil rights until he acquired property and entered the guild of his craft. He then could set up on his own account and employ journeymen and hold apprentices. By custom and law he was held to be a man of an inferior caste, and the unfortunate stigma has followed him down through the centuries.

At this time the capitalist, or lord, was not actuated by hostile feelings, nor did he in any way seek to oppress him, but as the serf was virtually his property he protected him for the sole purpose of avoiding his loss. Wages was a pretext for a quarrel at any time, just as it is to-day.

In 1349 a terrible plague swept over Europe from the orient, and in England its devastation was horrible. The "Black Death" marked the era of freedom for the serf. Nearly one-half of the entire population was swept away, and labor assumed the phase of being the most important element in the kingdom. Laborers demanded quadruple pay and dictated their own terms. The historic "Statute of Laborers" was passed, and then began the antagonism between capital and labor.

In 1381 the Peasants' war broke out and the insurgents captured the city of London. They demanded of the king: "We will that you make us free, our heirs and our lands, and that we be no more bond, nor so reputed." The king promised them freedom, but when parliament met it sternly refused to fulfill the promise. In an unanimous vote they declared "they would rather perish altogether in one day." The strife continued and coercive laws were constantly passed. The laborer was forbidden to leave his place or travel without a passport, and in 1391 parliament was petitioned to forbid the children of the base-born to attend the schools. The land-owners finally gave up the attempt to employ serf labor, and rented small farms to tenants for a fixed rent to be paid in money. At the end of fifty years serfdom was a thing of the past, and the statutes which had been passed for the regulation of wages became obsolete.

The wages of workmen soon became more than enough for a comfortable support, and his day of work was eight hours. With the close of the reign of Henry VIII, after a period of about one hundred and fifty years, legislation again oppressed him, and for two hundred and fifty years he struggled against laws which tended only to the interests of the rich. An extravagant royalty swallowed millions of money, and the prosperous workman became a beggar with a starving family. In 1601 the English Poor Law was passed, but it failed to accomplish a benevolent end.

Meanwhile the discovery of America had electrified the old world, and settlements were made here. During one hundred and twenty-five years following the discovery of America in 1492, the territory of the Atlantic states and the West Indies were infested by adventurers. Their purposes were the gathering of the precious metals, trading with the natives for furs, and the locating of fishing banks from which food might be obtained for Europe. The Basques, from France, and other Celtic nations, visited the banks of Newfoundland to fish, several hundred years before the time of Columbus.

In 1607, Jamestown, Virginia, was occupied by the English, and developed into a permanent settlement in 1610. Colony after colony secured footholds on the Hudson, along the coast of New England, and in what are now the Atlantic states. Religious and political oppression in Europe stimulated the tide of emigration, and the new world began to live. Up to this time actual industrial settlements had not materialized. The class of people who first came to America were those who sought gold, or conquest, and the majority of them were banished criminals. Later during the seventeenth century, people of a different stamp were driven to seek a new home across the Atlantic, and the colonists gained a new element of thoughtful and religious cast.

The French and Indian war came and passed, leaving the Virginian colonists aware of the weakness of English troops in the peculiar warfare incident to the border, and the feeling was prevalent that the colonial Assembly was composed of strong and fearless men. The colonists although loyal, desired to conduct their affairs in their own way. Conscious of their strength they felt their own importance and were quick to resent any acts of interference on the part of the mother country. Parliament sought to maintain a standing army, to enforce certain navigation laws and to tax the colonists to contribute to the financial burdens of the empire. The execution of these laws in the way of the stamp act, and other revenue laws, led to the union of the scattered colonies, resistance to England, to war and to the successful upholding of the Declaration of Independence. In this country the white workman has never been subjected to the hardships and deprivations which disgrace the pages of England's history, but has always been politically the peer of any one. Land was free to all and it rested upon himself whether he occupied and made use of it for his support. He quickly learned to rely upon his own efforts and grew self-reliant and independent with the exercise of his natural rights. Unhampered by the fetters of conscienceless legislation, and with the pride and knowledge which is inseparable from full citizenship, the workingman developed the germ of American independence, and the spirit which prompted the determination to throw off the English yoke was given birth.

The colonial era laid out the plan of the American land system, which began with royal claims, and ended with speculation and actual conquest. The chief feature of the land polity seemed to be, that each man strove to get as much land as he could, and if he chose to retain his possessions, his family should inherit it. Tenure was based upon privilege and human rights were a secondary consideration, yet the spirit of liberty was strong, and the system did not take on the Old World form of primogeniture. In England the feudal land-owners struggled with the chattel-holders, and their differences were carried to the colonies. It was from these materials that American tenure was molded.

Had no aristocracy existed in England slavery would not have been introduced in America. Indigent dependents of aristocracy sought riches, and being unwilling to work themselves, and unable to employ free labor, they took the negro. Labor was wofully scarce, and as the expense of securing it from England was great, the natural consequence was the cheaper course of importation of slaves. Slavery, however, did not materially interfere with free labor in other than the cotton, cane and tobacco districts, and never secured noticeable foothold north of the Ohio river.

After the close of the Revolutionary war still a better class of people came from Europe who brought with them the pioneer spirit which has always marked American enterprise. Statistics show that the wages of the workingman began an upward tendency and his welfare made decided progress. The discounted Continental money was replaced by a valuable circulating medium, and financial confidence was resumed. As late as 1780 labor was not organized, nor at that time was organization demanded. The undeveloped resources of the vast area of tillable land, at no great distance from the seaboard, continually drew the surplus population from the growing cities and towns, and high wages was the natural result. The farm constituted an admirable regulator from a wages point of view. The tide of immigration steadily flowed on toward the great western prairies, the valleys west of the Alleghanies became thickly settled, and the workingman prospered everywhere.

Amid this era of peace two irreconcilable theories of government clashed, and the great war of the rebellion began. While the fierce contest was in progress, hundreds of thousands of men were taken away from the factories, the farms, and from all kinds of business. The armies drained the country of its labor, and the inevitable sequence was that wages fluctuated with each succeeding day. At the close of the war labor prospered. In 1866 over six hundred millions worth of public lands were sold, and a large part of our population was engaged in preparing for substantial prosperity. A protective tariff gave an immense impetus to manufacturing industries, and in the eastern states their development was remarkable. The eastern states not having the fertility of soil found in the west, capital instinctively gravitated toward profitable manufacturing, and soon found mechanical industry, backed by tariff, to be the most reliable and satisfactory of investments. Farm life in New England gave way to life in the factory, and we now see our Atlantic seaboard transformed from an agricultural into that of a manufacturing region. This method of centralizing capital has in a great measure taken labor from the farm to the workshop, and a constant premium has been offered to the mechanic. To this fact may be attributed the prodigious growth of cities during the past twenty-five years, and it is especially noticeable in New York, Chicago, Philadelphia, and Boston. Everywhere it may be seen that the planting of a factory, or mill, is followed by the erection of a cluster of houses which grows into a village, then a town is formed, and the town finally becomes a city.

High pay to workingmen surely follows the growth of cities. Since 1752 the mechanic's pay has increased from thirty-three cents per day to one dollar and forty-five cents per day, but the farm worker has always been paid at a lower rate. An examination of the following table will give the reader a good idea of the fluctuation of the prices paid during the last one hundred and thirty-four years:

Year.	Farmwork Wages.	Mechanical Wages.	Year.	Farmwork Wages.	Mechanical Wages.
1752	$ .33	$ .33	1845	$1.00	$1.25
1756	.33	.48	1860	1.06	1.50
1763	.33	.35	1864	1.12	1.33
1770	.33	.34	1870	1.15	1.50
1781	.41	.46	1875	1.00	1.35
1790	.33	.40	1878	.94	1.21
1801	.57	.61	1880	.90	1.20
1810	1.00	1.10	1884	.92	1.30
1820	.75	1.00	1886	.96	1.45
1826	.78	1.00			

The foregoing tabulated statement unerringly shows the effect of the investment of capital upon the rate of wages paid in cities, and lays open the secret of their constant increase in population. There are now thirty-six cities in the United States with inhabitants numbering over fifty thousand.

One great result of the civil war was to bring free labor to its present condition and rate of wages, by doing away with the antagonism incident upon cheap slave labor. It was first thought the South was hopelessly involved in ruin, but the contrary has proved true, and that region is securing larger returns to-day for the amount of capital invested than it did under the control of wasteful and brutal overseers. The period following the war was one of excessive inflation. The greenback dollar reached its lowest value in 1864, at which time a gold dollar could be sold for $2.85 in paper, but it gradually ascended in value, and in 1879 it reached par, and since has been worth a dollar in gold, through the resumption of specie payment.

In 1866 the Granger movement began, and had for its object the financial benefit of the farmer. It combatted the monopolies of railroads and corporations, and so popular was this agitation that in 1875 the order had nearly 800,000 members. The rapid increase of the power of capital in America is without parallel in any other country in the world, and the manner in which gigantic syndicates and railroad corporations have pursued their objects has been watched with much solicitude by the farmers, workingmen, and others, whose interests have been prejudiced. The fact that an enormous amount of money, gained by dishonest financiering, has been invested in transportation industries, and as the earnings of this vast amount of capital finally come upon the workingman and farmer to pay, they have become dissatisfied. Watered stock and jobbing pools have created a burden under which the bone and sinew of the nation are restive, and they have combined against it, as was evinced by the events of 1886, in the great southwestern strike on the Gould system of railroads. The Knights of Labor have been rapidly perfecting their organization throughout the United States, and as the order is seeking redress of grievances by means of legislation, the outlook is that they will act as a powerful factor in shaping the industrial welfare of the country during the next few years.

CHAPTER II.

LAND AND TAXES.

LAND MONOPOLY THE BANE OF THE WORLD—ITS EFFECT IN THE PAST—EGYPT'S DOWNFALL—GOLDEN BABYLON CRUSHED BY LAND-OWNERS—THEY RUIN THE ROMAN EMPIRE—IMPROPER MANAGEMENT OF OUR PUBLIC DOMAIN—VAST TRACTS OF VALUABLE LAND GIVEN TO CORPORATIONS—TWENTY MILLIONS OF ACRES HELD BY FOREIGNERS—POWDERLY ON BONANZA FARMS—HENRY GEORGE'S THEORIES—HIS BOOK, "PROGRESS AND POVERTY"—HIS POSITION DEFINED—THE UTOPIAN IDEA OF CONFISCATION—PROF. W. T. HARRIS ON GEORGEISM—GROUND RENT—STATISTICS—CAPITAL'S GRIP AT THE THROAT OF LAND PROPERTY—TAX THE RICH AS WELL AS THE POOR—HOW JUST ASSESSMENTS MAY BE MADE.

The right to the soil is as much an inalienable right as that of working for bread. Depriving a man of either, is a violation of both moral and secular laws. Land monopoly is shown by history to be the bane of the world. Great nations have risen, ruled and fallen, and in each instance the lesson has been taught, that when such burdens have been laid upon the masses, and were deprived from earning bread from the soil, their doom was sealed.

Back in the dim distance of time we see Egypt the proudest and most powerful nation on the globe. She excelled in mighty undertakings, and to-day we marvel at the ruins of her vast structures which have withstood the crumbling touches of scores of centuries.

The great pyramid of Gizeh is the grandest monument of human history, the mightiest building on earth and the oldest—in structure a miracle, in extent almost incomprehensible. Forty centuries have looked upon its glittering sides, and the tooth of time during all these rolling centuries has not been able to eat away the grandeur of the pile.

An oppressive land monopoly rule worked the fall of Egypt. One per cent of the people owned all the land, and ninety-nine per cent of the people owned none—were tenants, serfs and slaves. Then Egypt died, and her death-dirge rings yet in the ear of the world.

The golden glory of Babylon, with its city the most magnificent man ever built, was cursed with a class land monopoly which was its death warrant. Two per cent of the people owned all the land, and ninety-six per cent of the masses owned none, and were tenants, slaves and serfs.

In a speech recently delivered by Hon. Jesse Harper, he said:

"The founding, growth and glory of the Roman

empire has been the wonder of the world. Begotten in myth, fed upon the ferocity of the wolf, led by intellect of man, she grew to be at last the palladium of law and the legionry war. Her 'Twelve Tables' underlie the codes of all civilization to-day. Her military prowess has been the admiration of mankind. Her works in every department of human thought and action are unsurpassed. Acqueduct, temple, forum, each stand unparalleled. Theater, hippodrome, drama—in these she leads all.

"Rome has been termed 'The Eternal City.' From that center has gone forth blandishments, political chicanery, ecclesiastical Jesuitism, and they for ages upon ages have ruled the world.

"Rome in her highest glory, was simple in habit and austere in manner. There was but a slight distinction between the people. 'Citizen' was the name of man. Equality of fortune, generous distribution of land was the law of common consent, and the legal enactments of the state also.

"So rich in achievement was she at one time, that eighty-five per cent of the people had title in land. Then the legions were heroes beyond conquering; then Rome was founded on a rock. She but followed the course of the great empires which had preceded her. In the incipiency of them all justice ruled and mercy reigned more largely than at any other period of their life. But as the nations before her turned from those true principles of equity and justice, in the day of their degeneracy, so did Rome.

She traveled the same road to the same death, to certain destruction. In what way?

"Her volume of money at the commencement of this era was about $1,800,000,000, made up of brass, copper, and other metals. This was doomed to destruction. She determined to shrink the volume and make the lesser volume of a finer metal. So she shrunk the volume to $200,000,000. A long time was consumed in doing it, but the road was passed over, the goal reached.

"The fatal effect upon the empire came at last; and Rome fell by reason of this very shrinking of the volume of money. The lands passed out of the hands of the people into the hands of the few millionaires, so that when death's great ford was reached, where civilization was to die, we see that two thousand people owned all the land in the Roman empire. Less than one per cent of the people owned all, and more than ninety-nine per cent owned none."

Land monopoly, a shrinking volume of money and class legislation made up the decree of national dissolution. History chronicles a repetition of such events, but there lies in experience an opportunity to avert them in the future.

During the past two decades there has been no proper management of public lands, but our national legislators have actually given away to corporations, in a spirit of prodigality without parallel in the world's history, more land than is contained in the states of Illinois, Iowa, Ohio and Michigan combined. Only a few years ago the line of statesmen now retiring, gave to one corporation in America forty-eight millions of acres of land.

There is, in the state of Iowa, but thirty-five millions of acres; in the state of Illinois but thirty-six millions of acres. And yet, there was given to one corporation forty-eight millions of acres of land. And that, too, in the face of the fact that within a score of years we will have on this continent one hundred millions of human beings. We have sixty millions now; we will have a hundred millions then.

The tendency has been to throw large estates into the hands of a few people, and to dispossess the poor, the small land owners of the country.

Millions of acres comprising the best agricultural land on the earth have been thus disposed of, until there is over twenty millions of acres held by foreign capitalists. Ireland's pitiful condition to-day was brought about by a similar course of events.

General Master Workman Powderly says: "In the United States, although scarcely out of its squatting era, we already have an incipient landholding aristocracy, which is by no means confined to the bonanza farms of the west, where work is to a great extent done by machinery and a horde of tramp agricultural laborers. There are in this country over one million five hundred thousand of capitalists, or speculating owners, who have their farms tilled by hired workers. Nearly one hundred thousand of these land barons hold from five hundred to thousands of acres each. We have one million tenant renters, almost as many as there are in Great Britain, cultivating one-fourth of our farms, and three million three hundred and twenty four odd thousand wage workers who do not even rent land. Of the one million five hundred thousand of real farmers who either wholly, or in part, themselves cultivate their holdings, it is estimated that forty per cent have their farms mortgaged to such an extent as to really pay a rent in interest. In many industries we already have a system of pooling and combination to which the much-denounced union tyranny and that of the terrible walking delegate can not hold a candle. Until lately, in all but a few, even the best organized workers could hardly counteract the terror of the ticket-of-leave-plan, by virtue of which it was impossible for the blacklisted unfortunate to obtain employment."

Among the numerous writers on the land question, Mr. Henry George has attracted much attention. In his admirably written book, "Progress and Poverty," he has endeavored to show that the great cause of the inequality in the distribution of wealth lies in the unequal ownership of land. In all probability Mr. George wrote his book between the years of 1873 and 1879, when he saw the evil results of over-importations together with a contraction of our currency. Unfortunately he erred in divining the causes of the country's depression and thereby erred in the remedy he advocates. There can be no doubt that ruin will throttle the nation if our broad acres fall into the hands of a few landlords, but that time will never come. Even though certain speculators and corporations have succeeded in securing an illegal right to vast acres of land, there is no danger o their being able to work other than local inconvenience.

He asks, "Why, in spite of increase in productive power, do wages tend to a minimum which will give but a bare living?" The question is an idle one, for wages, salaries and remuneration of all kinds have steadily risen, notwithstanding fluctuations. At the end of each decade during the past century there has been more and more to divide—that is, when no temporary causes overcame the general cause of financial events. Wages do not tend to a minimum but we find them generally on the increase, and to his proposition that "where population is densest, wealth greatest, and the machinery of production and exchange most highly developed," we say there is not "the deepest poverty, the sharpest struggle for existence and the most enforced idleness." This is clear the moment we compare the workingman of fifty years ago, with the workingman of to-day.

One of the essential ideas of the Georgian theory is, that in as much "as in the nature of things unequal ownership of land is inseparable from the recognition of individual property in land, it necessarily follows that the only remedy for the unjust distribution of wealth is in making land common property."

Mr. George proposes to tax land to its full rental value, and defines his position as follows:

"Let me declare plainly and distinctly, for this is a point on which there is much misapprehension and misrepresentation, that we do not propose to have the state take the land from its present owners and divide it up or rent it out; we simply propose to make such a change in our fiscal system as will shift the burden of taxation from labor and the products of labor, to land values—the value attached to land, irrespective of the improvements upon it; the value attached to land, not by reason of what the occupier has done, but by reasons of the growth of the community. We propose to reach by this easy and gradual change, the end at which we aim, and that aim is, that the man who enjoys the privilege of holding a piece of land that the growth of the community has made valuable, shall pay to the community what the special privilege is worth, and thus all citizens be placed upon an equal footing. When this is done, or even as we approach it, it will become unprofitable for anybody to hold land without using it, in the expectation of becoming rich by the value which attaches to it from the growth of the community. Land will become profitable only to those who want to use it. Thus the dog in the manger will be choked off, and from the vacant lots of our eastern cities to the great tracts held on speculation in the far west, opportunities for employment will be thrown open to labor and forestalling be prevented."

The Utopian idea of confiscating or nationalizing land, is shown in its true light by Prof. W. T. Harris, who exposes the sophistry of this Georgian theory, and demonstrates that the claims concerning the advantage to be gained by taxing land excessively, are false and hollow. He says:

"Mr. George evidently supposes that a revenue equal to the total land-rent of the country would constitute a vast fund, for he says: 'There would be a great and increasing surplus revenue from the taxation of land values, for material progress, which would go on with greatly accelerated rapidity, would tend constantly to increase rent. This revenue arising from the common property could be applied to the common benefit, as were the revenues of Sparta.'

"Mr. George is bound to suppose that the aggregate amount of ground-rent is a very large sum, because he has come to the conclusion that land absorbs, in the form of rent, all the increased production of labor, aided by capital in the shape of labor-saving inventions. If ground-rent produces poverty, by robbing capital and labor, its confiscation would restore enough to labor and capital to remedy the evil. What is the actual amount of this item of rent in the United States?

"The reader of 'Progress and Poverty' is struck with the fact that the book contains no statements derived from painstaking inquiries into the statistics of land values and rents. The book is eloquent and effective, its author evidently an earnest and disinterested philanthropist. But his theories all relate to numbers of population, rates of wages, prices of food, amounts of rent, and the ratios of these numbers to one another. These are not a priori questions, but matters of statistics. There is not only no investigation of statistics in 'Progress and Poverty,' but there is not even an attempt to make definite estimates, although there are occasional references to isolated data. If it should be found that the total ground-rent is an insignificant item compared with the total income of the nation, it would be necessary to conclude that Mr. George is mistaken in supposing that private property in land exercises a power to rob capital and labor.

"The United States census for 1880 gives the total assessment of real estate and personal property, as determined in the several states of the Union, at $16,902,993,543, of which $13,036,766,925 stands for real estate, distributed in such a manner that more than one-half of the amount is assessed in New England and the middle states (about $6,714,-600,000). 'Real estate,' of course, includes land and improvements. The United States census does not give the items for land alone, but the state of Massachusetts publishes an aggregate of property and taxes showing the separate items, 'land exclusive of buildings' and 'buildings exclusive of land.' The former item (land) is $587,824,672; the latter (buildings) is $752,669,001, land being to buildings nearly 44 to 56. This ratio may be assumed to hold good for the entire eastern and middle sections of the country, giving $3,766,000,000 for buildings and $2,948,000,000 for ground. In the southern section it may be assumed that the ratio is reversed, and that the $1,671,000,000 of real estate assessed there represents $671,000,000 as value of buildings and $1,000,000,000 as value of land. In the Western States and Territories, likewise, the total of $4,644,000,000 of real estate may represent at least $2,000,000,000 as value of buildings and not more than $2,644,000,000 as value of land. This will give a total of $6,437,000,000 for buildings and $6,592,000,000 for building sites and agricultural land. The rate of assessment for taxes is usually fixed at two-thirds of the market value. Allowing for this the actual value of all land in the United States owned as private property must have been somewhat less than ten billions (10,000,000,000) for the year 1880. Counting the rent on this land at 4 per cent we have less than $400,000,000 per annum, making an average of nearly $8 for each inhabitant, or a little more than two cents per day.

"The result surprises us. Two cents per day, or $8 per year, added to their income would not bring ease and luxury to those who are struggling with

RICHARD GRIFFITHS,
General Worthy Foreman, K. of L.

poverty. Nor would it amount to a vast revenue in the aggregate as a tax. Four per cent—and it is fair to estimate the return in rent as under this figure, because, when land yields more than this amount in rent, the valuation is at once raised—would give the government only $400,000,000, a sum only slightly in excess of the amount annually paid for local taxes (state, county, township, and district), while the total of taxation, national and local, amounts to nearly $800,000,000. To pay all taxes, both national and local, ground-rent would have to be increased to 7½ per cent.

"To understand the bearings of this, it is necessary to consider the actual annual income of the total population. This income is estimated by Mr. Edward Atkinson, in his 'Distribution of Products,' at the round sum of $10,000,000,000. Mr. Mulhall estimates the total productions of the United States at £1,420,000,000 sterling, or about $7,100,-000,000. The items used for these estimates are given by Mr. Joseph Nimmo, Chief of the National Bureau of Statistics for the year 1884, in a letter to Mr. Atkinson, as follows:

Agriculture	$3,600,000,000
Manufactures	5,369,579,911
Illuminating gas	30,000,000
Mining	236,275,408
Forestry	455,000,000
Fisheries	43,046,053
Meat, and wool clip on ranches	40,000,000
Petroleum	44,000,000
Total	$9,817,900,652

"But in the above estimate the manufactures are given the gross annual value of manufactured goods for 1880, and of course there are repetitions of the same item under different heads. For example, lumber appears as product of saw-mills, and again in the items of wood manufactures and buildings, as well as in the inventory of products of forestry; wool and cotton appear first among the agricultural items, next in the textile productions, and lastly as items in the value of manufactured clothing. Hogs are called a manufacture under the names of pork, lard, and bacon; cattle appear as beef, tallow, hides, leather, horns, hair, glue, and the bones and blood as fertilizers.

"Deducting the materials from the aggregate of manufactures, as given in the census report, the net total is $1,972,755,542. Moreover, in Mr. Nimmo's statement the agricultural product is increased by the total of live stock, which is rather a product of three years than of one—an over estimate of $1,-000,000,000. Besides this, all the hay crop and three-fourths of the Indian-corn crop go to the raising of live stock and are already reckoned in the increase of the live stock. Deduct for these items and the total annual product appears as about $6,000,-000,000. But there is a large amount of produce consumed in the farms that does not get reported in the census schedules. Add to this the manufactures done at the homes, a considerable item, and the earnings of the railroads in so far as they enhance prices by bringing productions to the place of consumption, and the actual annual income may be safely placed at a little over seven and a quarter billions—say $7,300,000,000. This would give 40 cents per day, or $146 per year, for each inhabitant. The total taxation, national and local, takes four and one-fifth cents per day, one-tenth of the average income. The ground-rent amounts to only one-eighteenth of the total average earnings. If this would make any great difference in the wages of the poor, it is certain that a small grain of economy would go much further.

"Capital has its hand at the throat of land property, contrary to the theory of Mr. George, who supposes that land is throttling capital and labor. Capital frees labor from the tyranny of land, and the present ratio of land to the total wealth of the United States is less than one to four. In the United Kingdom it forms only one-fifth of the total wealth, being only £1,737,000,000 sterling, with an annual rental of £65,442,000, while the total wealth is £8,720,000,000.

"Wages seem to be fast receding from that 'minimum that will give but a bare living.' But it is the wages of the skilled mechanics and manufacturers that have increased most. The wages of farm hands are much below the wages of those engaged in manufacturing industries. As there is one wage-earner to three persons, or, more accurately, to 2.9 persons, it is clear that all laborers who get over $1.35 per day, or $34.80 per month, get more than they would get if the total annual production were divided equally among the wage-earners without allowing anything to capital or land.

"By this it will be seen that all our skilled laborers, and a considerable number of common laborers, are paid now at higher rates than a socialistic division would give them. All who are receiving over $34.80 per month in wages are on the side of the 'bloated bondholder' already, and cannot complain of land or capital as robbing them of the products of their labor. Skilled labor in the mechanic industries gets from twenty to eighty per cent more than this average. But the farming population of the country get from twenty to eighty per cent less. And it is on the farming population that the burden of a high land tax would fall with the utmost severity. A seven per cent tax on land would destroy our agricultural interests, all except the market gardening. No grain could be exported, and, without a protective tariff, none could be raised for the home market."

To assess all taxes upon real estate would give the government immense revenues during periods of fluctuation and excitement, the use of which would tend to evil results, and leave it without necessary revenue during times of depression and when disbursements would be most beneficial. The present laws of taxation are not without genuine merit, and were they executed according to their intent, a just and adequate revenue would be secured. Any and all evils which may be current, arise from the fact that true assessments are not made. When property is justly assessed every man will pay a proper tax, and a sufficient revenue will be the result. The capitalist will pay as great an amount, in proportion to his possessions, as the middle class, or the poor man.

The chief obstacle to a fair assessment is perjury. Many a man who passes for honest in a community will swear to a return which he knows is false, if a sworn statement is necessary to get his valuation down to a notch satisfactory to himself. The amount of this kind of crime committed is appalling. The instances of punishment are so very few that the fear of the penitentiary is too remote to be a deterrent.

A large latitude is allowable for variation in estimates, but where a stock of goods, for example, which would inventory at $20,000 is sworn to be worth only $1,000, the perjury is too flagrant to escape conviction upon a fair presentation of the case to a jury. The vigorous prosecution of such criminals would do more to reform the revenue than all the legislation devisable. The first step in this reformatory direction should be taken by these town boards of review, either as boards or individually. The order of proceeding is not important. The knowledge that such perjury has been committed, however obtained, should reach the grand jury—or, to be more exact, the grand jury should have sufficient ground to suspect perjury to occasion a call for the sworn statement, the examination of which should be followed up by an investigation.

Let it once be understood that the law means something when it prescribes a punishment of from one year to ten years in the penitentiary for perjury in an assessment return, and an era of reform will follow in its train. The boodler who steals the public money has a fellow-criminal in the property-owner who evades by false return the payment of his fair share of the common tax, and no cloak of respectability should shield either from the penal consequences of his crime. In a word, the town review should be supplemented by a grand jury review, with all the subsequent proceedings naturally following in the train of grand jury work faithfully done.

CHAPTER III.

THE GREAT QUESTION OF MONEY AND LABOR.

THE PROBLEM WHICH ALL NATIONS ARE CONSIDERING—WEALTH RIGHTFULLY BELONGS TO THE PRODUCER—ECONOMISTS AND THE PRECIOUS METALS—CHARACTERISTICS OF MONEY—MONETARY STANDARDS OF DIFFERENT NATIONS—THE GOLD STANDARD—THE SILVER STANDARD—THE DOUBLE STANDARD—HISTORY OF BANKING—RISE OF THE NATIONAL BANKS—OPINIONS OF STATESMEN—LABOR AND CAPITAL—THE WAGE FUND PRINCIPLE—PROFITS AND WAGES—THE ATTITUDE OF LABOR—INFLATION OF CURRENCY—HON. ALFRED TAYLOR'S REMARKS—DANIEL WEBSTER ON LABOR—MONEY THE GREAT HUMAN BLESSING—VOLUME OF MONEY—LINCOLN'S IDEAS—HORACE GREELY—BURKE—THE NEW ISSUES OF TO-DAY.

The greatest question in political economy is that of money and its distribution. It is now the problem which occupies the attention of the statesmen of England, France, and Germany, and it is destined to be the great question in this country.

Political economy designates the laws which govern the accumulation of money, but its distribution depends largely upon legislation and custom. Wealth created by the workingman in these times has a decided tendency to accumulate in the coffers of individuals and corporations, where it is often used for the oppression of the laborer. Naturally wealth belongs to the person who produces it, to the workingman, but he is obliged to give up the greater portion of it to the non-producer, or capitalist.

The primary idea of capital is, that it is obtained by giving a service whose market value is equal to the capital. But what service has the man who has accumulated a hundred million dollars in his own lifetime performed which can be compared in value to the wealth which he has gained? There is no comparison between the service and the pay of such men, and this is becoming more and more clear to the laboring millions. The man, woman or child, who earns a livelihood by manual labor gets too little, and the smart man who wins a fortune by dexterity gets too much. The wealth of the world is too unevenly distributed, and the laborer is finding it out. What if he should make a new distribution in some future day as the common people of France did in 1793?

At present there is little fear of any such thing in this country, because of the vast domain of unoccupied free land which the laborer can have by settling it. But the lands will by-and-by be occupied, and at a not very distant day, and then problems will arise in this country more difficult to solve than have ever yet arisen in Europe; for when the European hive becomes too crowded, the surplus laborers can come to America where all may secure a farm; but when there is no more land to grant, then will come the pinch.

There are certain characteristics upon which the majority of political economists agree, as being essential to substances used for money. These characteristics are attributed to the precious metals—gold and silver.

They have intrinsic value, besides their use as money. When either of these metals are demonetized their value diminishes.

Good authorities hold that being simple substances, and easily transportable, that they are universally of the same value. This is denied, however, by eminent writers, and it is obvious that money must vary with the scale of usual prices.

They have great value in small bulk.

These metals are indestructible, and they wear but little with constant use.

They are of universal use, and are capable of being stamped as to mark their value.

It is not known where coinage began, but it is fairly decided that it was in Asia, about 880 B. C. Although the precious metals have been most employed for money, many other substances have been used, viz., paper, iron, leather, wheat, tobacco, wood, shells, beads, skins, bark, etc.

The monetary standard has always been subject to change, and is an open question. Some countries have fixed upon gold, some upon silver, and others upon both.

Years ago Germany adopted silver, and has recently changed to gold. The single standard of silver is the rule with Russia and Austria, though they have no specie payment. Nearly all of Asia uses silver as a standard, as do a few nations on the American continent—in all about one-third of the population of the world.

The Latin Monetary Union—France, Italy, Belgium, Switzerland and Spain—adhere to the double standard, though the coinage of silver has been restricted, and for a time enjoined. About thirty years ago Holland adopted silver, but now has a gold standard.

England was the first nation to try the experiment of the gold standard, sixty-nine years ago, and it now exists in Australia, South Africa, Egypt, Turkey, Portugal, and in the Scandinavian kingdoms. The United States adopted gold in 1873, but returned to the double standard in 1878. In all these countries silver is made a legal tender for a small amount, and is used as a subsidiary coin.

As early as about two hundred and sixty years before the Christian era, a banker of Sicyon, a city of Peloponnesus, is mentioned by Plutarch in his life of Aratus. His business appears to have consisted in exchanging one species of money for another. The money-changers of Judea, who were driven out of the temple by Christ, were most probably of the description mentioned by St. Matthew in the parable of the talents—that is, such as made a trade of receiving money in deposit, and paying interest for it. St. Luke, in his relation of the same parable, expressly alludes to a banking establishment.

From Judea the institution of banks was brought into Europe; and the Lombard Jews are said to have kept benches, or banks, in the market places of Italy for the exchange of money and bills. The Bank of Venice, which was the first foundation upon an enlarged scale that we are acquainted with, was established about the year 1171, under the appellation of the Chamber of Loans (la Camera degl' Imprestiti), and the contributors to a forced loan, that had been raised to meet the exigencies of a Venetian war with the emperors of the East and West, were made creditors of the Chamber, from which they were to receive an annual interest of four per cent.

At what period the knowledge of banking was introduced into England is unknown, though it may reasonably be conjectured to have been within a short time after the conquest. There can be little doubt of its having been first practiced here by the Italian merchants, all of whom, who were engaged in money transactions, were distinguished, both in France and in England, by the name of Lombards, or of Tuscans. These merchants being dispersed throughout Europe, "became (says Anderson) very convenient agents for the popes, who employed them to receive and remit the large revenues they drew from every state which acknowleged their ecclesiastical supremacy. Hence, and from their being employed to lend the money thus gathered upon interest, they are called by Matthew Paris "the Pope's merchants." We learn from the same historian that some of the English nobles availed themselves of the same agency, and " sowed their money to make it multiply."

Henry III, in his twenty-ninth year, forbade his subjects to borrow money from any foreign merchants. This was on account of the great exactions which they are said to have committed. In the fourteenth century the business of banking was carried on by the drapers, at Barcelona, in Spain; as it was in after ages by the goldsmiths of London. Banking began in Italy, by Lombard Jews, in the year 808; that of Genoa, 1345; of Amsterdam, 1609; of Rotterdam, 1635; of England, 1694; of Hamburg, 1710; in the East Indies, 1787; in America, 1781, at Philadelphia. Bankers, on their first establishment, allowed to those who entrusted their money in their hands a moderate interest for the same. Thereby their business was very considerably increased.

The first bank in America was established by Mr. R. Morris, the Superintendent of Finance, and a delegate to the Continental congress. In May of that year congress gave its sanction to the plan of a national bank, and the Bank of North America had a legal existence. The hostility to national banks began with their organization, and in 1829 President Jackson condemned the renewal of their charters in his first annual message to congress. In 1833 President Jackson removed the government deposits from the United States Bank, and placed them in state banks, which were called "State Deposit Banks." A large number of local banks were then organized with the result of effecting an enormous amount of speculation and overtrading, and "wild cat" banking became rampant throughout the western states.

In 1836 the surplus money belonging to the United States treasury was distributed to the state banks, and to check speculation in public lands the President prohibited the receipt of anything but silver and gold in payment for land sold by the government. A year later the panic of 1837 paralyzed the nation. The funding of greenbacks into six per cent gold bonds was revoked in 1863, which rendered them irredeemable, and credit became so expanded under excessive issues of paper money, that the abuse of credit became general. The great paper bubble burst in 1873, and a general panic was the result.

The vexed question of the proper adjustment of financial matters is the source of several theories, and their discussion has always been foremost in legislative halls.

Our leading statesmen have frequently changed their opinions of the financial policy of the land. In 1791 James Madison opposed the first United States bank, and in 1816, when president, recommended the second United States bank. The same course was pursued by Henry Clay and Daniel Webster. Thomas Jefferson acted likewise. General Jackson and Mr. Van Buren favored state deposit banks in 1833, and four years later changed their minds.

The business world has been centuries in learning that wealth is not money, but consists of the abundance of those things which command money. Money is only the instrument of exchange for the articles comprising wealth. Some nations have been so carried away with the opposite notion, that it became the object of legislation to prevent exportation of the precious metals, as such was thought to diminish the wealth of the country.

The rich and the poor are two classes which are antagonistic, notwithstanding all that has been said and written about their mutual dependence. The history of man does not present a picture like that of the present, nor has the combination of circumstances seen to-day ever existed in the past. The invention of printing, telegraph, steam engine; the use of labor-saving machinery; the great increase of monopolies and the intellectual development of the masses have created a new era. The people are beginning to think and are beginning an attempt to better their condition.

It is often said that capital and labor are dependent upon each other, but it is also true that labor can secure many of the advantages held by capital, by combination or co-operation. Labor is undoubtedly the true source of capital. Under the present system the power of capital to accumulate exceeds the power of labor to produce. This fault lies in unjust legislation.

The riotous events and the exciting strikes of late years have elicited much thought and attention. In brief, it is a new phase of our history as a nation. It is a lesson which will bear good fruit. America with its millions of acres of yet uncultivated land, hundreds of inexhaustible mines yet unworked, is far from being cramped in resources, but unjust laws continually cast the pall of hard times upon the productive classes.

In the beginning of the present century about seven-eights of our population were farmers, while the last census shows a balance against agricultural pursuits. New trades and employments have sprung up, and the divisions of labor have multiplied. Out of this new order of things trades unions have come into life, and the natural differences between capital and labor have been brought out in intensified contrasts. Labor has hitherto been entirely ignorant of the economic laws which govern the conditions in which it exists, but to-day education is enabling it to comprehend them better. It is not to be denied that money is the great and only true basis of our social condition.

The grievance of labor does not lie on a social plane. Labor seeks to be treated humanely, irrespective of wages, and not like a machine or a brute. The fate of the workingman's wages is placed between two causes—that which reduces the competition of labor, and that which produces capital. The wage-fund principle teaches that the wages labor will receive, at any time or in any trade, is simply a question of division; capital may be called the dividend, the number of workingmen the divisor, and the quotient that amount which each workingman receives as wages. There are but two ways of increasing the latter—either increase the dividend or decrease the divisor. In each case wages increase.

Labor is interested in high profits as much as capital, for capital employs labor. How to increase capital has been a problem which all modern peoples have industriously attempted to solve. When labor and capital demand each other equally, happiness, peace and plenty result.

There have arisen various theories and conflicts between them in regard to commerce, free trade, protection, agriculture and manufactures, and partisans are urging their policies with zeal and all the ardor of positive conviction, and they say the prosperity of the country lies in the adoption of their theories. Many of these have arisen from local causes, and are doomed to defeat through lack of national importance.

In the use and misuse of profits lies a great power in the industrial world. Labor has a well grounded complaint in the abuse of capital, yet it is impossible to direct how wealth shall be spent by its owner. The investment of capital in productive industry advances the interests of the workingman, and profits inure to both capital and labor.

The workingman is not entirely without blame in the matter of ill-spent money. The amount of money spent for tobacco and liquor exceeds that expended for any other two articles, and in this he is wrong for he injures no one so much as himself.

Labor is grieved and angry at the injustice with which it feels that capital oppresses it, and in defense, it has organized the greatest labor order the world has ever known. In truth, there should be no antagonizm between capital and labor, for labor produces capital. If there were no capital there could be no industrial labor. One is helpless without the other. Should labor cease for forty-eight hours capital would take flight and want would stalk the earth. Labor needs the guidance of honest leaders rather than the violence of scheming demagogues.

It is probable the present conflict between labor and capital originates in a misunderstanding: capital does not comprehend labor, and labor does not understand capital.

Hon. Alfred Taylor says: It is the duty of every

healthy person to be self-sustaining and contribute some good by his energy, either mental or physical, for the blessing he enjoys in his life. Everything that adds to the happiness of life is the result of somebody's mental or physical exertion, and to enjoy it without an equivalent is to be a drone and a sponger of another's toil. The scriptures inform us that in six days God made the heavens and the earth, and all things therein. Not only setting an example of an industrial life, but dignifying its mission. Those that plow the soil, sow the seed and raise the food and weave the cloths, and build the shelter and create a nation's wealth, should be rich and enjoy life instead of struggling for existence, as they now do beneath mortgaged homes and burdensome taxes and blighted lives. The larger the fortunes of the few, the greater the hardships of the many. A class of men who will neither work, fight nor pay taxes; who have inspired class laws in order to extort fabulous private fortunes, and thereby they have excited envy, jealousy and discontent on the one hand, and selfishness, aggression, tyranny and crime on the other. Sculptured palaces are the immediate parents of the distressed hovel. Must religion build extravagant churches, trade its costly warehouses, wealth its long streets of sculptured mansions, and luxury flaunt its voluptuous trappings in the face of the industrial poor, debasing manhood, forcing them into vice and crime? President Lincoln said in his second message: "Labor is prior to and independent of capital. Capital is only the fruit of labor and could never have existed if labor had not first existed. Labor is the superior and deserves much higher consideration."

Webster said in his speech in 1837: "The interest of this great country, the principal cause of all prosperity, is labor, labor, labor. The government was made to protect this industry; to give it both encouragement and security, to that very end, with this precise object in view, power was given to Congress over the currency and over the money system of the country."

Let us swear to make labor profitable and respectable, whether it be hand work or brain work. Labor and capital are joint partners in the production of wealth. Capital is to labor what the skillful hand is to the useful tool. Interest and profit determines what each shall have. Then there would be no antagonism, unless one extorted from the other and brought on the conflict.

The claims of labor can be no more forcibly shown than wealth in a state of nature. Trees in the forest, rock in the quarry, iron in the mountain, bricks in the clay, or glass from sand on the sea shore. In their primitive condition they are almost worthless. Built into a mansion they furnish most of the comforts and luxury of life, whose value is increased a thousand fold and ought to receive the first attention of its legislator.

Men in affluent circumstances having no occasion for temptation claim superior nature, honesty, which keeps them from crime, when, in fact, it is only fortunate circumstances in life. Upon scanty allowance, coupled with hard work, they would be frequently ugly and criminal. A prominent divine once told his congregation of merchants, bankers and speculators that he was on too high a plane to be affected by a temptation to steal. He was then getting $20,000 per annum for his talk.

Money is an instrument susceptible of being the greatest blessing human ingenuity ever invented. Money to commerce is what blood is to the system; money to commerce is what water is to navigation, or freight cars to railroad traffic. To shrink their quantity clogs the channels of trade. All the political economists from Richards to Mill, admit that expansion of money is life, that contraction is death, and that the amount of money in circulation controls and fixes values and prices of all commodities, including land and labor. We have but two kinds of dollars in this country, one of gold, the other of silver. All others are a promise to pay a dollar, or be redeemed in coin. Any circulating medium whether of coin, or paper, that is not a full legal tender for public or private debts, is a fraud and a cheat. The control over the volume of money is mainly in the hands of the national banks, together with the right and profit of issue. A usurped sovereign power they will never surrender, because of its profit, until compelled to do so by law.

The volume of money in the United States as

shown by congressional speeches, is from $12 to $13 per capita. Subtract what is on deposit and held for redemption purposes, and there will not be left more than $9.70 per capita available for actual business. Great Britain, thirty times smaller in area, and only about two-thirds our population, has $23.70 per capita. France with her 200,000 square miles of territory, has $43 per capita and her people comparatively out of debt. Such are the facts, as unwelcome as they may be.

Those countries are densely populated as compared with ours, and the facilities of exchange far more convenient than in a country as expansive as this, and because of its wide distribution, payments of debts cannot proceed with the same rapidity.

The bank of England was established in 1794, and is 93 years old. It was originated by a London merchant by the name of Patterson, and was first chartered for eleven years. It has suspended specie payment eleven times, one of which lasted twenty-six years, each time tearing down the columns of British commerce and spreading financial distress, not only in England, but frequently in other nations. With all its boasted pride of gold redemption, its bank notes have been 41 per cent below par. Its mode of resumption has been invariably over the road of contraction, the path of gloom and despair, where nothing flourishes but poverty and crime.

Abraham Lincoln expressed to an intimate friend

a short time before he was assassinated, that he very much doubted whether there was moral virtue and patriotism enough among the controlling classes to perpetuate our institutions.

Mr. Greely upon his death bed said. "TheTribune and country are gone, and I am going."

The permanence of the government can only be secured by such property qualification as will prevent those who have no interest in the country from voting and controlling its affairs, shouts Hugh Mc-Cullough, ex-secretary of the treasury, the prime criminal of modern times. Government authority never shows its weakness and demoralized condition so much as when it resorts to physical and brute force to carry its ends.

Cæsar said: "The ides of March have come." When they had passed he was lifeless at the foot of Pompey's statue. Bloated wealth can never comprehend the suffering of the poor. Mary Antoinette, when told that the fisherwomen were revolting because they had no bread, replied in her confused ignorance with the insult, "Why don't they eat cake?" When Paris was in a wild tumult the king played locksmith to avoid the danger, and wrote in his diary, "Nothing in particular happened to-day." Yet they had moved the foundation of his monarchy. Charles I, with contempt for the people, said: "France needs mowing," and asked, "What can these round-heads do?" and he told them to go and eat grass. In one week from that time they were carrying his head on a pole. Rousseau wrote a book pleading for honesty and purity in the French government, which was treated with contempt by the aristocratic class. Carlisle says the second edition of that book "was bound in the skins of the sneering aristocracy."

The gold standard, the swindling bond system, the demonetizing of silver, the funding and refunding of national debts, the changing of inflated paper debts to a gold standard, is not the work of statesmen; it is the work of cunning, crafty tricksters, who betray their exalted trust, and barter away the most sacred principles of a confiding people. They are traitors to the republican form of government, and clamor for the gold standard to pile up collossal fortunes, notwithstanding it is the prop of a monarchy, and leads to a centralized government of force, resting on a standing army.

Nothing can be permanent based on a sham. Our banking system is based on debt, while debt and interest mean bankruptcy and the transfer of labor and property, without an equivalent.

To illustrate, I cite the following as only one of hundreds that took place in the years 1863 and 1864: $10,000,000 of United States bonds were sold in New York in 1863 when gold was $2.57 in greenbacks, which cost the bondholder in gold about $3,900,000; during the last fifteen years the interest amounted in gold, when the bonds were called and paid, to $9,900,000; and the principal, $10,000,000, making a total of $19,900,000; subtract purchase money, $3,900,000, and this leaves a net profit of $16,000,000.

King Philip said he had "no faith in the patriotism of any class of men who would be made to do wrong for a jackass load of gold." To first impoverish and then enslave, has been the history of the downfall of all republics. Do not imagine for a moment that our languishing industries and low price of agricultural commodities, is the lack of wisdom in legislation. Far from it. It is the work of a well-organized conspiracy, well known and long practiced in Europe, and forced upon this country by long-headed foreign tricksters. We have already paid the cost of the war in interest, the principal of which is over double in amount to-day, considering the price of labor and its commodities, as compared with what it was at the close of the war. A statesman has said that were it not for the the energy and enterprise of the people and fertility of the soil, American society would pine away beneath the blighting influence of marasmus. If national debt brought about by inflated paper currency was ever settled upon a gold basis, history fails to record the fact.

Burke says: 'It is to the life and property of the citizens, and not to the demand of the creditor of the state, that the original faith of society is pledged. The claim of the citizen is prior in time, paramount in title and supreme in equity.' The bondholder demonstrates why should a United States bond be guaranteed against all loss by storm, pestilence, war, and famine, exempt from taxation, principal and interest payable in gold and for ever afterward a lien upon everybody's property. Before the shrinkage in values took place, the long-headed men sold their property, invested it in bonds, moved into the towns and cities of the country and commenced clipping coupons, occasionally giving one to a gold-basis editor, who shouts the delusion that a national debt is a national blessing, the financial questions are settled, and gold and greenbacks are par.

Political parties have their birth, growth and maturity by first serving the people with fidelity on the vital questions of the day. When they have accomplished their mission and become rich and powerful, they boast of by-gone issues and fight battles over where they have once won a victory, and use their historic fame by appealing to the people for a new lease of power to acquire private fortunes by discriminating laws. No love or hate of old party issues, no pride or prejudice born of old conflicts should control your vote. New issues are upon us, and new ideas and new votes must pave the way for industrial emancipation, and then comes the tangible reality."

CHAPTER IV.

GOVERNMENT LOANS TO THE PEOPLE.[1]

MAN SHALL EARN HIS BREAD BY THE SWEAT OF HIS BROW—INTEREST AND USURY—THE MOSAIC LAW—THE POWER OF INTEREST—ILLUSTRATIONS—LOANS TO THE PEOPLE A FEASIBLE PROJECT—THE GOVERNMENT LOANS TO THE BANKERS—LOANS TO THE PEOPLE AT A LOW RATE WOULD BE A BLESSING—HOW THE FARMERS WOULD SECURE PROSPERITY—MILLIONAIRES AND PAUPERS ARE INCREASING—REGULATION OF THE VOLUME OF MONEY—GARFIELD'S THEORY—TOTAL NATIONAL DEBT—HYPOCRITICAL POLITICIANS—USURY NOTHING MORE THAN ROBBERY.

"It is a decree of heaven that every man shall earn his bread by the sweat of his brow," and no man will deny that it is just and proper. Furthermore, it will not be disputed that every man has a right to the product of his own labor. Under the present order of things men do not get the benefit of that which they produce, neither is it the practice for all men to earn the bread they eat. The rule

---

[1] By Hon. W. D. Vincent, L. A., 3797, K. of L.

FREDERICK TURNER,
General Treasurer, K. of L.

now is, and has been, that the man who earns the most gets the least, and he who earns the least gets the most.

A careful study of the subject of interest will convince any reasonable mind that it has been one of the leading causes in bringing about this state of affairs. Usury or interest upon money (which is one and the same thing), has been condemned by the better class of thinking men in all ages of the world —God himself condemns it. "Thou shalt not lend thy brother money upon usury." It was strictly prohibited by the Mosaic law; and for many years after Christ established the new order of things, any person in the church who was known to pursue or defend the practice of usury was subject to expulsion. It was prohibited because it was wrong. If it was wrong then it is wrong now. From no process of reasoning can we conclude that it is any nearer right now, than it was when Christ drove the money changers out of the temple.

Every state in the union has enacted laws against the taking of interest above a certain per centage. True, these laws are not enforced, but the fact that they remain on the statute books is proof that the law-makers themselves know that high rates of interest are bad for the people. It is impossible for anyone who has the welfare of his country at heart to uphold a system that will enable men to exact high rates of interest. On the other hand, it is equally unjust to oppose any reform that would lower the rate of interest. As before stated, the existing usury laws are not enforced, and under the present system it is absolutely impossible to enforce them.

The only way to form a proper idea of the power of interest to absorb is to make our estimates for long periods of time. Laws should be made, not only in the interest of all the people and on the principle of "the greatest good to the greatest number," but they should be made for the people of the next generation, as well as those who are now living.

We have no right to enact laws that will be detrimental to our children, or to oppose any measure that will be beneficial to them. We have no right to uphold customs which, even though they may not materially affect us, will eventually make paupers of a majority of our people. Three hundred years is a very short time in the history of a nation, yet if this government should give its note to-day for one dollar due three hundred years from date, at 10 per cent compound interest, the debt at maturity would be four times greater than the present assessed valuation of all the property in the United States.

The farmer mortgages his place to-day for $1,000 at 12 per cent compounded annually, and leaves the debt for his grandson to pay one hundred years after date. At the end of the time the young man finds a debt of $84,675,000 on his hands. If the three generations have done well and worked hard, the farm is worth $50,000. If sold, it will pay less than one mill on the dollar.

One dollar put out at interest—2 per cent per month compounded annually—if allowed to run one hundred years would amount to the enormous sum of $2,551,797,404. In silver dollars this would weigh 89,612 tons.

Two young men, James and John, start out in life at the age of twenty-one, with $1,000 each. James invests his money in a farm. At the end of twenty-five years, if he has no bad luck—if drouth and grasshoppers have not visited him too often, and if he has been able to stem the tide of periodical panics, he is worth $40,000. He has accumulated this by hard work and the strictest economy, together with the increase in the value of his farm.

John settles in town and establishes a "loan agency." He is very shrewd, and manages to keep half his capital loaned out all the time at 2 per cent per month, compounded every three months. At the end of twenty-five years he is worth $170,000. He has performed no labor except to drive a good bargain when he could. James, the farmer, has worked hard through heat and cold, from early morn till late at night. He has been trying to keep up with his friend John, and has not taken the time to read good books and study finance. He has neglected the art of "addition, multiplication and silence." But he has produced something. He has helped develop the country, and has added something to the world's wealth. Yet he is worth $130,000 less than John the money loaner, who has done nothing and added not one dollar to the resources of his country.

Now we claim that this order of things should be reversed. If any one has the advantage, it should be the man who chooses to labor and build up the country, and not the man who decides to do nothing but accumulate the products of other men's labor. One of the greatest means for the accomplishment of this end is, for the government to loan money, in limited quantities, at a low rate of interest—the rate to be determined after proper deliberation. I am aware of the prejudice that exists against new ideas, and the proposition for the government to loan money to poor people, is a new idea. The proposition has never been thought of, or agitated by the people to any extent. This will be one of the arguments used by our opponents. They will tell us that it is an experiment.

I answer that government control of the postal system was once a new thing, and an experiment.

Is that any reason why it should not be adopted? It is an admitted fact that the people derive more benefits from the postal service, as administered by the government, than from any other service of a public nature, as compared to the cost. And it will not be denied that if this system were operated by private individuals and corporations, it would be made a means of oppression and extortion, equal to that which is now carried on by railroad, telegraph, standard oil and moneyed monopolies. Every function that is now performed by the government, was once performed by individuals, and that unfortunate state of affairs would exist to-day, but for experiments and new ideas. Government itself was a new idea. Republican form of government is an experiment to-day, and yet I dare say the people do not wish it to be abandoned. The threshing machine, the printing press, the railroad, the telegraph and the telephone are among the fruitful effects of experiments and new ideas. This is an age of progression, and none but the antiquated "fogy" will adhere to old opinions because they are old, or oppose new ones because they are new.

Our government has been in the loan business for almost a quarter of a century. For twenty-three years it has loaned out to national bankers over $300,000,000 at one per cent a year. Instead of loaning it out to poor men who needed it most, it has been loaning to a wealthy class who have needed it least. During all this time while all these rich men have been borrowing at one per cent they have been loaning the same money to their poor neighbors at from 12 to 24 per cent. This is a fact so well known and an injustice so glaring, that no argument is necessary to demonstrate its truth or evil effects. The system under which this outrage is permitted is so contemptibly wicked, that I dare say that its defense will not be undertaken.

It is a self-evident fact that if the banker gets money of the government at one per cent, the farmer ought to get it at the same rate, if he can furnish as good security. No one can possibly deny this, unless he takes the position that our government should be run in the interest of the rich at the expense of the poor. On the contrary, I claim that the government should loan only to the poor. The rich man can take care of himself. But, if he cannot, if he finds this life too great a burden because of his riches, let him follow the Bible injunction, and give what he has to the poor.

What harm can possibly arise from government loans? Suppose the people get the money at three per cent interest. One per cent to go the county, in which the loan is made; one per cent to the state, and one per cent to the national government. In this way the people as a whole, would get back every dollar of interest paid by individuals. These several governments—county, state and national—would be benefited to the extent of every dollar of interest paid. Whatever benefits the government, under a just system of laws, benefits the people.

The men who are now loaning money from 12 to 48, and a few as high as 60 per cent, would be compelled to come down to 3 per cent, or go out of business. The consequence would be that most of them would quit the business, and take up some other calling. This of itself would be a blessing. There are to-day thousands of men who are making their living, or a greater part of it, by loaning money. Many of them do nothing else, and they are rapidly accumulating wealth. These men are positively not doing one thing toward developing the country. They are not adding one dollar of wealth to it. They do not even earn the salt that goes in the bread they eat, They consume as much as the producer, or more, but they pay for it with money that has been wrung from the producer by an unjust system. These men are living on the products of other men's toil.

And yet we cannot blame these men. They are not responsible for the system, and without a change we could hardly get along without them. They are not, as a rule, more selfish than other men. They are virtually nothing but public paupers, but if the people have no more judgment than to support them, by keeping up the system, they should find fault with no one but themselves. We are apt to choose a calling which we think will bring us in the greatest returns.

Every man in one sense of the word, is free to choose for himself with this exception. No man can go into the money-loaning business, if he has no money. The man who is now loaning money might have chosen to be a farmer, and the farmers might have decided to loan money, but this does not correct the evil. It is no proof that men should come into possession of that which they do not earn. If by some means men were compelled to change conditions—if those who are now poor should become rich, and those who are now rich should become poor, the fact would remain that one class of society would be getting the benefit of the hard earnings of another class. The injustice and hardships would be just as great.

That we all have equal chances is the language of the professional gambler. This he offers as consolation to his poor victim, and the deluded wretch will go off and repeat it. And while we often find the men who are suffering most from the curse of usury defending it, yet the fact remains that it is a curse. John Brown was the best friend the African slaves ever had, and yet they were among the first to resist him when he sought to free them. Verily, ignorance and prejudice cover more sins than charity.

We expect to hear from the opponents of this measure a great deal of talk about "an army of paid clerks"—that the people do not need a guardian. In the absence of argument they will offer for your consideration a long list of high sounding words and phrases. Ridicule will doubtless be resorted to, as that is one of the means used in fighting every just measure. When a lawyer has a weak case he invariably resorts to ridicule or abuse, and sometimes both. If they are consistent they will tell you that it is not the government's business to look after the people—that "we are not our brothers keeper." Forgetting that this language was used first by a murderer who was trying to conceal his crime.

Who can estimate the benefit our country would derive in one hundred years time from this vast army of men, if they were compelled to engage in some useful occupation? If they could get but 3 per cent for their money, they would prefer to invest in some factory or other enterprise, for the employment of labor. This would increase the demand and price for labor. Their money would soon be in circulation in the hands of the people, without their having to pay one cent of interest. One or two men would be able to do the work of these men, and in a short time the postmasters at the different county seats would be able to do it in addition to their other duties.

People would become so prosperous that few would want to borrow, even at 3 per cent. The farmer who is now paying these high rates of interest can lift the mortgage on his place with 3 per cent money, and gradually get out of debt. If it is expected that he will ever get out of debt, by paying the present rate of interest, it must be admitted that he can get out sooner at a lower rate. It must also be admitted, that the less interest money he is compelled to pay, the more prosperous he is. His increased prosperity enables him to pay—compels him to pay—an increased price for labor. In this way the poor man who has no property to put up as security, derives a benefit from government loans.

The men who now own their farms will be able to keep them. They will not be compelled to sell them to keep the sheriff from making a sale. How many of the men who owned farms fifteen years ago own them now? I venture to say not more than one in twenty. What has become of the other nineteen? Most of them were compelled to sell out. Old Shylock had a death grip on them. They have gone further west where land is cheaper.

In a few years from now, many more of our farmers will have to travel the same road. In fact they are traveling that road to-day. We are told that this is a benefit to our country. That wealthier men are taking the places of the poor ones, who are moving away. This is true, but it only proves that poor men are being crowded to the wall for the benefit of those with greater capital. But this is not a matter of such serious consequence so long as there is plenty of vacant lands. But "Uncle Sam" will not always be rich enough to give us all a farm.

When the government land is all occupied, which can only be a few years at the longest, and these poor wretches are no longer able to find cheap lands, what will be the result? They will become tenants, subject in time to eviction and all the attendant evils of a British landlord system. But we are told the American people will never submit to it. They would have been compelled to submit to it, ere this had it not been for our boundless resources, and unlimited area of public land.

Our country has prospered. Indeed it has. Our resources and natural advantages are greater than those of any other nation on earth. America is still the best country in the world and, as good patriotic citizens, we should strive to keep it so. We have prospered in spite of bad laws and wicked systems, but not because of them. We even prospered in spite of African slavery, but that prosperity was not due to slavery. Neither is our present prosperity due to the usury system. While our material wealth has increased at a wonderful rate, it has been, and is being now, concentrated in a few men's hands. Millionaires and paupers are also increasing. There must naturally follow hundreds of paupers for every millionaire.

"There are two things," says Socrates, "which the magistrates of Athens will be careful to keep out of our city—opulence and poverty. Opulence because it engenders effeminacy; poverty because it produces baseness; both because they lead to revolution."

It has well been said that these two evils go hand in hand. One cannot exist without the other. They are the two extremes of one evil.

Another consideration of government loans will be the regulation of the volume of money. As the law now stands, the bankers can expand or contract the volume of money to almost any extent. It was only a few years ago—1878—that they gave us an illustration of their power, withdrawing $19,000,000 from circulation in a few weeks' time, almost producing a panic, and compelling the president of the United States to veto a law of congress.

About that time, the bank journals of the east openly boasted that the banks, by concerted action, could in a short time defeat any measure of congress that was detrimental to their interests. We all know the effect of contraction and expansion of the volume of money. The price of every day's labor, and every bushel of grain, is regulated by it. By this means the bankers have it in their power to make low prices or high prices, and they never fail to use this power in their own interests. In a speech in congress, Garfield said, "Whoever controls the volume of our currency is absolute master of the industries and commerce of the country."

With government loans, under proper regulations, this power would be taken out of the hands of the bankers and placed in the hands of the people. It may be said that if it is wrong for individuals to loan money, it is wrong for the government. But this is not true. The government may properly—and must necessarily—do many things which would be improper for individuals to do. The government makes money, but if the individual undertakes it, although he may use the same material and make a perfect imitation, he is sentenced to state's prison.

CHARLES H. LITCHMAN,
General Secretary, K. of L.

Then again, the people as a whole, get every dollar of money derived from government loans.

Under the present system a favored class get it. In the one case the people get the benefit; in the other, a few rich speculators derive all the benefits at the expense of the poorest class in the community. We have only to choose between these two classes. Which shall be rewarded, the poor laborer or the wealthy idler?

It is often said that men have the same right to receive pay for the use of money, that they have to receive pay for the use of a horse. Again there is a difference. Money is not only a public necessity but it is a medium of exchange, an implement of trade and, in one sense, a measure of values. It is the only legal tender for the payment of debts. To be in debt is to be a slave, and he who controls the one thing that can legally cancel a debt is the master. And as Mr. Garfield has said, is absolute dictator over our industries and commerce.

We have already seen how the wealthy—and by the way, one of the most "dangerous classes"—may control it by means of usury. One dollar, or even one cent, placed at the lowest possible rate of interest, if allowed to run long enough, will absorb every dollar in the world. This fact of itself, is proof that usury should be prohibited. It is possible with the aid of a few other wicked customs and laws, for a few men to own every dollar in the United States.

These means have been used to a greater extent than war, to bring about the conquest of nations.

It is estimated that the total amount of indebtedness, both public and private, in the United States, is about twenty billion dollars. Every dollar of this is drawing interest, and every dollar of this interest is paid by labor. There comes a time every few years when the interest falling due on this enormous debt, amounts to more than every dollar in circulation. The result is a financial crisis—a panic. Sometimes it is temporarily postponed, but it is just as sure to come, as effect follows cause.

The men who control the currency—the one thing with which this interest can be paid—will not let it out. They draw it in as fast as possible to hoard it up. The law gives them this power and they use it. They make money by it, and that is what this class of men live for. It is their sole object in life—the summit of their ambition.

They demand the pound of flesh and get it, but they laugh in their sleeves to think that their poor victims have not the manhood, patriotism—not even the good sense, to resist it. Men are thrown out of employment. Prices go down. Money is hard to get. Men are compelled to part with their property for less than it is worth—even less than it cost. Paupers, tramps and criminals increase. Law-suits and other calamities which naturally follow in the wake of hard times, come in their order.

Hypocritical politicians, claiming to be statesmen,

have educated the people to believe that a panic once in eight or ten years, is a necessary consequence of good government. Sensible people absolutely entertain this foolish notion. Some of them believe this from the same reason that they hold on to many other absurd opinions regarding finance—because their fathers before them believed it. The thought never enters their minds, that they are the result of the manipulations of selfish and designing men.

There is another difference between the hire of a horse, and the hire of money. The horse must be fed and attended. This is not necessary with money. The horse will wear out; money will not. The horse will grow old; money will not. Money is just as valuable as it was before. The horse is not. The argument which applies to one, does not apply to the other.

Our opponents will tell you that if all the wealth of the world was divided equally among men, it would not be long before a few men would again have it all. This is an "old song," and some men have repeated it so often they really believe there is argument in it. We admit that this would be the result, if the cause is not removed. The same cause will invariably produce the same effect. Abolish usury, and other wicked systems, and the result will be different. This is what every just man should try to do—remove the cause.

We admit that some men will grow rich faster than others under a perfect system of laws. The man who is more industrious than his indolent neighbor ought to receive more pay; but let us bear in mind that there is a difference between the industrious man and a miser. The man who hoards his wealth, and whose whole object in life is the accumulation of wealth, is a ten times greater curse to society than the indolent man.

There is another class of men who will always grow rich faster than their neighbors—the sharp unprincipled men. Because nature has given them the advantage of their fellows is no reason why the laws should step in and give them still greater advantages. These are the strong men. They need no special legislation in their behalf. The object of law is supposed to be the protection of the weak against the oppressions of the strong. Blackstone defines law as "a rule of action, etc., commanding that which is right and prohibiting that which is wrong." Any law for the effectual abolition of usury will be a means of enforcing this principle.

But it is not asked that there shall be a division of property. We would not have one dollar of Shylock's ill-gotten gains taken from him. We only ask that he be restrained from further robbery. Communism in any form is bad, but that particular form which takes from all and gives to all, is certainly no worse than that which takes from the many and gives to the few.

There is but one just rule to govern in this matter, and that is this: That every person should receive and enjoy the full value of the product of his own industry. This is impossible under the present system, as has been demonstrated. If it be true that every man has a right to the product of his own labor, it is equally certain that no other man has a right to it. It is an undisputed fact that men do get more, and they get it by the practice of usury. If there is any way except through government loans to cut off this practice, it has been beyond the wisdom and intelligence of man to discover it.

CHAPTER V.

THE NATIONAL BANKING SYSTEM.[1]

THE MONETARY CHANGE DEMANDED BY WORKINGMEN—AIM OF THE KNIGHTS OF LABOR—SOULLESS CORPORATIONS HAVE NO PITY—ATTITUDE OF BANKING CORPORATIONS—"SPECIE BASIS"—"INTRINSIC VALUE"—"HONEST MONEY"—MONEY IN ANCIENT AGES—IRON, BRASS, TIN, CLOTH, LEATHER AND WOODEN MONEY—GREAT FINANCIERS ON METALIC MONEY—HOW THE NATIONAL BANKS ABSORB THE NATION'S WEALTH—DEBT THEIR FOUNDATION—HOW THE BANKERS SECURE DOUBLE INTEREST—ENORMOUS SUMS OF MONEY WITHDRAWN FROM JUST TAXATION—THE IMMENSE EARNINGS OF THE INDIANAPOLIS NATIONAL BANK—WHAT WORKINGMEN SHOULD HAVE.

The Knights of Labor demand at the hands of congress a change of the present monetary system, whereby money shall issue directly to the people, and that all of the national money shall be legal tender for all debts. No other clause in their platform is so far-reaching in its influence, or one that

---

1 By J. W. Gaul. S. W. F., L. A., 2691, K. of L.

more nearly touches the vital interests of the people.

Of one thing we may rest assured, that so long as the financial legislation of the country is left to be controlled by a class whose interests lie in the direction of increasing and perpetuating the indebtedness of the country, as may best suit their own purposes, so long as that class retains the control, they will continue to wield it for their own aggrandizement, utterly regardless of the periodically returning panics that sweep over the land like cyclones, leaving ruin and desolation in their track, and just so long will the toiling millions of our brothers be deprived of the full, just fruits of their labor, and remain the veriest dependents, the "hewers of wood and drawers of water" for soulless corporations that have no heart and no pity.

The necessities of the people are their opportunities. The greater their extremities, the more inflexible are they in their demands. Those who control the money of a country control all else that it contains, and recognition of that fact, on their part, is sufficient explanation of the stubborn fight they make to retain it. To-day we are confronted with just such a spectacle.

In this boasted "land of the free," a moneyed obligarchy, composed of some 2,400 national banks, boldly and openly assume it as their right to dictate as to the volume of our currency, the nature of the material that shall compose it, and the source from which it shall be issued. They deny the right and power of the people to supply themselves through the agency of the government: deny that the law can create money, except its material be gold, or such other metal as their unscrupulous greed may determine. As one means of perpetuating their power they strive to surround the whole subject with mystery by the use of terms invented to blind and mislead, thus making fraud and rascality less easily understood. They have succeeded to a most lamentable extent in deceiving the producing millions, whilst they themselves are not deceived.

"Specie basis," "Intrinsic value," and "Honest money" have been dinned into our ears unremittingly, and industry lies prostrate, millions starve, ruin stalks through the land, crime increases, strikes and riots prevail and blood is shed—all this while "great financiers" and "wise statesmen" quibble about a few grains more or less of gold or silver to the dollar.

Let us turn to the pages of history and see if, from the practice and experience of the past, we cannot learn some lessons that will serve to expose the falsity of the ideas they have so assiduously instilled into the public mind. Centuries before Christ, money was found to be necessary. The Jews used many forms, substances or materials for money. For a long time they held it by weight, considering the stamp of no value. They did not seem to have any confidence in any form of government they could adopt, or in its durability, nor did they have confidence in themselves sufficient to take each others notes or obligations without collaterals. They demanded property for property, taking nothing on credit except accompanied with a bond which would hold the debtor in slavery, even to death, for the benefit of the creditors. Services were paid for in female children, in cattle, sheep or asses.

For a long time cattle were held as ready money by the ancient Romans and Grecians, and were declared a legal tender for the payment of debts. In Rome seven hundred years before Christ, by edict of Pompilius, the legal tender money was made of two materials, wood and leather. The leather was the most valuable, while small pieces of wood, resembling button moulds, constituted the small change.

Pompilius refused to place his stamp, by which money was created, upon gold and silver, considering them too expensive to be used for such a purpose. He established a treasury department and gave his chief officer of finance the right to fix the stamp of the emperor upon pieces of white leather, and burn it upon circular pieces of the hardest variety of wood that could be obtained. Both kinds were legal tender for all debts. It was given by the king to all who served him, or furnished property. The man receiving it could pay it to the man he was indebted to, and by law it settled the debt. Thus it passed from hand to hand, until it came, through the tax collector, back into the treasury, when it was again paid out, and after due time again taken in. This was the money of Pompilius during his reign.

Had he been as wise as our modern financiers, and as anxious for the interests of the people, when the wooden and leather money had reached the treasury, he would have refused to re-issue it, but would have "contracted the circulation" by destroying it, and have given to the holders interest bearing non-taxable bonds. He was not far-seeing enough to appreciate the blessing he would have conferred upon the people and their posterity, by plunging them into debt. He was woefully blind to the great truth—"A national debt is a national blessing."

Had the kingdom of Pompilius been a republic, intended to endure forever, with no break in the law or power, with the people electing the presidents and the successors to administer the one direct, non-elastic law, there would have been no demand for other money, because property of all kinds could be accumulated with money made of wood and leather, as well as upon money made of gold or silver.

The national banks deny the power of this sovereign government of the people to create money of paper. They persistently refuse to recognize the greenback as absolute money, but name it as a debt to be paid in gold. They insist that money must have "intrinsic value" in its material, and that "intrinsic value" makes it money, and not the stamp, decree, edict, or, if you please, the "fiat" of the law. What made the wood and leather of Rome, money—"intrinsic value?" No, it was the edict, the "fiat" of Pompilius, as expressed and certified by the stamp of the royal seal, affixed thereon by his decree.

Woe would have been to the traitor who had dared to deny it. With it the commerce of Rome was carried on, her armies were equipped and maintained, her public buildings were erected, her internal improvements achieved; with it her children were educated, and all her citizens fed, housed and clothed. With money of wood and leather, Rome prospered, and pursued steadily her onward march to imperial greatness.

The first sixty millions of treasury notes issued by the government of this country, were legal tender at their face value, for all debts without an exception, and never for one hour, from the date of issue to the present time have they been less valuable than gold, but actually commanded a premium over gold on account of their greater convenience. The bankers recognize that fact, and acknowledged them to be money, in the fullest sense of the term, by the very haste they made to obtain possession of, and hold them, and the frantic clamor they raised to prevent further issue of the same kind. Like Demetrius, the silversmith, they perceived their craft was in danger.

The Carthagenians, for several generations used leather money, until there was such an abundance of gold and silver among the people that they did not know what to do with it, and so used it under the stamp of government as money. How was it that their "cheap" leather money did not drive all the gold and silver away? That is what our "financiers," with owl-like gravity, say would be the effect of our issuing "cheap" paper money.

In 1158, Frederick Barbarossa, during his contest with Milan, carried on war and afterwards the industries of peace, with leather legal tender money. During this period gold was demonetized; was simply property. King John of France, in 1360, issued an immense quantity of leather money. William I, of Sicily, during periods of time between 1154 and 1156 compelled the Sicilians to surrender their gold and silver and receive in exchange leather money, which was not redeemable in gold or silver, but possessed of full legal tender power. This broke up the gold ring of that country and gave the people a respite from usurers, so they became prosperous. The continued issue of them would have annihilated the gold ring here, and have forever emancipated labor from its burdensome and infamous exactions.

Spain and Italy used leather money as late as 1574. China, in the thirteenth century, used the middle bark of the mulberry tree stamped with a mark representing the signature of the sovereign

HON. W. D. VINCENT.

who issued it. It was death to counterfeit or refuse it. In 1574 the Hollanders used pasteboard. In 1635 the colonists of Massachusetts used wampum, as full legal tender, and musket balls as small change at a farthing each, and legal tender in sums under one shilling. Slaves, land, iron, bronze, brass, tin, pieces of cloth, and numerous other things have been used as money, at various times and places. All served as, and were, money just as long as the law declared they should be legal tender for all debts.

The republic of Venice for over four hundred years issued paper as its sole currency. It passed the world over, and commanded a premium of twenty-eight per cent over the money of any other country, never for one moment depreciating. Venice received it, as she issued it, for all dues. History through all the centuries past, brands as false the wilful statements and juggling sophistries used in behalf of "intrinsic value" money, and conclusively proves that money is an absolute creation of the law, and "fiat" alone is the power that confers full debt paying quality.

Charles Moran, a distinguished French writer on political economy, says: "Metalic money whilst acting as coin is identical with paper money in respect to being destitute of intrinsic value. Coin, so long as it circulates for the purpose of buying and selling, for the time loses its intrinsic value. As commodities, gold and silver are capital, but as money they are mere representatives of value." Of paper money, he says: "The simplest and most perfect form of currency is that which represents transferable debt—paper money with no intrinsic value. It is only when states have reached a high state of civilization that they adopt this perfect sort of money."

Such men as Baron Rothschild, Fanchette, Isaac Buchanan, A. H. Gaston, Franklin, Jefferson, William H. Harrison, Daniel Webster, and Buckles' History of English Commerce, might be quoted as to the effects of contraction, the unsuitability of a metalic currency, the power of the government to issue paper currency, etc.

In speaking against the proposition to establish a United States national bank, Henry Clay said: "I conceive the establishment of this bank as dangerous to the welfare and safety of this republic."

"Specie basis," is another bugbear flaunted before us. Let us see what it amounts to. Bonamy Price, the English economist, says that the business of England is done with ninety-seven per cent bank checks, drafts, bills of exchange and notes; two and one-half per cent with paper currency, and fifty cents gold to every one hundred dollars of the aggregate business transactions. The same holds good in this country, yet our bankers speak of "specie basis," and affect a horror of inflation of cheap paper in face of those facts.

The interest of money loaners and banking syndicates is to have money scarce; to have it of material the most costly possible: and if by any means it is likely to become otherwise, they will immediately exert every effort to have it substituted with another kind. A strenuous effort is being made to suspend coinage of silver, in short, to drive it out of our monetary system. The mono-metalists insist that its presence there is dangerous to the business interests of the country, and that a wise regard for the preservation of those interests, and of course the prosperity of labor, demands that it be practically demonetized. Hundreds of thousands of poor dupes swallow the bait, and believe in the sincerity of their motives.

Baron Rothschild understands finance quite as well as our financiers, and says: "The suppression (demonetization) of silver would amount to a veritable destruction of values without any compensation." M. Wolowski, a European financier, says: "If by a stroke of the pen, they suppress one of their metals (gold or silver) in the monetary service, they double the demand for the other metal, to the ruin of all debtors." The truth of these statements is self-evident. President Harrison, in his inaugural speech, made the following remark: "If there be one measure better calculated than another to produce that state of things where the rich are daily getting richer, and the poor are daily getting poorer, it is a metalic currency."

What is this national banking system? Its foundation is the interest bearing, bonded indebtedness of the people, and upon the perpetuation of that debt its existence depends. The full legal tender power was taken from the treasury notes; they are not received for custom dues, or interest on the public debt, and they must be paid in gold. A law was passed to authorize the issuing of bonds, bearing interest, into which we can convert, or by which we can redeem the greenbacks.

The foundation was now laid for a perpetual debt, to be saddled upon industry and serve as a basis for the banking system. Congress authorized the establishment of a national system of banking upon the basis of depositing the bonds with the United States treasurer, as security for our circulation: the bonds thus deposited to continue drawing interest, and to be exempt from all taxation. A national currency was supplied to constitute our circulation, at the rate of ninety per cent of the face of the bond deposit.

On the sale of bonds from 1862 to 1868, embracing seven issues of six per cent, and one of five per cent bonds, according to a statistical table prepared, the people lost, and the bondholders gained, the enormous sum of $678,551,460. In fifteen years, labor paid as interest on bonds, nearly $1,700,000,-000, and also paid to bankers and money lenders during the same period, as estimated by the National Banking Association, over $5,000,000,000. In twelve years of that time it was directly taxed over

$1,200,000,000, the amount of currency taken from the channels of trade and converted into idle, untaxed bonds. The money so taken from circulation, was, at the behest of this grasping money power, never reissued, but cancelled and consigned to the flames.

For further illustration, let us take the report of Hon. Wm. E. English, retiring from the presidency of the First National Bank of Indianapolis: "I congratulate the officers and stockholders of our enterprise. The bank has been in operation fourteen years under my control, with a capital of $500,000. In the meantime it has voluntarily returned $500,000 of capital stock back to its stockholders, besides paying them in dividends $1,496,250, a part of which was in gold. And I now turn it over to you, with a capital unimpaired, and $327,000 of undivided earnings on hand. To this may be added the premiums of United States bonds, at present prices amounting to $36,000, besides quite a large amount for lost or destroyed bills."

Total amount of profit in fourteen years, on half a million dollars capital—$2,383,250!

The whole burden rests upon the shoulders of labor, since labor alone can supply the means of paying the enormous tribute so pitilessly exacted. The cause of labor demands that the bonds be paid, that congress shall not delegate the control of the currency to any one class of citizens, or issue interest bearing obligations, and that a purely national currency shall issue directly to the people, based upon the credit of the people, a legal tender sufficient for commerce and productive industry.

CHAPTER VI.

TRANSPORTATION.[1]

GOVERNMENT PREROGATIVES DANGEROUS IN THE HANDS OF CORPORATIONS—NO ONE CLASS INDEPENDENT—CORPORATIONS NOT ENTITLED TO DISCRIMINATION—THE COUNTRY SUFFERING FROM RAILROAD EXTORTIONS—WHAT THE BALLOT SHOULD ACCOMPLISH—THE TELEGRAPHS—TELEPHONES—RAILROADS—THE GOVERNMENT'S SUCCESS WITH THE POSTAL SYSTEM—THE POWER OF SYNDICATES AND CORPORATIONS—THEIR IMMENSE WEALTH—DANIEL WEBSTER'S GREAT WARNING.

The opinion of the workingmen upon the subject of transportation, is fully expressed in the eighteenth section of the preamble of the principles declared by the Knights of Labor. In a recent address, Mr. J. R. Sovereign made the following remarks:

To delegate any of the prerogatives of republican government to private individuals or corporations,

---

1 By J. R. Sovereign. L. A., 2116, K. of L.

is dangerous to national liberty and personal security. That the operation of the great agencies for transporting intelligence, passengers and freight, is clearly the duty of the government, can scarcely be doubted. For when we consider the fact that they control the destinies of the nation; that they are the mighty cords which bind us together as one people, we can only conclude that the rights, the liberty and the happiness of every citizen depends upon the operation of such agencies in such a way as will preclude the possibility of private interest menacing the public welfare.

It is a great truth that no part of this nation produces all the necessaries and comforts of life, and that no man produces with his own hands a sufficiency to feed, clothe and house himself and those dependent upon him. Every toiler, then, marches to the music of machinery and the hum of industry, upon the hope that he can produce more of one particular article than he wants for himself, and that he can distribute his surplus productions among men engaged in other vocations, and receive in exchange a just proportion of their productions.

For instance, it is by this means, and this alone, that the farmers of the West are permitted to wear the clothing made in the East, and the weavers and clothing makers of the East are permitted to eat the bread raised in the West.

In fact, the prosperity of every people may be measured not alone by their power to produce but by their opportunities to distribute as well. It is, therefore, one of the first duties of government to see that nowhere on the great highways of distribution, shall the people be subjected to rank discriminations or unjust exactions. This principle is the corner stone of republican government, and the bed-rock of American society. With faith in the enforcement of this principle, the people have penetrated the dark forest and the unbroken waste, reared great cities, built homes, erected factories and developed industries.

How is this principle of justice to be guaranteed to every citizen of this great nation, and every stumbling stone which greed and avarice has erected upon the avenues of transportation to be removed?

There is but one method that will embody all the safe guards of justice, and that is for the government to become the owner and operator of all telegraphs, telephones and railroads.

Ah! but says some one, there is an easier way and shorter road to a remedy for all these evils. Let the corporations continue to own the telegraphs, telephones and railroads, and the government control them by statutory enactment.

Municipal law, says a great jurist, is the rule of civil conduct prescribed by the supreme power in a state, commanding what is right and prohibiting what is wrong. And while I hold this definition to be true, yet there is not a teacher in jurisprudence, there is not a practitioner at the bar, nor a judge on the bench, who will not freely confess that to combine private interests with government functions and public agencies, jeopardizes liberty and places the administration of justice outside of the pale of statutory enactments.

To combine corporate interests with public institutions always involves the government in an irrepressible conflict and a never-ending struggle for supremacy, and is always a question of doubt with the people, as to whether the government controls the corporations, or the corporations control the government. Viewed in the light of history, this doubt is dispelled by a preponderance of evidence showing that corporations control the government.

In solving the powers of government, we must not forget that there are impossibilities in law, and the benefits of a law depends upon the power of a government to enforce it in spirit, without giving life to others and more dangerous evils.

To-day our people are suffering from railroad extortions. Let our government pass a law prohibiting such extortions, and, if need be, enforce it with the strong arm of the military, and who will prevent the railroad companies from retaliating with a proportionate reduction of the wages of their employes. Who will prevent them from wreaking their vengeance upon the law by discharging free American laborers, and contracting in a great measure the mechanical operation of the roads with Polish, Italian and Hungarian serfs? It is folly to say we can prevent such an evil by prohibiting the importation of foreign serfs, for the serfs are already here in countless numbers, and are ready to bow at the bidding of corporate greed.

Let our government enact a law preventing railroads from discriminating against persons and localities, and who shall have authority and power to prevent the railroad companies from engaging in mining, manufacturing and other industries, and put their own products on the market at such prices as to force into bankruptcy all opposition. Ah! says one, under such circumstances could not the government resort to the Missouri law, and the laws of other states, prohibiting railroad companies from engaging in any other business than the operation of their roads? Yes, we could resort to a great many farces. How often has this power of government been tested and found too tardy to meet the demands of justice? Nearly a quarter of a century ago our law-makers framed out to opulent and arrogant corporations, the monetary prerogatives of the nation. In that law is combined private gain with the functions of government. But the government sought to control it in the interests of the people by statutory enactment, which provided among other restrictions that no national bank should charge or receive a greater rate of interest than that prescribed by the laws of the state in which the bank was operated, and that no national bank should receive real estate security for the loan of its notes. How is that law respected and obeyed?

As an expression of their defiance of law and the expressed will of the people, a little office adjacent to nearly every national bank in the land, is appropriately furnished, and in these private offices you will find the cappers of the banks who loan the funds of the banks under the pretense of private account, at from one to two per cent per month, and on real estate security. Here is a striking illustration of the inability of the government to control public institutions when combined with private interests. They have defied law, they have clasped their icy fetters about the throats of presidents, and now openly boast that, on a single day's notice, they can act together with such power that no act of congress can resist their demands.

Let our government attempt to control telegraphs, telephones and railroads while they are permeated with corporate greed, and who shall be the giant to march forth upon the plain of equal and exact justice, and wring out the four billion dollars of watered stocks which the confederate monopolies of to-day are using, as an instrument of torture and a harbinger of slavery, that their own coffers may be filled with ill-gotten gains? Legislate to control these agencies, and leave the ownership where it now is, and what power under heaven will prevent them from becoming the bulwarks of every political contest? While this remains a free govern-

HON. HENRY SMITH,
State Master Workman, K. of L., Wis.

ment, what law can prevent them sending a hired lobby of cunning sharpers to the council chambers of the nation, to corrupt courts and bribe legislatures. It is the first duty of government to obtain possession by purchase of all these agencies.

Let us turn our attention for a moment, to one of the avenues of public distribution from which the government has served private ownership. Reference is made to the postal service. During all the time the government has operated the mail routes, we never hear of postoffices combining to harangue the people in political contests, except the mere clamor for office. We never hear of a postoffice lobby in Washington. We never hear of the postoffices charging more for a "short haul" than for a "long haul." We never hear of the postoffices watering stocks. We never hear of them discriminating against localities. We never hear of them sending abroad for the paupers of the old world to take the place of free labor. We never hear of them spending millions of dollars per year, to subsidize the press and deceive the people.

And now comes the question: Is the transmission of human intelligence upon paper, any more the duty of government than the transmission of life and property?

Is human thought more sacred when inscribed upon paper, than when upon the electric wires it flashes across the continent in the twinkling of an eye.

During all the time the government has operated the postal service you never heard of the employes of that department going on a strike. On the other hand you never heard the people complain of excessive rates or extortionate charges in the transmission of the mails. But how different is the feeling and the situation, when applied to the railroads, the telegraphs and the telephones, everything is confusion and dissatisfaction. While the employes are striking for increased wages, the people are threatening confiscation, or a return to the old stage coach system, as a possible refuge from the grasp of monopoly.

Nowhere is there a single instance where the government has succeeded in controlling a public institution in the interests of the people while it embraced private ownership.

This government started out in life on the basis that a white man could have ownership in the flesh and blood of a black man, and all that was necessary was to control it by law, but that evil corrupted legislation, and defied the will of the people, until it costs millions of lives and billions of treasury to subdue it.

In 1791 our government started a bank with $10,-000,000 capital. Four-fifths of it was private property, and it nearly choked the life out of the government. It had to be abolished to save our free institutions.

In 1816 our law makers were induced to try the

experiment again, and another bank was established with $35,000,000 capital, four-fifths of which was private property, but it darkened American freedom and became so oppressive that in 1832, Jackson had to put his foot on the neck of the monster and crush the life out of it. Then that function of the government was turned over to state banks, and they nearly bankrupted the nation.

The national banks of to-day have become so haughty and powerful, that they can grasp the arm of the president of the United States, as they did a few years ago, and compel him to veto a bill which was passed in the interest of the people. But what has all this to do with the operation of the railroads, or the telegraph and telephones. It shows the weakness of the law and the power of corporations, and the dangers which threaten the liberties of the people, when private interests are combined with public institutions. Our government has gone further than the mere attempt to control a railroad. A few years ago our government formed the acquaintance of a railroad magnate and his company, and the government gave them a strip of land forty miles wide, extending from the Missouri river to the Pacific coast, then the government loaned them $16,000 on every mile of road they built. Then the government released the lands and bonds from taxation. Yet, with all this public charity, that railroad has become a robber of the people and an oppressor of the poor. Not only that, but they nearly annihilated the government's claim, by slipping a first mortgage under it, and for years they have refused to pay even the interest on the loan the government gave them, and to-day more than $50,000,000 of interest remains unpaid.

Their last great act of charity that came under my personal notice, was when the leading officers crossed this country in their gold mounted cars, and drank their fine wines and whisky under the dazzling banners which bore the motto of "Victory." Under the present administration, we have a railroad law that the angels in Heaven cannot tell what it means, and we have five railroad lawyers to execute that law.

Give us statesmen who have the honor, and the will, to spurn the flattery of these corporations, and can damn their devilish treachery without flinching.

For many years past it has been the custom of the people to donate large sums to aid in the construction of railroads. In many localities the people have taxed themselves poor for this very purpose. Millions upon millions of dollars have gone into the pockets of railroad companies from this source. But no sooner did the railroad companies receive these donations, than they rated them with their own capital stock, and as soon as the roads were in running order the people were forced to pay dividends on their own donations. It is not just that a man who donates $100 to aid in the construction of a railroad to-day, shall be assessed to pay a dividend on that same $100 to-morrow, and when he is dead and gone, his children to be assessed on their father's charity. But what is worse, the railroads no sooner get the $100 you donate them, than they water it 100 per cent, and assess you to pay a dividend on $200, when you only donated $100.

It is, therefore, clear to every investigating mind that there are scores of evils growing out of the present mode of operating the public agencies of distribution, which cannot be remedied except the people take them in their own hands.

The best results the people can hope for, under any attempt to control by law the agencies of transportation without government ownership, is that they will be put on the same commercial basis with mining, manufacturing, agriculture and other industries. Put the telegraphs, telephones and railroads under such restrictions only, and the same tendencies towards centralization from which we suffer to-day will still continue. And why? Simply because these agencies are public institutions—they are of such a character that sixty millions of people are by force of circumstances compelled to patronize them, and they are owned and controlled by the few. Thus we have every element of concentration. Give a man the exclusive ownership of the postal system, and place it on the same remunerative basis with other industries, and in less than fifty years he will own nine-tenths of the wealth of the nation, and nine-tenths of the people will be his servants and he will be their master. Private gain must not be the motive for operating a public institution. For so surely as it is, will Daniel Webster's great warning be realized, "Liberty cannot long endure in any country where the tendency of legislation is to concentrate wealth in the hands of the few."

CHAPTER VII.

"OVERPRODUCTION."[1]

THERE CAN BE NO OVERPRODUCTION WHEN MONEY IS PLENTY—SCARCITY OF MONEY PRODUCES STRIKES AND RIOTS—WHY MONEY IS WITHDRAWN FROM CIRCULATION—LINCOLN'S WARNING IN 1861—OVERPRODUCTION DOES NOT STARVE CHILDREN—INTEREST ON BONDS A GREAT VAMPIRE TO THE NATION—BONDS TAXED IN ENGLAND AND FRANCE—GEN. WEAVER ON TAXATION—THE INTER-STATE COMMERCE LAW—REPORT OF THE SILVER COMMISSIONERS—PLAIN FACTS—SHOWING MADE BY UNITED STATES TREASURER IN 1887 OF THE NATION'S MONEY—IDLE CAPITAL MAKES IDLE MACHINERY AND THE WORKINGMAN SUFFERS.

THE cry that "overproduction produces these hard times," is a farce. There would be no overproduction of cereals, clothing or any other commodity, if we had a sufficient amount of money in circulation. If men are on the verge of starvation —half-paid and large families to keep, how can

---

[1] By Hon. William Baker.

they get the money to buy a sufficient amount of clothing? If clothing, cereals and produce are not bought for the want of money among the laboring class, then overproduction must follow.

With wages hardly enough to support families and nothing to buy clothing, manufactures must stop, or if they run on half-time and at reduced wages, then dissatisfaction is followed by strikes and riots. If laborers get good wages they are generous with the distribution of their money. Instead of mending up old garments they get new. There never was "overproduction" with plenty of money in circulation. Not more than one-third of the money in the country is in circulation. Over five hundred million dollars are locked up in the United States treasury, the rest is in the banks, and in the vaults of insurance companies, to loan at usurious rates. When money is scarce, interest increases—when plenty, it decreases. As long as men can loan their money at from 6 to 10 per cent, they will hoard their money to loan.

If a law was passed, allowing only four per cent interest, money would leave its hiding places. It would invest in realty, manufactures and other channels of trade, wages would go up, and the busy hum of industry would be heard throughout the republic. Nothing pays as well as money at a high rate of interest. The capitalists know this, and do all they can to cramp the money market so as to create a higher rate of interest. If farmers borrow money at over five per cent it will eat them up, as farming as a rule will not pay over three per cent. Much is said about paying the national debt. The debt cannot be paid under the present national banking system.

Let the government cease to issue any more bonds to the banks, issue none but legal tender money. Call in the National Banks' money as soon as their charters lapse, reduce by law the rate of interest to four per cent, keep the circulation up to fifty dollars per capita. Do this, and panics will be unknown—strikes a thing of the past, and prosperity and contentment will cease only with the Republic.

Venice had one hundred dollars per capita, and for six hundred years down to the time that Napoleon crossed her Lagoon, and destroyed a republic which had kept the civilized world at bay for thirteen hundred years, she never had a failure. England with her irredeemable currency and a large per capita circulation, during her Napoleonic war of eighteen years, enjoyed a prosperity she never had before or since. Failures were unknown, the hum of industries was heard throughout the day, and the midnight sky was brightened by the glow of hot furnaces. "Each day a link is forged in the change which makes labor subservient to capital."

Abraham Lincoln in 1861 warned the people to watch, lest capital be put above labor. He said:

"I bid the laboring people beware of surrendering a power which they already possess, and which surrendered will surely be used to close the doors of advancement to such as they, and fix new disabilities and burdens upon them until all liberty is lost." We must be on our guard. We hear the muffled sounds of discontent. We had better heed the warning voice of Lincoln, and not stand like abject slaves and tremble before the marble face of power.

The laboring class are battling for their rights. "It is billions of money against millions of men." The people must settle their difficulties through the ballot, not by the bayonet, and their strikes by arbitration, not by riots. Unity of action is indispensable to success. Let not cunning Catilines mislead you. Select those whom you can trust to defend your cause. Rare scholastic attainments and brilliancy of mind are not required. Good judgment, and a clear perception of right and wrong, is a better equipment for a public officer than eloquence or polished manners. No nation can prosper with our limited circulation, cornered as it is by demagogues, to raise the interest, cramp the people, and to sell their homes.

We want no more such scenes as red flags in the sheriff's hands, as pitiless for humanity as the black flags of the pirates. We want no more to see children driven from their homes, with bony hands extended heavenward, with sunken eyes, pallid cheeks, but gnawed by the pangs of hunger, piteously exclaiming, "We've got no home! Oh, God, we've got no home!" We want, with the keys of Justice, to unlock the coffers of the nation, by paying the bonds now almost due, that times may ease and happy homes and comfort once more reign.

We must either have an income tax, so as to compel the untaxed bondholders to help the poor liquidate the enormous taxes, or pass a law not to allow over four per cent. The capital which seeks hiding places for the purpose of contracting the currency, so as to increase the rate of interest, would then pass into the channel of trade. If those in power will not do that, then recall the bonds. We have paid them over and over again.

In a speech in 1870, delivered by Hon. Daniel Voorhees, he said: "I think it safe to say, that up to the present time the bondholders have realized in bonds and interest, not less than $4,000,000,000. There is nothing parallel to it in the history of constitutional government. In what government, or land, governed by written law, will the explorer of other countries find such a wholesale plunder of the people. Where else, than in this land of professed equality, has wealth ever committed a crime against industry and liberty, of such huge proportions as towers up in our midst, and darkens the homes of our people with its cruel and unjust demands? The funding of the bonds though the interest be lessened, will not relieve labor of its oppressive taxation. The mortgage of the bondholder on all their homes and farms will still continue. Their children, and their children's children will be subject to the same undiminished burdens. Interest, interest, with its frightful accumulation will compel the tax payer to pay it over and over again, and yet it will never be cancelled. The principle of funding, established an inexhaustible mine of gold for the bondholders, and an eternity of hopeless toil for the people. On the chancery side of the court, there is always relief to be found against an extortionate transaction. This is a well known principle between individuals. It will hold good also in behalf of a whole people. They have been imposed upon, and defrauded in the creation of the debt, and they may justly and without breach of contract appeal to the greater equity of the case. Do we live in the days of the Medes and Persians, when it was an offense punishable with death to repeal a law once enacted?"

In this land of boasted freedom, the moneyed power imposes laws upon the working class more unjust, than those of France or England. Heath says: "In both England and France, the government obligations are taxed pro rata with all other investments, and have to bear their proportions of the public burdens, while in America they are exempt from all taxation, thus throwing their entire burden upon those who reap no profit from them." Is it not a disgrace that such a law is not repealed? Is it any wonder that the people are oppressed? Statistics show that our mortgages aggregate $800,000,000,

J. R. SOVEREIGN,

that the average interest is 8 per cent, which per annum amounts to over six hundred million dollars.

General Weaver says "that we are in debt twenty billions of dollars, out of say, six billions of dollars of wealth, that the lowest average tax is 6½ per cent, and that on twenty billions of dollars, it is one billion three hundred thousands of dollars of simple interest, say nothing of compound interest, that the people are paying on national, state, corporate, municipal and private indebtedness, that the annual net increase of wealth of this nation is scarcely 3 per cent, but call it three, and that on sixteen billions of dollars is one billion, eight hundred thousand dollars, and you pay in usury alone, simple interest, one billion, three hundred thousand dollars of it to money loaners, then add interest, then extortionate charges of railroads, then add the enormous rentals paid by the laboring poor, and you find you haven't a farthing left to add to the wealth of this country as a whole."

There is another power we need to fear besides the banks and bonds, a power that by the stroke of the pen can increase or decrease the price on every thing we eat or wear. It is the railroads with their power of wealth. To hush the general cry on such abuse which railroads have imposed, congress passed an inter-state commerce law that would have raked the brains of Coke, Blackstone, Kent, Grotius, Vattel or even Mucius Scævola, the greatest lawyer then in Rome, whose pupil was the great Cicero, who once did wield the palm of eloquence, to decipher it. The law says: "Shall not charge more for a short haul than a long haul under substantially similar circumstances and conditions over the same line running in the same direction." If a poor man is injured, what chance has he in the upper courts, he must then perchance to five commissioners appeal, who in a Trojan horse perchance will sit, with paid retainers to favor my lords, the kings of railroad fame.

In 1874 the United States senate committee on transportation routes said: In the matter of taxation there are four men representing the four great trunk lines between Chicago and New York, who exercise power which the congress of the United States would not venture to exert. An additional charge of 5 per cent per bushel on the transportation of cereals, would have been equivalent to a tax of forty-five millions of dollars on the crop of 1873; that the day is not far distant, if it has not already arrived, when it will be the duty of the statesmen to inquire whether there is less danger in leaving the proper and industrial interests of the people thus wholly at the mercy of a few men who recognize no responsibility but to their stockholders, and no principle of action, but personal and corporate aggrandizement, than in adding somewhat to the power and patronage of a government directly responsible to the people and entirely under their control."

General Weaver says, "That Iowa and in Illinois

farmers are yearly losing money that the enormous rates of transportation has made them poor, and that the railroads make out of every dollar of their gross earnings, thirty-six cents out of every dollar, which represents actual profit." Where is there a farmer who makes annually over four per cent? The national banks themselves are dangerous. They hold the purse that means the sword. They tell the government that if they dare to make laws against their rights, they will make such a combination that panics will ensue. No more right have they to thus hold the purse and sword, than brigadier generals the right to make war or peace. Besides that, these railroad kings have 1,800,000 employes under their command, six times more than Napoleon had, when he disposed of crowns and kingdoms, and made all Europe tremble. Forty times more than Alexander, or Cæsar, or Pompey commanded. This shows the wealth which they possess.

People, and those who ought to know better, repeatedly exclaim, "Oh! there is as much money in the country as ever." If they would take the trouble to examine Secretary Bristow's statement under the head of Destruction Account, they would be shocked at the amount of money destroyed. General Logan in 1874, said in congress, that the circulating medium had been diminished $1,018,167,784. To show the terrible effect the contraction of the currency has had, take the report of the silver commission of the second session of the 44th congress, which commission consisted of Messrs. John P. Jones, Lewis V. Bogy and Geo. M. S. Boutwell, of the senate; Randall L. Gibson, Geo. Williard and Richard Bland, of the house of representatives; Hon. W. Groesbeck, of Ohio; Prof. Francis Bowen, of Massachusetts; and Geo. M. Weston, of Maine. They said:

"The loss which this country sustains by the "shrinking of money is awful. The depression in pro-"ductive industries will become more deathly, and "the number of idle laborers will indefinitely in-"crease. The loss which this country sustains by "the enforced idleness of three millions of persons, "who although idle, must still, in some scanty way, "be supplied with food, clothing, and shelter, is in "aggregate, very great. If it be estimated at one "dollar a day, for each laborer it would amount in "two years to a sum sufficient to discharge the na-"tional debt. It would pay the interest at 5 per "cent per annum on eighteen thousand millions of "dollars. It would be a sum more than sufficient to "supply anew each year, the circulating medium of "the country. It would amount in four years to a "greater sum than the world's entire gold produc-"tion, in the last fifty prolific years. It would ag-"gregate in ten years far greater than the value of "the world's entire product of both gold and sil-"ver, for the last hundred years. It would amount "in four years, to a sum more than sufficient to du-"plicate, and stock every mile of railroad now in "the United States. No more fatal blow, therefore,

"could be directed against the economical machinery
"of civilized life, than one against labor, and that
"blow can most effectually be delivered through a
"policy that strikes down prices. If all debts in
"this country had been doubled by an act of legisla-
"ture, it would have been a far less calamity to the
"debtor and to the country than the increase of their
"real burden already caused by a contraction in the
"volume of money. Indeed this country could bet-
"ter afford, in an economical view to support one mil-
"lion of soldiers in the field, than to support its
"present army of three millions, that fallen prices
"have conscripted into the ranks of non-producers.
"Without money, civilization could not have a be-
"ginning with a diminished supply, it must languish
"and unless relieved finally perish. It is a volume
"of money keeping even pace with advancing pop-
"ulation and commerce, and in the resulting steadi-
"ness of prices, that the wholesome nutriment of a
"healthy vitality is found. The highest moral, intel-
"lectual, and material development of nations is
"promoted by the use of money unchanging in its
"value."

One can see from the above report what money does and the power it has. In 1865 we paid the government in taxes three hundred and thirty-two million dollars. Last year three hundred and thirty-six million. What means these figures? We are told the debt is being quickly paid and fourteen million dollars more of taxes than in 1865. We have over five hundred million dollars in our national vaults, and manufactures stopped, and money scarce, and working men crying for bread. Still it flows in, three hundred and thirty thousand dollars a day, ten million dollars in one month, and in one year, at least, one hundred and twenty million dollars more than used for expenditures and appropriations. Without stand the grinning Shylocks, like the one at Rialto, demanding his pound of flesh, amid this cry of hunger and of woe. Look in the vaults with a prophetic eye and see what they contain.

The Iowa Tribune says, "On the 18th of July, 1887, the statement of the United States treasury showed gold, silver, United States notes and other funds in the treasury, as follows:

Gold coin and bullion	$178,719,037
Silver dollars and bullion	215,716,600
Trade dollars redeemed	7,025,852
Fractional silver coin	26,808,959
United States notes	28,618,442
National bank notes	203,993
National bank notes in process of redemption	2,363,899
Deposits with national bank depositories	28,295,798
Total	$577,752,580

CERTIFICATES OUTSTANDING:

Gold	$ 96,764,067
Silver	143,278,781
Currency	8,750,000
Total	$248,792,848
Balance available cash	$328,959,632

"That sum enables the Secretary to redeem at once the $250,000,000 of four and one-half bonds now outstanding, and $50,000,000 of the fours. The four and halfs have four years to run, and the annual interest is $11,250,000, to redeem them would save the people $45,000,000. The interest on $50,000,000 fours is $2,000,000 a year, and they run twenty years, so the saving on them would be $40,000,000. These two items foot up $85,000,000, which Secretary Fairchild can save the people of the country, besides relieving the pressure in money matters, by putting $300,000,000 out of the vaults of the treasury into circulation. The law authorizes this act."

Any one can readily see what this country would save by the redemption of the bonds. It would not only lessen taxes, increase trade, but make times good. Idle capital is like idle machinery. When idle, neither produce anything. We not only lose the interest of the money in the vaults, but what it would produce if put into circulation, besides making homes once more bright and happy, seeing every arm once more employed, and all the avenues of trade exulting with the shouts and peans of victorious labor.

CHAPTER VIII.

HARD TIMES.

THE KNIGHTS OF LABOR AT RICHMOND—A COMMITTEE ON HARD TIMES—THEIR REPORT—THE INTRICACIES OF DISTRIBUTION OF WEALTH—AN ANALYSIS OF THE SUBJECT—SENATOR SHERMAN'S IDEAS IN 1869—JOHN A. LOGAN'S THEORY—THE UNITED STATES TREASURER IN 1820—JOHN STUART MILL, THE GREAT ENGLISH ECONOMIST — SIR ARCHIBALD WILSON — SECRETARY M'CULLOCH — BOUTWELL — THE BURNING OF $100,000,000—PETER COOPER ON INDUSTRIAL DEPRESSION—THE FLUCTUATION OF FINANCES THE CAUSE OF HARD TIMES—A STEADY STANDARD A FIRM FOUNDATION.

AT the general assembly of the Knights of Labor held at Richmond, Va., October, 1886, a committee was appointed to investigate and report upon the question of hard times. The committee was composed of able men, chosen from five states, viz.: John Davis, Kansas; Richard F. Trevelick, Mich.; J. R. Sovereign, Iowa; John H. Conner, La.; and James Collins, Pa.; and their report contains interesting matter upon the financial and industrial depression which the workingmen find is laid heavily upon them. The report is a succinct commentary on the general situation, and may be justly termed a chapter of practical political economy. They reported as follows:

In examining our subject, we discover that the more civilized nations of the earth, including the people of the United States, find themselves face to face with the problem of their existence and continued progress.

The problem of savagery is plain and simple. It comprehends physical force and personal prowess only. It means "to the vicious belong the spoils," and death or slavery, to the vanquished. The problem of civilization is more complex, yet the statement of it is short. The great Victor Hugo, of France, has stated the problem of civilization in these words: "The creation of wealth and the distribution of wealth."

The people of the United States, England and other civilized nations, create wealth magnificently, but they distribute it badly. So perfect and so rapid is the creation of wealth in recent times, that the first half of the problem of civilization may be considered solved. The last half of the problem is still before us, as much unsolved as in the crudest conditions of savagery. Among the more civilized nations, including the people of the United States, we find whole classes of the creators of wealth suffering in a state of the most abject poverty and want, while other classes that are not creators of wealth at all have accumulated such enormous amounts of the earnings of labor, that their presence in society has become absolutely dangerous to the liberties of the people.

What, then, are the intricacies and difficulties connected with the distribution of created wealth in civilized society? Let us analyze the subject. The distribution of created wealth consists of two parts: The change of place of commodities, and the change of title to commodities. What are the agents and implements in the performance of these functions and transactions? For the change of place of commodities we use wagons, boats and cars; for simplicity, let us say, we use wheels. For the change of title, we use dollars.

Now suppose that in the transportation of commodities from producer to consumer, there are wheels enough in existence and in motion; the transportation goes on smoothly and normally. In the midst of this felicitous and prosperous condition of things, let some unseen power withdraw or suppress one-half, or one-fourth of the wheels. The result is disastrous in the extreme. Producers cannot deliver their commodities, and suffer in consequence; consumers cannot receive the commodities, that they desire, nor the necessities that must sustain their lives. Society is afflicted with congestion and paralysis in all its parts; and, if the unseen interference continues, confusion and suffering must continue.

What is the remedy? Plainly this: Restore the wheels and, for the future, add wheels as the exigencies of transportation shall require.

On the matter of the change of title to the commodities, suppose that a requisite number of dollars are in existence and floating, and that the buying and selling of commodities is proceeding normally and smoothly—that the requisite change of title to commodities is practicable, in accordance with the necessities of society. Now suppose that some unseen power shall withdraw one-half, or one-fourth of the dollars, what is the result. The same as that seen when part of the wheels were withdrawn. There can be no general change of title to commodities, except upon the most disadvantageous terms. There must be a general over-loading of the remaining dollars which is recognized as a general reduction, or fall of prices. Falling prices means general depression of trade and industry; and loss and distress among all classes engaged in changing title to commodities are the inevitable results. As titles to articles cannot be safely exchanged, change of title must cease, or proceed under very adverse circumstances, and so imperfectly that society must suffer the most severe distress.

So insidious and so deceptive are the processes and results of the withdrawal of the money of society, that your committee beg leave to introduce authorities on this important part of the subject. First, we refer to the language of the United States

HON. WILLIAM BAKER.

monetary report of 1877, respecting the depression of industry then existing, as follows:

The true and only cause of the stagnation in industry and commerce now everywhere felt, is the fact now everywhere existing of falling prices caused by a shrinking volume of money. This is the great cause. All others are collateral, cumulative, or really the effect of that cause.

Speaking of the progressive contraction of the currency then going on, Senator John Sherman, in 1869, said:

The contraction of the currency is a far more distressing thing than senators suppose. Our own and other nations have gone through that process before. It is not possible to take that voyage without the sorest distress; to every person except a capitalist out of debt, a salaried officer, or an annuitant, it is a period of loss, danger, lassitude of trade, fall of wages, suspension of enterprise, bankruptcy and disaster. To attempt this, is to impose upon our people, by arresting them in the midst of their lawful business, and applying a new standard of value to their property, without any reduction of their debts or giving them any opportunity to compound with their creditors, or to distribute their losses, and would be an act of folly without an example of evil in modern times.

Speaking of the long continued and disastrous depression existing in 1874, Senator John A. Logan said: "It is a money famine and nothing else."

In his great speech of March 17, 1874, Senator

Logan quoted approvingly **from Hon. Isaac Buchanan,** of Ontario, Canada, as **follows:**

It is seen that the question of money, and the question of labor, are one and the same question, the solution of one being the solution of the other; plentiful, and therefore cheap money, being a convertible term for plentiful and well paid employment.

Wm. H. Crawford, secretary of the United States **treasury, in 1820, said:** "All intelligent writers on **currency agree that when** it is decreasing in amount, **poverty and misery must prevail."**

John Stuart Mill, a great English economist, states:

If the whole money in circulation was doubled, prices would double. If it was increased one-fourth, prices would increase one-fourth.

Ricardo, of England, **says:**

That commodities would rise **and fall in** price in proportion to **the** diminution of money, I assume as a fact that **is** incontrovertible; that such would be the **case,** the most celebrated writers are agreed.

Your committee **have** been absolutely overwhelmed **and** embarrassed by the volume **of** testimony **accessible,** showing that, **as** tersely stated by President **Grant,** "Prices keep pace with the volume of money;" and, with this mass of available material, we have selected only the best known American and English authors.

We call special attention to the following additional testimony from the report of the United States monetary commission, 1877:

Primarily, then, prices must have been entirely controlled by the volume of money unaffected by credit. There can never occur a universal fall in prices, and a general withdrawal of credits, without a preceding decrease in the volume of money. As the volume of money shrinks prices fall. When money is decreasing in volume prices have no bottom except a receding one, and they are inexorably ruled by the volume of money. In the whole history of the world, every great and general fall in prices, have been preceded by a decrease in the volume of money. At the Christian era the metalic money of the Roman empire amounted to $1,800,000,000. At the end of the fifteenth century it had shrunk to $200,000,000. During this period a most extraordinary and baleful change took place in the condition of the world. Population dwindled, and commerce, arts, wealth and freedom all disappeared. The people were reduced by poverty to the most degraded condition of serfdom and misery. The disintegration of society was almost complete. The conditions of life was so hard that individual selfishness was the only instinct consistent with self-preservation. All public spirit, all generous emotions, all noble aspirations of men shriveled and disappeared as the volume of money shrunk and prices fell. That the Dark Ages were caused by decreasing money and falling prices, and that the recovery therefrom, and the comparative prosperity which followed the discovery of America were due to the increasing supply of the precious metals, and rising prices will not seem surprising, or unreasonable, when the noble functions of money are considered. Money is the great instrument of association, the very fibre of social organization, the vitalizing force of industry, and as essential to its existence as oxygen is to animal life. Without money civilization could not have had a beginning —with a diminishing supply it must languish, and, unless relieved, finally perish.

Sir Archibald Allison, the great English historian, corroborates the foregoing testimony to the fullest extent, and says:

The two great events in the history of mankind have been brought about by a successive contraction and expansion of the circulating medium of society. The fall of the Roman empire, so long ascribed in ignorance to slavery, to heathenism and to moral corruption, was, in reality, brought about by a decline in the silver and gold mines of Spain and Greece. And as if Providence intended to reveal in the clearest manner possible the influence of this mighty agent in human affairs, the restoration of mankind from the ruin this cause had produced was owing to the directly opposite set of agencies being put in operation. Columbus led the way in the career of renovation; when he spread his sails to cross the Atlantic he bore mankind and its fortunes in his bark. The annual supply of the precious metals—of money—for the use of the globe was trebled; before a century had passed the price of every species of produce was quadrupled. The weight of debt and taxation insensibly wore off under the influence of that prodigious increase; in the renovation of industry society was changed, the weight of feudalism cast off and the rights of man established.

No earthly force can withstand the enginery of the financial autocrats. Thomas H. Benton said: "All property is at their mercy."

In view of the transcendent importance of the quantity of money afloat, we now proceed to inquire as to the usual manner and processes of reducing its volume. Prior to 1861, the usual and very successful plan for suppressing the currency of the country was by a run on the banks. This plan not only destroyed the money in the pockets of the people, but, by the sudden and complete contraction of the currency, it almost entirely destroyed the prices of all property.

After 1865 the old plan of contraction was not practicable; but, in 1866 a law of congress was passed for the material reduction of the volume of currency, and Secretary McCulloch advised that: "The process of contracting the government notes should go on as rapidly as possible without producing a panic." The same secretary reported, in December, 1866, that he had during the year, "counted and retired $211,000,000."

In 1872, Secretary Boutwell reported that he had cancelled, "by burning," $100,000,000. The continued contraction of the currency produced the disastrous depression of 1873, which continued until the remedial measures of 1878 were passed. One of these remedial measures forbade the further retirement of United States notes; the other provided for the coinage of silver, and the issuing of silver certificates. They added to the money facilities of the country and gradually, and partially, relieved the financial and industrial depression.

Since 1878 suppression of currency, by burning, has not been lawful or practicable, hence a third plan has been adopted; the policy of hoarding, or locking up, the money of the country in the treasury, and, by various excuses and devices, the amount of available assets in the public treasury is unprecedented. From 1865 to 1882, a period of eighteen years, the average available assets in the treasury was $160,000,000. In 1882 the treasury hoard began to permanently increase, and has since continued to do so. The amount now reported monthly by the United States treasurer has, for several months, ranged above $550,000,000.

This material contraction of the currency by locking up, has afflicted the country with falling prices, compelling all business men and investors to hoard in self-defense. Thus we see piled up in the great money centers unusual amounts of money, belonging to individuals, waiting a change from the continually receding prices of the products of labor and the commodities of commerce. And, as in all cases of suppression of the money, and consequent falling prices, we hear on all hands the moans and cries of distress, and the earthquake rumblings of threatening revolution and anarchy. Such scenes and dangers were witnessed under similar circumstances during the years 1873 to 1877.

The great Peter Cooper stated, that during his long business life, he had witnessed ten disastrous industrial depressions, always from the same cause; always and uniformly from a destruction, or suppression, of the money of the country. And British history informs us that a law for the suppression of the currency of that country was passed in 1820. At that time the country was prosperous and the British people were employed and contented. Under the influence of the Peel contraction bill, four-fifths of all land-holders of England, through bankruptcy and forced sales, lost their lands. The people were without employment, and were suffering everywhere for the commonest necessaries of life. The suffering country was relieved by five money bills introduced in a single night by Lord Castlereagh, and passed under a suspension of the rules as matters of urgent necessity. Every bill was designed to increase money facilities. The relief was sudden and effective.

Your committee now submit, that the primal and general cause of financial and industrial depression, is a suppression of the means of changing titles to the products of labor, and that this blocking of the means of distribution should be remedied by a restoration of the currency of the country. We agree in this report, that the general government should resume its exclusive sovereign right to coin and issue the money of the country, and that all money so issued, whether metal or paper, should be receivable by the government for all dues, and a legal tender for all debts and taxes. That the money so issued shall be gradually increased to the volume per capita that existed in 1865, before the law for its suppression was passed; that it be floated from the treasury in payment of the interest-bearing debt, and other liabilities of the government, giving bond holders their option of coin, or paper, in such payments.

And we further report, that such volume per capita should be substantially maintained forever hereafter, by the issue of new coin, or treasury notes, in accordance with the increase of population; said money to be circulated through the usual disbursements of the government. To shield from the evils of falling prices through the hoarding of money, or other causes, your committee suggest the creation of a Bureau of Prices. Said Bureau should have a central head at the seat of the general government, with branch offices in the principal commercial cities of the country.

It should be the business of the branch offices, to observe and note the daily prices in their respective cities, of all the important products of labor that are the commodities of commerce. Each branch office should make a full monthly report to the head office in Washington, where the average price of each commodity, and of the aggregate commodities, must be arranged and published monthly. Then if these monthly reports show an average monthly fall in the sea level of general prices, the per capita additions to the currency must be increased. But, if three consecutive monthly reports show a rise in the general sea level of prices, then the per capita additions to the currency should be smaller.

It is the opinion of your committee that the volume of the money should be maintained as nearly as possible unfluctuating, and that the general average, or sea level of prices, should be maintained as nearly as possible the same.

In discussing the general and bottom cause of financial and industrial depression, your committee does not forget that there are many collateral and cumulative causes. We recognize the grievances that continually arise between the money earners and their employers, but we know that the interests of both parties are best served by steady prices, and an unfluctuating money market. We know that strikes and lockouts occur oftenest, and are most difficult of management, when the volume of currency is shrinking and prices are falling. We know that individuals and syndicates may lock up money, and bring down prices, as well as the United States treasurer; but our Bureau of Prices will correct that. We know that there is still left for discussion the land, labor and transportation questions, in a hundred varying forms; yet we believe that the asperities and afflictions on the body of civilized society, may be smoothed down and healed with greater ease, and certainty if the circulating medium of society is normal. We believe that our Bureau of Prices, in its monthly reports, will reveal the fact and locality of corners in the products of industry, and may lead to the discovery, exposure and punishment of the criminals. We know that the gold corner of Black Friday, 1873, became a possible and accomplished fact, after a period of seven years of suppression of money and falling prices.

We do not believe that an unfluctuating system of finance will cure all the evils of land monopoly, but it is a historic fact that every money panic has caused thousands of the homes of the people to pass into the hands of the money lords at merely nominal prices, through sheriff's sales and foreclosures of mortgages. We do not believe that the adjustment of the money question will heal all the differences between capital and labor, but it may be safely stated, that ninety per cent of the strikes and troubles in this line have occurred during a period of falling prices. At such times the capitalist has the advantage in these fights, while, on a steady, or rising market, the employes usually gain easy victories.

We do not, either as a committee or as individuals, claim that all the ills of society can be cured through the manipulations of finance. We do believe that all reforms, and all adjustment of troubles, may be easily accomplished if we have at all times steady, unfluctuating financial ground to stand upon. In our opinion, he would be a very foolish man who, designing to build an enduring edifice of masonry, should select a volcanic region where the earthquakes beneath his feet would continually change the level of his foundations.

We think he would be a very unwise man who, when navigating the broad ocean, should choose as his guiding star a fluctuating and moving planet, instead of the polar star of fixed certainty. So, in the construction of an enduring civilized society, that is expected to live through the ages, dispensing justice and protecting the liberties of all its citizens, the system should be erected on a steady and unfluctuating foundation, and its founders should be guided by the fixed and unchanging principles of justice. Such a system cannot be established on the shifting and treacherous sands of a fluctuating medium of exchange, but must stand on solid ground, where all citizens may meet on equal terms for the adjustment of their grievances, and the enjoyment of citizenship.

CHAPTER IX.

HARD TIMES—Continued.

THE DIFFERENT CLASSES OF SOCIETY—MONEY EARNERS AND MONEY USERS — THE PREDATORY STRATUM — LAWS FOR THE CONTRACTION OF MONEY VOLUME— 7 YEARS OF SHRINKAGE IN THE UNITED STATES—THE PRACTICAL QUESTIONS OF TO-DAY, LAND, LABOR, FINANCE AND TRANSPORTATION — THE DECISION OF JUDGE GRESHAM IN THE WABASH RAILROAD CASE— THE KNIGHTS OF LABOR AN ORDER OF PEACE AND EDUCATION.

In connection with the report of the committee on Financial and Industrial depression contained in the previous chapter, Mr. John Davis, the chairman, made the following illustrative remarks, which may be properly considered with the report.

He said, for the convenience of discussion, civilized society in the United States may be divided into four classes: Two useful classes, devoted honestly and earnestly to the creation and distribution of wealth; and two predatory or vicious classes, adding to the burdens and misfortunes of society,

A MINER'S COTTAGE.

hindering the creation of wealth, blocking its distribution, and, in a thousand ways, making themselves a clog and a menace to civilized communities.

The useful classes embrace the men who labor and earn money on the farms, in the mines and in the factories. Also the men of business who have money or borrow it, and employ men in all the departments of industry and commerce. The two useful classes of society embrace all the men and women engaged in the creation and distribution of wealth, in all the existing forms of labor and legitimate business. They may be defined as "The money earners" and "The money users."

One of the predatory classes of society undermines, steals and debauches from the bottom, and the other attacks from the top, endangering the very existence of free institutions.

The substratum class embraces the indolent and vicious who decline to labor for a livelihood, living and dying as parasites and burdens on society. They are usually without visible means of support, and spend much of their time in the hands of the police and peace officers of society. They are the thoroughly discouraged wrecks of humanity, destitute of courage or hope; the debauched offal of societary misfortunes. During periods of industrial prosperity this substratum of vicious indolence is not large in America. Its numerical volume is reduced to a minimum, and ultimately, with continued industrial prosperity, it would cease to be of observable importance. But during periods of industrial depression, this substratum class grows rapidly in volume, becoming very burdensome, and sometimes absolutely dangerous to the peace of large communities.

The upper society embraces men who live not by earning money, nor by legitimately using money, but by the usury of money, and by gambling and speculating on the necessities and misfortunes of society. Since they thus live and fatten, it is to their selfish interests that society shall have as many and as great necessities and misfortunes as possible. Hence they are devoted, body and soul, to the business, not of creating and distributing wealth, but to creating societary necessities and misfortunes. They desire high and usurious rates on their loans to men, to states and to the nation. Money being dear in proportion to the limited supply, they favor and procure scarce and dear money through legislative action for its contraction and suppression.

The laws for the contraction of money are always passed in the interests of these usurers and speculators. Scarce money makes borrowing compulsory and usury high. It reduces the price of all property and makes the payment of money obligations difficult or impossible. Then when foreclosures and sheriff's sales occur, the usurers become the owners of landed estates and the creations of labor at nominal rates. Scarce money and falling prices offer unusual opportunities to stock gambling and the monopoly of the necessities of life, and of everything that money can purchase.

During five years of shrinking money in England, four-fifths of freeholders of England lost their homes, and those independent English farmers became the tenants of the money vultures of the country. During a period of seven years of shrinking money in this country, from 1866 to 1873, the people of the United States passed from a state of abounding prosperity to a condition of deplorable bankruptcy. In 1866 they were virtually out of debt; in 1873 the red flag of the auctioneer floated on every street in all the cities; farmers gave up their homes to the holders of the mortgages, and invaded the western wilderness to begin life anew. Men of enterprise who had been using money in the creation and distribution of wealth became bankrupt, and their former employes became idle, discouraged and vicious, swelling the substratum class to dangerous proportions, tramping everywhere for a living, as dangerous marauders on society.

These deplorable conditions of society are periodically produced at the bidding of the usury classes who are interested in scarce and dear money, and who prey on the necessities and misfortunes of civilized society.

What are the remedies? There are two. One is legitimate, safe and effective. The other, illegitimate, unsafe and ineffective. The legitimate and safe plan is public enlightenment on financial and industrial subjects as taught by the Knights of Labor, and to be consummated through the ballot box and wise legislation. The illegitimate and unsafe course is that taught and practised by the advocates of violence for legislative evils, and consummated in the flames of burning cities and the general destruction of property and human life. In fact they are anarchists, through their persistent violations of the very principles of all just government. They not only engage in anarchy, in their high sphere, corrupting the sources of law and justice; but are logically and certainly the parents and producers of the less harmful anarchy found in the vicious substratum of society.

Paid exorbitant rates for building railroads and telegraphs, in bonds, lands and money, they still hold them as their own property, and tax the public to whom the lines rightfully belong, "all the traffic will bear." The remedies for these evils are not the tearing up of railroads, the burning of cities, or the destroying of property. But public enlightenment on the practical questions of the day—on the subjects of land, labor, finance and transportation. Public enlightenment will beget public action. It will procure the repeal of class laws and the prompt arrest, trial and punishment of great criminals as well as small ones. The use of dynamite in Chicago was the violence of thoughtless anarchy.

The enlightened vote for Henry George in New York, and the just and patriotic verdict of Judge

Gresham in the Wabash railroad case, have changed the tone and course of a thousand newspapers, and have almost revolutionized the sentiment of the entire country. The decision of Judge Gresham actually wrung from Jay Gould, our great American anarchist, a real shriek of pain! These results of enlightened and patriotic action demonstrate and illustrate the practical superiority of the ballot as compared with physical violence. The dew and the sunshine are creators of wealth, while the blind cyclones only destroy. Enlightened labor will always accomplish happy results by the use of peaceful, lawful and civilized methods; while the blind, violent methods of savagery can only end in chaos from which spring individual and class usurpations of power and public oppression.

It was the object of the committee at Richmond to point out the central and main cause of industrial depression and public distress. It is our object now to point out and classify the principal agencies at work in civilized communities, for both good and evil, and to further illustrate the subject.

From what is here stated it will be seen that there should be no fight between employing capital and labor—between the money earners and the money users; yet such fights are common from the fact that suffering and uninformed men usually strike those nearest them; or because employing capital finds itself amid falling prices with no profits on the products of labor; or because employing capital, not satisfied with legitimate profits, enters the field of speculation and gambling on the products of labor. These questions must be solved, understood and peacefully settled. Herein is the mission of the order of the Knights of Labor. It is an order of peace and education.

In all mention of capital we should bear in mind the important distinction between employing capital and speculative or gambling capital—between the class of so-called "capitalists," and the capital-using, wealth-creating business men. And, in our mention of labor and laboring men we must remember the important distinction between sober and industrious wage-earners, and the idle, vicious class of parasites who avoid labor as much as possible. These distinctions between the useful and the predatory classes will materially aid us in understanding each other.

CHAPTER X.

WAGES.

WAGES A SUBJECT OF VAST IMPORTANCE—GREAT NATIONS ARE NOW DEALING WITH IT—THE ECONOMICS OF WAGES — INDUSTRIAL CONDITIONS INCESSANTLY CHANGE—A TABLE OF STATISTICS—THE PROGRESS OF WAGES—ECONOMY DOES NOT DEMAND LOW WAGES—WHAT HIGH WAGES WILL DO—HON. WILLIAM WALSH ON WAGES — INCREASE OF CAPITAL DEMANDS INCREASE OF LABOR—TO PROTECT LABOR A SACRED DUTY—DR. PARKER ON REGULATION OF WAGES—CO-OPERATION THE ULTIMATUM OF PRODUCTIVE INDUSTRY.

THE question of wages, as one of the phases of the labor movement, is of vast importance to the workingman. All who have investigated the subject are irresistibly driven to the conclusion that indications point to a contest in every civilized nation.

We read daily reports of the proceedings of the English parliament upon her land system and the struggles of her Irish tenantry; sensational accounts of Russian nihilism startle the world; Austria and

Germany are kept in a continual state of fear lest the death of Bismarck will leave them helpless; and everywhere there are unmistakable signs that an undercurrent is agitating the masses. This agitation assumes various phases in different localities. At one place it is a difficulty between mill-owners and their operatives; in another it lies between the rich and the poverty stricken; again, it is between land holders and peasants, and between privileged classes and the proletariat.

Wages, or the compensation for work performed, is that proportion of the value of any product to which each contributor to that product is entitled. This proportion may be either nominal or real. Nominal wages is the amount of money paid for a certain amount of work done, and real wages refers to the quantity of the commodities which the money received for the work will purchase. The two great forces which are engaged in the production of the substances which comprise food, fuel, shelter, or the materials which may be converted into capital, are labor and capital. Land is worthless unless labor and capital render it valuable. It is by the co-operation of these two forces that an annual product is brought into existence, wherefrom wages may be obtained.

A careful review of the economic development of the United States during the last fifty years, leads to the conclusion that the workingman has secured results for a given amount of labor which have gradually increased. The industrial conditions have been in a perpetual movement, and this movement has been controlled by artificial encouragement and restrictions. It is, therefore, difficult to trace the economic progress with exactness, and almost impossible to accurately determine the situation at any given time.

In the tenth annual report of the Massachusetts Bureau of Statistics of Labor, 1879, will be found a comparison between the wages of 1860 and those of 1878. The returns from 63,515 workingmen tended to show that the weekly wages were twenty-four and four-tenths per cent higher in 1878 than they were in 1860. A comparison made by Mr. Carlisle shows that between 1850 and 1860 wages advanced seventeen per cent, in gold, and only four per cent in purchasing power, but in the next ten years wages declined ten per cent in purchasing power. In the next decade they fell ten per cent, but increased eighteen per cent in purchasing power. By taking the average annual wages in cotton, woolen and iron industries in each census year, and the cost of living, the following comparison table was obtained:

Year.	Currency.	Gold.	Purchasing power.
1850	$244.83	$244.83	$244.83
1860	287.00	287.00	255.32
1870	358.12	306.55	230.83
1880	277.00	277.00	272.91

Similar estimates from labor statistics of other

states show a like increase in the rate of wages, despite the gradual centralization of capital.

It is not the amount of money received for wages that determines whether labor is cheap or dear, but the rate is fixed by the amount of valuable product secured by the money paid. An employer may pay two dollars for one man's work, and one dollar and a half for that of another, but the higher priced may be the cheaper. The two dollar man may be able to do twice the amount of work as the one who is paid one dollar and a half. Low wages are often the cause of poor labor, and it is from this point of view that capitalists may see that an apparent sacrifice may result in their ultimate advantage.

Economy does not demand the lowest priced labor, but the labor which produces the most at the least expense is always the most profitable. It is certainly clear that the employer who engages the man who is vigorous, intelligent and in best physical and mental condition, will profit more by high wages paid, than for low wages paid to a miserable, ignorant and half-starved animal.

E. P. Smith, in his Political Economy, says: "Looking upon a human laborer, then, as we would upon a steam engine, we see that the amount of force which he is capable of creating depends upon the amount of food supplied to him; a part of it answering the purpose of the coal which gives heat, another answering to the water which is converted into steam and generates motion. A sheet iron jacket put around the boiler prevents the waste of heat in one case, just as a woolen jacket about the body of the laborer does in the other. But food, clothing and shelter, are supplied to the human machine in the shape of wages. To stint them, and to keep the laborer down to the lowest point that will induce him to live, without deterring him from propagation, is precisely the same kind of economy which would keep the steam engines of a nation at half their working power to save wood, water and sheet iron. The rate of wages which such considerations would demand has been attained in very few regions of the world. Suppose it anywhere to have been reached: the laborer is only brought up to the condition of an ox."

At a Knights of Labor celebration in 1887, Hon. William Walsh, among other remarks, said:

"Wages arise where one is paid for his labor or services to another. Profit arises where one puts his capital at risk in production of some beneficial kind, and what has been gained after paying wages, rent, interest and other expenses, is profit.

"Labor is to some extent capital, because it requires a good deal of capital to bring an infant to manhood and educate him for the occupation he is to follow. It cannot justly be treated as a mere commodity. The workman cannot be separated from humanity, and the rights and duties that environ him as a man and a citizen, and I regard all who labor with hand or brain as workmen. All who think, plan, direct, record, invent, who contribute to whatever sustains, enlightens, graces, human life, are workmen. Every increase of capital creates an increased demand for labor of some sort; for capital will generally seek profitable use. It is only the weak and ignorant who bury their talent. Hence we are all interested in the increase of capital, and desire to give all the safety to its investment that may be consistent with the welfare of society in reference to the great objects for which society is organized.

"We all are interested with wages and profits. Between these two poles the labor questions chiefly play. While the rate of movement in population and in capital, and the fluctuation in the cost of necessaries have effect on wages, yet it is recognized by all economists, and is a truth which the workingmen should stand firmly to, that the standard of living is one of the chief foundations to establish good wages upon.

" 'Is man's life cheap as brutes?' is a vital question in this discussion, which Shakespeare puts in the mouth of one of his characters. Universally wherever the standard of living has been kept high, wages have been best maintained. Wages will never go higher than the point where profits cease. The capitalist will quit the business ultimately if profits cease. Fair profits then give the upper limit of wages. The standard of living is the lower limit. Keep this standard high and let it become traditional, bred in the sentiments and habits of the people, and wages will never go below it. The capitalist will withdraw when his profits vanish. The worker must cease to work and retire from the field when the wages offered will no longer furnish himself and his family with means to procure comfort and respectability, and make his home a place of sanctity and endearment.

"Workers must start from a high point of self-valuation, and never go below it. In a political sense, the high standard of living is a chief requirement for the preservation of our republican institutions. And it is a public duty of the most sacred kind to protect the workingmen of the country in all means and all natural and civil rights to secure a high standard of living. They are American citizens, and the safe guarding of liberty and public virtue is entrusted to their charge. The high standing of living has saved the labor of Switzerland from degradation, though the country is not rich in capital. The low standard of living has produced the degradation of labor witnessed among the Orientals. The low standard, if once allowed, will be further reduced until man's life will be cheaper than the brute's. In the slave days, a Southern master asked his servant to do a piece of work attended with danger. He said to the master: 'You had better let John (the white man) do that.' The master asked him why. The colored man said: 'If I go up there and fall I will be killed, and you will lose $1,-

500; but if John falls you will lose nothing.' The master saw the point and sent John. The freeman must look out for himself, and all are now free.

"The tendency of the fierce competition between capitalists, the multiplication of machinery, the over-flowing tide of emigration, woman labor and child labor, to reduce wages may be largely resisted by the elevation which a high standard of living communicates to the sentiments and expectations of the wage earners and to wages. If this standard is lowered the American workmen would in time be prostrated to the level of the degradation which may be seen among the toilers of the eastern world. American citizenship would be debased, and the arrogance of wealth and the insolence of its satelites and dependents would dominate over us. We would have proved ourselves unworthy of freedom, because we were unable to preserve that elevation of sentiment and dignity of character which are essential to the permanence of our American freedom.

"The capitalist fights everything that resists cheap production and lessens profits. He regards labor as a commodity. He sees no law but that of supply and demand. He forgets that the laborer is a man, a citizen and Christian, that he raises a family, and that families make the state, and that the state will reflect the elevation or degradation of the families that compose it. He takes no account of the ten commandments, nor of the grandeur and glory of the state.

HAPPY TOILERS.

"If labor submits to a low standard of living, low wages will prevail, and the workingmen will find poor, low priced goods and unhealthy tenements prepared to suit their fallen condition. Workingmen should never buy adulterated food or drink, shoddy or sizing clothes, or occupy filthy tenements. They should boycott these and stop the production of them, because they will be produced to meet the lowered condition of wage earners.

"There is one method of elevating wages that capital could not possibly resist, but it will take time and sacrifice from wage earners to place themselves in the condition to apply it.

"The capitalist treats labor as a commodity. He is governed solely by the law of supply and demand. He encourages by emigration, long hours, spasmodic activities, and suspension of production, and other means, a surplus supply of labor. Labor has no capital ahead. The workingman and his family must have food and shelter from day to day. He cannot withdraw his labor from a low market, as the capitalist can his productions. Providence has arranged that crops come in annually to encourage prudence, foresight and economy among men. The man that has saved enough to support himself and family for one year is independent. Production cannot stop for one year. And if wage earners would determine as rapidly as possible to save and accumulate one year's living, they would be absolutely independent of the fluctuations, artificial or otherwise, of the excessive supply of labor. They would be able to withdraw their labor from the market until the wages come up to the American standard of high living.

"It is one of the few well-established doctrines of political economy, that increase of wages never comes off the consumer, and must come out of profits. Good wages reduce the profits of the capitalist, but do not inhance the price to the public. The rule is, that it is the quantity of labor required to produce an article that increases its price to the consumer, and that the value or cost of the labor cannot in the workings of economic laws, be transferred to the consumer. But, even if high wages did not come out of profits alone, but enhanced the price of the commodity, the community would suffer infinitely more from the moral and political degeneracy which must inevitably result, and always and everywhere has resulted, from low wages and low standard of living than it would lose by any cheapening commodities effected by lowering wages. Our institutions are priceless, and must be maintained and handed down to all the generations that are to spring from the present. We cannot barter them away for cheaper goods.

"The wealth of the world would be no compensation to freemen for the degeneracy of their manhood and the debasement of the uplifting spirit that animates our glorious republican institutions. The constant increase of machinery, steam transit, and the whole tendency of the present industrial system is to release capital, dispense with the quantity of labor required in production, increase the surplus of labor, and lower wages down to the starvation line, and far below the standard of respectable, dignified and decent living, without which the days of our freedom and glory will rapidly pass away, and the great American Republic will die from the inordinate avarice of the few, and the lack of manly spirit and public virtue in the many.

"Freemen were never charged with a more sacred duty than now commands the American people to unite together and concentrate all the force of enlightened and patriotic public sentiment and opinion against low wages, and that inevitable degeneracy of the spirit of the people and institutions which have followed low wages always and everywhere."

In answer to a question as to the manner in which wages might be regulated, Dr. H. J. Parker replied as follows:

"It is all right and proper for workingmen to form unions and associations for mutual protection and improvement, but when they attempt to keep wages up on a par with the general advancement in other fields, without taking into the account the underlying forces of legislative enactments affecting money, commerce and labor, they are swimming against the current and will finally sink.

"Workingmen vote for men and parties that legislate for the Shylock money oppression, that permit high tariffs on articles of general consumption, and the free importation of labor to take the places of home laborers, and yet expect by some means to maintain a condition of labor superior to that of the European wage slave. It will be a failure. They may benefit themselves locally and temporarily, and in a few instances may protect themselves during their natural lifetime, but it cannot be a lasting nor a general protection that in its efforts ignores legislation that alone and inexorably determines the destiny of a people.

"As our country becomes developed we must sink to the European level, unless we refuse to yield to the shaping of our institutions in the European channel.

"With the European money system, tax and land systems, with the same laws governing the production and distribution of wealth, it is only a question of time as to where we will go. Wages cannot be regulated arbitrarily. They must go with everything else sooner or later.

"Co-operation is the ultimatum of productive industry, the highest point to be attained in manufacture. Labor will have its reward when it gets what it produces. Then its reward will be regulated by the demands of consumption and will seek an equilibrium and its proper fields of action, according to the demands which may press from various quarters.

"Until co-operation is perfected we must regulate

wages by regulating incomes or capital, supply of labor, etc. If we have the right to restrict interest on money, we have the same right to limit incomes on money invested. Limit incomes of all enterprises to a given per cent, and let the balance go to a fund to be distributed pro rata to employes according to skill and time put in, and you have the scientific solution of the labor question, when considered apart from general legislation. This need not destroy the spirit of enterprise and will not. It will give an extra stimulus to the laborer, and make him contented and emulative. He will try to do something for himself, because he sees an opportunity for something in the future.

"Just how far this kind of legislation may be necessary, is the question to be solved by an intelligent ballot from time to time.

"We may remember that government itself or civilization itself is based properly on the premise of protecting the weak against the strong, the good against the bad."

All countries, whether commercial or manufacturing, are visibly affected by periods of adversity and prosperity, and are subject to changes of varying intensity. Laws regulating the hours of labor, the collection of revenue and the like, may alter conditions and situations to some degree, but there can be no permanent effect. In the long run wages will be highest in that country or locality where capital and labor fully co-operate and, at the lowest cost, together make up the greatest amount of product. As conditions change, labor may be displaced for a time, and poverty may ensue, but this poverty is brought about more from the destruction of capital and in rendering land valueless, than from other causes.

CHAPTER XI.

ORIGIN AND PROGRESS OF TRADES UNIONS.

THE DISCLOSURE OF HISTORY—ANTIQUITY OF COMBINATIONS BY WORKINGMEN—THE OLD GUILDS OF EUROPE—THE FIRST AUTHENTIC ORGANIZATIONS—THE POWER OF ORGANIZATIONS SIX HUNDRED YEARS AGO—THE CRUELTIES PRACTICED IN ENGLAND—THE SECRET OF THEIR STRENGTH—UNIONS HAVE ELEVATED WAGES—WORKINGMEN CANNOT BE TOO WELL PAID—UNION MEN THE BEST WORKMEN—LITERATURE FOR LABOR—UNIONS ARE EDUCATING WORKINGMEN—THEIR GREAT FUTURE.

It is a singular fact that history discloses a systematic oppression of labor in all ages, and from time immemorial there has been a constant resistance on the part of the laborer.

In attempting to trace the origin of combinations and organizations among workingmen and laborers, we find their beginning lost in the remote ages. The first authentic evidences of such organizations, according to Brentano, are found in the history of the northern German tribes of Europe, which were called guilds or gilds. Guilds were originally feasts and gatherings held in celebration of births, marriages and deaths. Other events, such as coronations, national assemblies and the like, were the occasion of similar banquets and deliberative assemblages. These guilds led to the formation of a kind of brotherly alliance between those of similar occupations or modes of life, and eventually the term guild expressed the idea of a common community or society.

The spirit of association naturally found its way into the ranks of labor, and as early as the eighth century the organization of guilds had become almost an universal custom.

These guilds assumed a general classification and were divided into Religious, Merchant and Craft guilds. The religious guild was the prototype of church denominations, the merchant guild the predecessor of corporations, and the craft guild the archetype of the modern trade union. The craft guild grew up among the old freemen hundreds of years ago, and to-day we see trades unions as combinations of workingmen united in common defense of their rights as against the oppressive tendencies of great capitalists.

It was in the twelfth century, during the reign of Henry II, that the first organization, akin to the present trade union, was formed in England, and since that time the general tenor of legislation has been much against the interests of the workingman, and proportionately, has been enacted in behalf of the capitalist.

The essence of the craft guilds was "mutual support, mutual protection, and mutual responsibility." Their exclusiveness widened the separation between the craftsmen and their employers, and served to give each different views and interests. In the fourteenth century the masons maintained a higher rate of wages than was received by other trades, solely on account of their organization, and in 1383 the authorities of London, alarmed at the power exercised by the unions, forbade all "congregations, covins, and conspiracies of workmen."

In 1396, a coalition of shoemakers was disbanded by the authorities. Notwithstanding the legislation against them, the workingmen continued to combine, but the history of the working classes during the next three centuries is a tale of suffering and sadness. They resisted in every way possible, but were met at every hand with brutal force and infamous laws. While Edward VI was on the throne, an act was passed to brand a man who refused to work at "statute prices," with the letter "V" (vagabond), and reduce him to slavery for two years.

Nearly all of the attempts of parliament to fix wages were failures. At the dawn of the eighteenth century, the combination laws were universally in operation, and the workingman worked sixteen hours out of the twenty-four. With the introduction of steam power, the domestic system of manufacturing declined, and trades unions perfected their organizations. The workingmen met the combinations of their employers to keep down the price of labor, with organizations to keep them up. Capital has heretofore been directed against ignorant and uneducated men, but the conditions have changed in the last fifty years.

In speaking of trades unions, Trant says: "They are built on a rock—a firm, sound, substantial basis. They cannot be annihilated. If they are done away with to-day, they would spring up again to-morrow the same as in the celebrated dispute with Messrs. Platt, of Oldham; when the men were starved into submission, and were obliged to give up their union, yet they rejoined as soon as they were at work."

It is evident that workingmen are everywhere becoming less and less indifferent to the caprice of their employers. When they demand just laws their request cannot longer be passed unheeded, because they are able to show that they are as competent as any other class to judge of their own needs and requirements.

One of the fundamental elements which go to make up a trade union, is brotherly sympathy. This admirable sentiment seems to be peculiar to workingmen. Prof. Rogers writes: "I confess that I look forward to the international union of labor partnerships as the best prospect the world has of coercing those hateful instincts of governments, all alike irresponsible and indifferent, by which nations are perpetually armed against each other, to the infinite detriment, loss, and demoralization of all."

One of the general results of unions has been a raise in the payment of wages. Usually, the relations between workingmen and their employers imply a pecuniary bargain, and when differences have arisen, the efficacy of organization has been shown in the securing of better conditions. A general review of the history of trades unions indicates a gain for them. It is, however, difficult to point out to what extent a raise in wages is due to the direct action of a union, because the elements of general progress and prosperity have much to do with the amount of product, therefore, with the amount of wages paid.

Few employers when unasked advance the amount of wages paid, and the workingman in seeking to better his condition cannot well strike singly.

If a strike fails, it shows that the men have the capacity to combine in such a way that the employer may well fear, and despite failure, strikes are often successes. The loss incident upon a strike renders future demands for just dues a more readily adjusted affair than the first difficulty. An ineffectual strike often proves to be one of general effect, for non-unionists invariably gain, to some extent, the advantages of the unionist.

The action of the trades unions in gaining an increase in the amount of wages paid, does not affect the purchasing power of their stipends. This stimulates trade in a general way, for the workingman and his family are ever willing to spend his hard earned dollars in pecuniary additional comforts for the household. A general rise in wages throughout the United States would increase our exports to an enormous amount, and every department of trade would feel an impetus.

There is no doubt in the minds of intelligent and candid thinkers, that trades unions are the source of material profit and a general increase of products, and employers have learned that union men are, as a rule, better workmen. Every manufacturer knows that a good workman, though paid high wages, is of more value to him than a poor workman at less wages.

"It seems strange that in this enlightened age," Trant writes, "there are persons who believe that men can have more wages than is good for them. There is no such thing as being too well paid. The men who think so are, as a rule, those who are plentifully provided with the blessings of this life, and who opposed the movement in favor of universal education, because they objected to workingmen being too well educated, as it would make them discontented with their 'station,' as if there was such a thing as too much education. . . . All that is maintained here is that, though some evil may creep in with a rise of wages, as it seems to do

COAL UNDER DIFFERENT ASPECTS.

with an increase of wealth, yet that good wages are a great blessing, and ought to be gladly welcomed by those who even have not yet reached that stage of morality of endeavoring to love their neighbors as themselves."

The great movement which has agitated every state in America has been the cause of the springing up of scores of newspapers which are wholly devoted to educating the rank and file of the workingmen. Newspapers are now seen in homes which never before were blessed with them, and public schools are showing a decided increase because of their influence. The men, too, show a general desire to improve in their respective trades. The better the workman, the sooner he leaves incompetent associates and becomes a unionist. All union men are not superior workmen, but very few experts are non-union men. Men outside the unions are generally inferior workmen employed at greatly reduced rates.

An iron manufacturer, in writing of the influence of unions on his men, said: "I have had twenty years of pretty close acquaintanceship with artisans and laborers of all kinds, and I know many of them have much sounder views of common-sense political economy than the middle classes in general hold. I look upon trade unions as admirable training schools for the workmen, where they will soon outgrow their heresies on the subject of capital and labor, whereas, if they are brow beaten and scolded in a violent manner, they will begin—as some of them, I fear, have already—to think that masters are to be regarded as their natural enemies, and treated accordingly.

"The uneducated workmen are, as a rule, a rather violent set of fellows, it must be admitted; but I can see that, under the training and leadership of the foremost men in the unions, these are fast becoming a very small minority, as they are very plainly and forcibly told that the old way of settling disputes with their employers is about the very worst that could be adopted. This, coming from men of their own class, they are daily becoming more and more ready to listen to with respect, which would not be the case if it emanated from the employers' class, whom they have good grounds for regarding with distrust and suspicion.

"I know enough of the unprincipled conduct of the employers, through their agents in our iron industry, to understand and excuse much in the conduct of the unionists that would be indefensible on any other grounds than those of extreme injustice and most heartless provocation—not that the employers had directly perpetrated such things personally, but they must be held responsible, seeing that they have seldom or ever taken the trouble to find out the rights and wrongs of disputed points; but in ninety-nine out of one hundred cases the underlings have been left to take their own course and represent their own case as, of course, decidedly angelic. The unions have done immense service in bringing about a different state of things, and to my certain knowledge, it has been due to the influence of the leaders of the unions that the system of arbitration has been adopted lately in so many industries; and this, bear in mind, in spite of the dogged resistance of many of the employers, who do not like the system as I have heard them say, because it puts a weapon into the men's hands to fight with, when a dispute arises about the rate of wages."

It cannot be gainsaid that the unions have a great future before them. The legitimate end of pure unionism is to allay the antagonism between labor and capital, and to bring the employer and workingman to a plane of mutual understanding and mutual benefit.

CHAPTER XII.

AMERICAN LABOR UNIONS.

The First American Trade Union — Journeymen Shipwrights — New York Typographical Society — First Labor Party — Franklin Society of Printers — National Typographical Union — The International — Hat Finishers — Iron Moulders — Mechanical Engineers of America — Brotherhood Locomotive Engineers — Locomotive Firemen — Cigar Makers — Bricklayers and Stonemasons — Patrons of Husbandry — Grange — Railway Conductors — Boot and Shoemakers — German-American Typographical — Horse-Shoers — Iron and Steel Heaters — Granite Cutters — Lake Seamen — Boiler Makers — Carpenters and Joiners — Hat Makers — Miners and Mine Laborers — Bakers — Switchmen — Tailors — Telegraph Men — Furniture — Coopers — Etc. — Etc.

Organizations and combinations of workingmen have existed in the United States over one hundred years. On the Fourth of July, 1788, there was a grand parade in Philadelphia, and all of the trades were represented in the procession. Those

THE VOICE OF LABOR. 185

of each trade were appropriately costumed and carried an emblematic flag.

The following crafts were in line: Carpenters, boat-builders, sail-makers, ship-joiners, rope-makers, cabinet-makers, brickmakers, painters, clock and watchmakers, weavers, bricklayers, tailors, carvers, turners, coopers, plane-makers, blacksmiths, nailers, coachmakers; these were followed by hatters, potters, wheelwrights, tinners, printers, glovers, saddlers, stone-cutters, bakers, silversmiths and jewelers, goldsmiths, coppersmiths, gunsmiths; foundrymen, tanners, curriers and upholsterers, engravers, plasterers, brushmakers, brewers, etc., etc.

The first American trade union was the New York Society of Journeymen Shipwrights, which was incorporated April 3, 1803. The New York Typographical Society No. 6, was formed several years later, of which Horace Greeley was the first president.

The present system of labor unions may be said to have formed in 1825, and during the administration of John Quincy Adams. During this period the first labor party had birth, and through its organs, "The Workingman's Advocate," Daily "Sentinel," and "Young America," promulgated the following platform:

1. The right of man to the soil—"Vote yourself a farm."

2. Down with monopolies, especially the United States Bank.

3. Freedom of public lands.

4. Homesteads made inalienable.

5. Abolition of all laws for the collection of debts.

6. A general bankrupt law.

7. A lien of the laborer upon his own work for his wages.

8. Abolition of imprisonment for debt.

9. Equal rights for women with men in all respects.

10. Abolition of chattel slavery, and wages slavery.

11. Land limitation to 150 acres: no person after the passage of this law to become possessed of more than that amount of land. But when a land monopolist died, his heirs were to take each his legal number of acres, and be compelled to sell the overplus, using the proceeds as they pleased.

12. Mails in the United States to run on the Sabbath.

These radical principles were enthusiastically endorsed by the workingmen, and were the basis upon which they founded the "Workingmen's Party," whose convention in 1830 nominated Mr. Ezekiel Williams for governor of New York. From 1830 to 1840 the labor movement was more active than at any time previous to the rebellion. A law which had been enacted in Massachusetts against unions was attacked in 1842, and a complete victory was won by the Journeymen Boatmakers.

The Franklin Society of Printers, organized at Cincinnati in 1827, was the earliest of the printers'

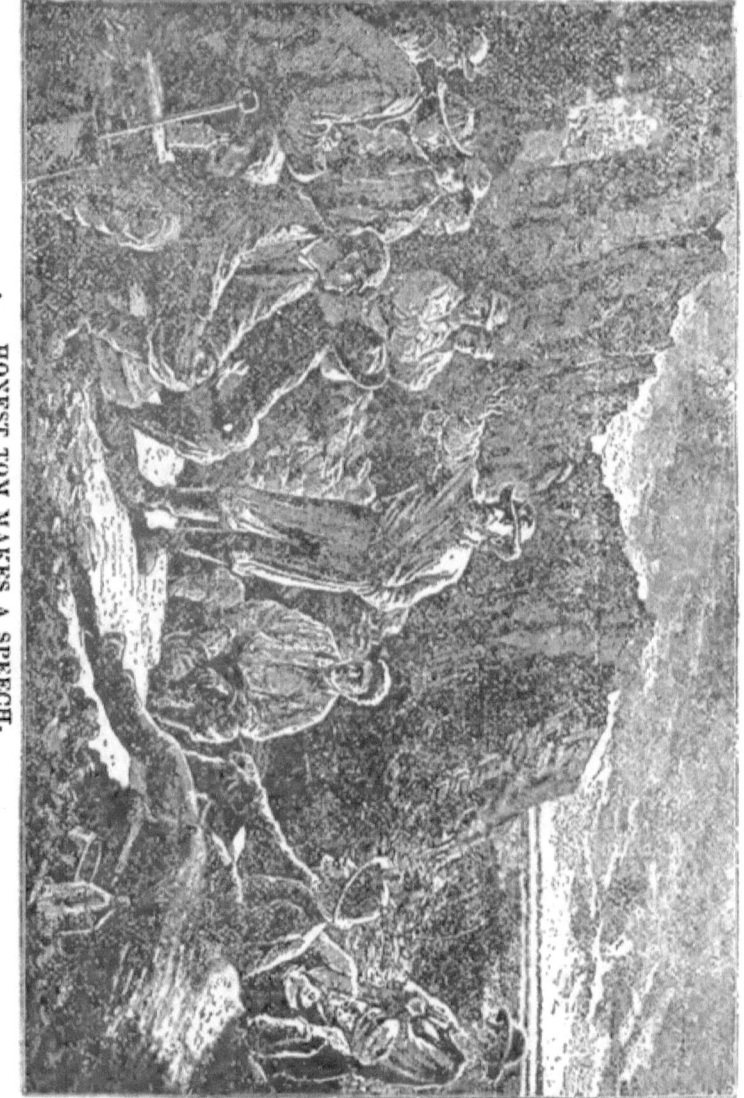

HONEST TOM MAKES A SPEECH.

unions. After a somewhat checkered career, a national call was made, and the National Typographical Union was formed in 1852. They became the International Typographical Union in 1869. They have over 355 local unions with a membership of over 18,000.

In 1854, The National Trade Association of Hat Finishers was organized. The hatters, in their various divisions, have about 10,000 members.

The Iron Molders' Union was formed in 1859: it now has 300 subordinate unions with a membership of 20,000.

The Machinists and Blacksmiths formed an organization in 1858. In the following year they received the first union charter granted by the United States government. They took the name of Mechanical Engineers of the United States of America in 1877. 10,000 members.

Despite serious opposition, the glass-blowers organized at Philadelphia in 1848. In the various divisions of their organization they now have about 30,000 members.

The Brotherhood of the Foot-Board was organized in 1863. The locomotive engineers have a membership of over 20,000, and now are known as "The Grand International Brotherhood of Locomotive Engineers." The locomotive firemen, also, have a brotherhood, with a membership of 17,000, which was formed in 1873, and is now known as "The Brotherhood of Locomotive Firemen."

The first union of the cigar-makers was formed in 1851, and since have acquired a combined membership of 30,000.

The bricklayers and stone-masons, organized in 1865, has a register of over 16,000 members, and is well organized.

In 1866, "The Patrons of Husbandry," otherwise known as the National Grange, was formed, and now has over 800,000 members. It is only rivaled by the Knights of Labor in size.

The railway conductors perfected their organization in 1879, and are now called the "Order of Railway Conductors." Membership about 8,000.

The boot and shoe men organized in 1869, but failed in the general strike of 1873.

The National German-American Typographical Union began in 1873, and now has a roll of about 1,200 members.

The union, from which the National Horse-shoers Union was formed, was organized in 1849. The present organization was perfected in 1874, and has 5,784 members.

The "Sovereigns of Industry" formed in 1874, and four years later had 180,000 members. The order failed in 1880, and in 1886 was re-organized. Its object is co-operation and to shut out the "middleman" in all departments of business.

The iron workers organized two unions in 1873, called the Associated Brotherhood of Iron and Steel Heaters, and the Iron and Steel Roll-hands' Union.

They combined with the Sons of Vulcan in 1876, and are now known as the Amalgamated Association of Iron and Steel Workers. They number in all, 60,000.

The Granite-cutters National Union was formed in 1877.

In 1878, the organization named the Lake Seamen's Union was organized, and now has a membership of 8,000.

The Lasters' Protective Union of New England was organized in 1879, has fifty-eight branches and 7,860 members.

The members of the International Brotherhood of Boilermakers, and Iron Shipbuilders and Helpers, have a membership of 20,000. These workmen first organized in 1880.

The Brotherhood of Carpenters and Joiners of America is the outgrowth of previous organizations, the first of which was formed in 1854. The present name was taken in 1881. It has about 42,500 members. There is also an United Order of Carpenters.

In 1883, the National Hatmakers' Union was organized.

The railroad brakemen formed their National Brotherhood in 1884, and now have 18,000 members.

The National Federation of Miners and Mine Laborers is a combination of various coal and mining organizations, and has a roll of 90,000 members. The present order adopted its name in 1885.

In 1886 the Journeymen Bakers' National Union was formed, and has a present membership of 25,000.

The Switchmen's Mutual Aid Association was organized in 1886. Its membership is 5,000.

The Custom Tailors' National Union has 18,000 members; the Telegraph Operators and Linemen have 10,000 members; the House Painters, 10,000; the Coopers' Union, 10,000; the Furniture Workers, 10,000; and the Mule Spinners (in the cotton factories), number 5,000. There are, perhaps, a score of other organizations whose membership is less than 5,000.

The most powerful organization of workingmen extant, is the Knights of Labor.

CHAPTER XIII.

THE KNIGHTS OF LABOR.

THE CAUSE OF THEIR ORGANIZATION—THE GREAT POWER OF THE ORDER—URIAH STEVENS, THE FOUNDER—EARLY HISTORY—STRUGGLES—ATTACKED BY PULPIT AND PRESS—ITS GROWTH—CHARACTER OF ITS MEMBERS—WHO THEY ARE—PRESENT NUMBER—A SEMI-SECRET ORDER—THEIR PREAMBLE AND PLATFORM OF PRINCIPLES—MANNER OF JOINING—WHO ARE ELIGIBLE—LAWS AND REGULATIONS OF THE KNIGHTS—LOCAL, DISTRICT AND GENERAL ASSEMBLIES—PASS-WORDS, SIGNS AND GRIPS—WOMEN AS MEMBERS—INTERESTING INFORMATION—BIOGRAPHY OF MR. POWDERLY—THE OFFICERS—THE EXECUTIVE COMMITTEE—A DESCRIPTION OF THE MANAGEMENT.

THE exigencies of the workingmen in the United States have been the cause of creating the largest and most powerful organization, wholly devoted to the interests of labor, that the world has ever known.

The history of the Knights of Labor, until the last few years, has not been sufficiently eventful to attract general attention, but the events of 1886 proved conclusively that organization of the workingmen throughout the land had been perfected upon an unparalleled scale, and that it had grown into the position of being one of the most potent factors of this decade as a social and industrial force. The growth of the order has been phenomenal, both in number and for reaching strength. Its history, and its influence upon industry, have become matters for the historian.

The originator of this vast organization was Uriah Stephens, a tailor by trade, of Philadelphia, who was born in Cape May County, New Jersey, in 1821.

In October, 1869, the "Garment-Cutters' Society" of that city grew discouraged, and its members determined to dissolve their society. Immediately after the close of their last meeting, Uriah Stephens consulted with James L. Wright, I. M. Hilser, R. C. McCauley, William Cook, R. M. Keen, and James L. Kennedy, upon the advisability of forming a new union. All of them were clothing cutters. The plan proposed by Mr. Stephens was discussed and met with hearty approval.

After several informal meetings, the men above named, with several others, met at Mr. Stephens' house on Thanksgiving day, 1869, and the association now known as the Knights of Labor was formed. The chief idea of their organization was a national union of wage earners of all classes.

The members were bound to secrecy, and the existence of their society was unknown outside of their own number for several years. Like all great enterprises, the order developed slowly at first, but it grew in strength and gradually gained a foothold in the estimation of workingmen.

The method adopted for calling a meeting was the marking of five stars upon the front of Independence Hall. This singular and mysterious sign never failed to bring together thousands of the working class, and it was the cause of much adverse comment, both from the press and the pulpit. Because the object and principles of the order were unknown and miscomprehended, the organization was bitterly condemned on all sides, and the Catholic church added its denunciation to the general deluge of adverse criticism.

At this time the order had 80,000 members, but during the succeeding five years their number materially decreased, and in 1883 the roll fell to 52,000 members. In 1871 their present name was adopted. Previous to the publishing of the objects of the order, its simple plan and general utility everywhere met with favor, and workingmen in all of the eastern and middle states were rapidly enrolled.

Amid this clamor of defamation the leaders decided to make public their aims and the ultimate object of the society. In June, 1878, Mr. Stephens, G. M. W., signed a special call for a meeting, at which he said they had met "to consider the expediency of making the name of the order public, for the purpose of defending it from the fierce assaults and defamation made upon it by press, clergy and corporate capital, and to take such further action as shall effectually meet the grave emergency."

There is a widespread opinion that the Knights of Labor are solely recruited from the ranks of laborers and mechanics, but this is not the case. Among their number may be found men and women of all producing occupations. The growth of the order has been such that over three hundred new assemblies have been formed in a single month. The total number of Knights, in the United States and Canada, is estimated to be over ONE MILLION.

There is not a branch of labor, trade or profession that exists, that cannot furnish material for a Knights of Labor assembly, and the occupations as are not organized are joined together in separate assemblies. This order is not only because of its numerical strength, but more especially on account of its almost certain future, the most important labor combination ever conceived.

The name may or may not be well chosen. Many of the Knights have expressed themselves to the effect that the term is too much like those of orders with which the Knights are distinctly at war. It was this feeling which prompted them to change the official name of their chief executive from "Grand" to that of "General Master Workman." Contrary to current belief, the Knights of Labor is only a semi-secret order. Members are not now oath-bound, but are simply obligated upon word of honor to keep silent as to the workings and proceedings of the organization. On the other hand, one Knight is not permitted to reveal another's connection with the order without the latter's consent. As a general rule, the work done by local general assemblies is done secretly, as expediency demands.

The preamble and platform of principles of the order, as narrated in their various organs, is briefly summarized as follows:

The alarming development and aggressiveness of great capitalists and corporations, unless checked, will inevitably lead to the pauperization and hopeless degradation of the toiling masses.

It is imperative, if we desire to enjoy the full blessings of life, that a check be placed upon unjust accumulation, and the power for evil of aggregated wealth.

This much desired object can be accomplished only by the united efforts of those who obey the divine injunction, "In the sweat of thy face shalt thou eat bread."

Therefore we have formed the Order of Knights of Labor, for the purpose of organizing and directing the power of the industrial masses, not as a political party, for it is more—in it are crystalized sentiments and measures for the benefit of the whole people, but it should be borne in mind, when exercising the right of suffrage, that most of the objects herein set forth can only be obtained through legislation, and that it is the duty of all to assist in nominating and supporting with their votes only such candidates as will pledge their support to these measures, regardless of party. But no one shall, however, be compelled to vote with the majority, and calling upon all who believe in securing "the greatest good to the greatest number," to join and assist us, we declare to the world that our aims are:

I. To make industrial and moral worth, not wealth, the true standard of individual and National greatness.

II. To secure to the workers the full enjoyment of the wealth they create, sufficient leisure in which to develop their intellectual, moral and social faculties; all of the benefits, recreation and pleasures of associations; in a word, to enable them to share in the gains and honors of advancing civilization.

In order to secure these results, we demand at the hands of the STATE:

III. The establishment of Bureaus of Labor Statistics, that we may arrive at a correct knowledge of the educational, moral and financial condition of the laboring masses.

IV. That the public lands, the heritage of the people, be reserved for actual settlers; not another acre for railroads or speculators, and that all lands now held for speculative purposes be taxed to their full value.

V. The abrogation of all laws that do not bear equally upon capital and labor, and the removal of unjust technicalities, delays and discriminations in the administration of justice.

VI. The adoption of measures providing for the health and safety of those engaged in mining, manufacturing and building industries, and for indemnification to those engaged therein for injuries received through lack of necessary safeguards.

VII. The recognition by incorporation, of trades, unions, orders, and such other associations as may be organized by the working masses to improve their condition and protect their rights.

VIII. The enactment of laws to compel corporations to pay their employes weekly, in lawful money, for the labor of the preceding week, and giving mechanics and laborers a first lien upon the products of their labor to the extent of their full wages.

IX. The abolition of the contract system on National, State and Municipal works.

X. The enactment of laws providing for arbitration between employers and employed, and to enforce the decision of the arbitrators.

XI. The prohibition by law of the employment of children under fifteen years of age in workshops, mines and factories.

XII. To prohibit the hiring out of convict labor.

XIII. That a graduated income tax be levied.

And we demand at the hands of Congress:

XIV. The establishment of a National monetary system, in which a circulating medium in necessary quantity shall issue direct to the people, without the intervention of banks; that all the National issue shall be full legal tender in payment of all debts, public and private; and that the Government shall not guarantee or recognize any private banks, or create any banking corporations.

XV. That interest bearing bonds, bills of credit or notes shall never be issued by the Government, but that, when need arises, the emergency shall be met by issue of legal tender, non-interest bearing money.

XVI. The importation of foreign labor under contract be prohibited.

XVII. That in connection with the postoffice, the Government shall organize financial exchanges, safe deposits and facilities for deposit of the savings of the people in small sums.

XVIII. That the Government shall obtain possession, by purchase, under the rights of eminent domain, of all telegraphs, telephones and railroads, and that hereafter no charter or license be issued to any corporation for construction or operation of any means of transporting intelligence, passengers or freight.

And while making the foregoing demands upon

the State and National Government, we will endeavor to associate our own labors.

XIX. To establish co-operative institutions, such as will tend to supercede the wage system, by the introduction of a co-operative industrial system.

XX. To secure for both sexes equal pay for equal work.

XXI. To shorten the hours of labor by a general refusal to work for more than eight hours.

XXII. To persuade all employers to agree to arbitrate all differences which may arise between them and their employes, in order that the bonds of sympathy between them may be strengthened, and that strikes may be rendered unnecessary.

The manner of joining the order and the forming of local assemblies is of interest, and the following comments are given for the benefit of the uninitiated:

Any female of the age of sixteen, or any male of the age of eighteen, whether manufacturer, employer of any kind, wage-worker or farmer, is eligible to become a member, except lawyers, bankers, professional gamblers, stock brokers, and any person who makes, or sells, or derives any of his support from the sale of intoxicating drink; but at least three-fourths of every local assembly must be composed of wage-workers or farmers.

No local assembly can be organized with less than ten members.

14

Assemblies may be formed of any particular trade or calling, or they may be composed of all trades. The latter are termed "mixed" assemblies.

Assemblies can only be instituted by regularly commissioned organizers.

The charter fee is $16, which must be paid to the organizer, and for which will be sent a charter, seal and supplies. The expenses of the organizer are not included in the charter fee, but vary according to the distance traveled.

Under the laws of the Order the initiation fee cannot be less than one dollar for men and fifty cents for women.

The amount of local dues is regulated by each local assembly, but cannot be less than ten cents per month.

The Order also has a Benefit Insurance Association, on the co-operative plan, which went into operation November 1, 1883. The membership fee is $1.25, and on the death or total disability of a member, an assessment of only twenty-five cents is made. Until the membership is sufficient to pay $500, the amount of benefits will be regulated by the receipts from assessments.

After a local assembly is formed, a candidate must be proposed by a member in good standing, who has an acquaintance with the applicant.

The Order of the Knights of Labor is not a mere trade union, or benefit society; neither is it a political party. Some of the specific aims and objects of the Order are set forth in the preamble and declaration of principles published from week to week, but any and every measure calculated to advance the interests of the wage-workers, morally, socially or financially, comes within the scope of the Order. To abolish as rapidly as possible, the wage system, substituting co-operation therefor; the settlement of all difficulties between employer and employe by arbitration; to educate the members to an intelligent use of the ballot, for their own benefit and protection, free from restraint of party or the undue influence of employers or monopolies; opposition to land, transportation, currency and all other monopolies that affect the interests of the masses, and the protection of all its members in the exercise of all their rights as citizens, are some of the principal objects of the Order.

Believing that these objects can be best secured through a thorough organization of all branches of honorable toil, those who are not already members are cordially invited, and if they approve of the Order, to secure the requisite number of persons to form a local assembly in their locality, an organizer will proceed to arrange a date for founding the assembly.

Five or more local assemblies in any locality, within a reasonable distance of each other, may form a district assembly, for the better protection and regulation of trade matters.

Local assemblies, located at any distance from

a district assembly, are attached directly to the general assembly.

The general assembly meets annually on the first Monday in October at such place as may be selected at each session, and is the highest tribunal of the Order. The general assembly is composed of general officers and representatives from the district assemblies and local assemblies attached to the general assembly.

The revenue of the general assembly is derived from the sale of supplies and a per capita tax of six cents per quarter for every member in good standing.

Each local assembly has control of its own funds, and local co-operative enterprises are encouraged.

The Order has a secret work, consisting of passwords, signs and a grip, for the protection of the meetings against those not members, and against expelled or suspended members.

Each member is required to take a pledge of honor, upon joining, to obey all the laws of the Order, and not to reveal any of the business or secret work of the Order. No oath is taken.

There is nothing in the laws or workings of the Order to interfere with the religious views of any member.

Each local assembly is known by a number, assigned by the general secretary. Each local will also choose a suitable name upon organization.

Local assemblies attached to the districts have to

URIAH STEPHENS,
Founder of the K. of L.

pay an additional per capita tax, of such amount as may be fixed by each district assembly, for the support of the same.

Women may become members of the Knights of Labor under the same laws and regulations as men, and may form local and district assemblies; but the charter fee of a local assembly, composed wholly of women, is $11. The initiation fee for women is fifty cents.

The Order has an official paper known as the "Journal of United Labor," published semi-monthly by the general secretary, and each local assembly is required to subscribe for at least one copy each year, as it is the organ of official communications from the general master workman and general secretary of the Order.

At the death of Uriah Stephens in 1879, the mantle of General Master Workman fell upon Mr. T. V. Powderly, of Scranton, Pa.

Terrence Vincent Powderly is of Irish parentage, and was born at Carbondale, Pa., January 24, 1849, and was the youngest son in a family of twelve children. Before reaching his majority he went to Scranton and entered a railroad machine shop, where he received $2.50 a day. While there he took a commercial course of study, became a member of a literary and debating society, and laid the foundation of his success as a public speaker and a convincing writer.

He soon joined the Knights of Labor, and became

a leader in the local labor committee of Scranton. Shortly afterwards he formed the personal acquaintance of Uriah Stephens: and was elected as the head of the organization at Scranton.

He urged pacific measures and moderation during the strikes of 1877, and his advice was the means by which much property was saved from destruction. He is an eloquent speaker, and his success as a leader of men is due to his broad and liberal ideas, combined with sincere purpose and clear judgment.

Under Mr. Powderly's control, the Knights of Labor has attained its present strength and importance. His mettle and aims are fully expressed in the preamble and declaration of principles of the order, which has been scattered broadcast throughout the land.

He has served as Mayor of Scranton, but has invariably declined to accept various political nominations which have been tendered him, among which was that for Governor.

Richard Griffiths, of Chicago, was elected General Worthy Foreman in 1879, and after serving as General Treasurer two terms, was elected to his present office October 13, 1886.

Charles H. Litchman was elected General Secretary in 1878, and has since held the same office. He has been a member of the Massachusetts legislature. He lives in Philadelphia.

Frederick Turner is General Treasurer, and has

held the office of Secretary and Treasurer since 1883.

The Executive Board of the organization is made up by the following gentlemen:

Thomas B. Barry, East Saginaw, Michigan; John W. Hays, New Brunswick, New Jersey; William H. Bailey, Shawnee, Ohio; Albert A. Carlton, Somerville, Massachusetts; Thomas B. McGuire, New York City; Ira B. Aylesworth, Baltimore, Maryland.

The officers of a local assembly are Master Workman, Worthy Foreman, Venerable Sage (retired Master Workman), Recording and Financial Secretary, Treasurer, Worthy Inspector, Almoner, Unknown Knight, Inside and Outside Esquires, Insurance Solicitor and three Trustees.

The officers of state assemblies correspond to those of the local assembly, and the general office term is two years.

CHAPTER XIV.

STRIKES AND LOCKOUTS.

A CAUSE OF RECENT STRIKES — WHY WORKINGMEN STRIKE—STATISTICS OF STRIKES IN 1880—SUCCESSES AND FAILURES—COMPLETE REVIEW OF THEIR EFFECT—AMOUNT OF LOSS INCURRED — AGGREGATE LOSSES IN APRIL AND MAY, 1886 — PUBLIC SYMPATHY FOR STRIKERS—POWDERLY ON STRIKES—GREAT THOUGHTS—THE POWER OF WEALTH GIVING WAY TO JUSTICE AND RIGHT — A NEW POWER DAWNING UPON THE WORLD—A BRIGHT FUTURE AT HAND—IDEAS FOR WORKINGMEN TO THINK AND ACT UPON.

ONE of the effects resulting from the rapid organization of the unions during the last decade, is an epidemic of strikes. It is needless to say, that sober and intelligent workingmen throughout the country do not throw down their tools and leave their benches without provocation. A week's wages is more to a workingman than it is to his employer, for the simple reason that it means a week's provision for himself and family, while his employer only suffers a diminution of his capital. The workingman strikes because he feels the weight of manifest injustice, and seeks thereby to secure redress for his grievances.

There is no doubt but strikes have been precipitated from causes that could have been removed by more pacific measures; often better results could have been secured. Instances can be cited where petty reasons and personal animosity have been the cause of strikes, but such cases are few. These movements, as a rule, have been efforts to better the condition of labor, and great good has resulted, notwithstanding the fact they have been generally unsuccessful.

Mr. Joseph D. Weeks, of the census bureau, says in a report on the strikes and lockouts of 1880, that it is evident that these labor disturbances are growing less frequent. The number of strikes in certain of the prominent trades, as given in the report, is as follows: Iron and steel industries, 236; coal mining, 158; textile trades, 46; cigar-making, 42; building trades, 36; transportation, 36; printing trades, 28; glass industries, 27; piano-making, 14; boot and shoe making, 11.

Much the greater proportion (71½ per cent) of the strikes and lockouts reported upon, were caused by differences as to rates of wages. A total of 503, or about 86 per cent of those relating to wages, or 62 per cent of all, were for an advance, and 77, or 14 per cent, of those relating to rates of wages, or 9½ per cent of all, were against a reduction.

Of 481 strikes—59 per cent of the whole—169, or 35 per cent, were successful; 85, or 13 per cent, were compromised, and 227, or 47 per cent, were unsuccessful. Of 307 strikes for an advance, 127, or 41 per cent, were successful; 62, or 20 per cent, were compromised, and 118, or 39 per cent, were unsuccessful. Of 45 strikes or lockouts against or for a reduction, 3 only were successful, 8 were compromised, and 34 were unsuccessful.

Of 20 strikes in connection with payment of wages, 11, or 35 per cent, were successful, 6 were compromised, and three were unsuccessful. Every strike in connection with hours of labor, of which the result is given, was unsuccessful. In questions relating to administration and methods of work, the strikes were, as a rule, unsuccessful. Of 813 stoppages by causes reported upon, 610, or 88 per cent, were strikes; 85, or 12 per cent, were lockouts.

Of 610 classified as strikes, the results of 369 are given. Of these, 143, or 39 per cent, were successful; 156, or 42 per cent, were unsuccessful, and 70, or 19 per cent, were compromised. Of 85 lockouts, the results of 52 are given. Of these 10, or 19 per cent, were successful; 34, or about 65 per cent, were unsuccessful, while 8, or about 15 per cent, were compromised.

In 414 strikes, the number of men idle were 128,262, making an average of about 310 men to each strike. Of these, 64,779 lost $3,711,097, or $57 each. The total loss in wages is estimated at $13,003,866.

When the strikes were successful, the additional wages compensated for a portion of this loss.

The theory and practice of strikes is greatly different to-day from that of the past. Intelligent leaders have perfected organization, and the workingman has never been better prepared to combat his wrongs and secure his just dues. Labor is now aware that in organization lies the true channel to a higher plane and a better condition, and with due regard for the law of the land, it is destined to accomplish a righteous advancement.

The following is a statement of the aggregate of losses incident upon the strikes in April and May, 1886.

	Wages.	Current Business.	New Business Stopped.
New York City...	$300,000	$300,000	$2,000,000
Philadelphia.....	60,000	50,000	5,000,000
Smaller Pa. cities.	70,000	50,000	....
Detroit, Mich.....	97,000	25,000	850,000
Cincinnati........	375,000	300,000	1,000,000
Milwaukee........	466,000	200,000	4,000,000
New England cities	275,000	....	6,000,000
St. Louis	75,000	....	....
Troy, N. Y.......	75,000	....	150,000
Washington, D. C..	54,000	....	2,000,000
Indianapolis.......	2,000	....	....
Pittsburgh.:......	30,000	75,000	300,000
Louisville. Ky....	23.000	5,000	500,000
Coal strikes......	200,000	500,000	Indeterm'e
Chicago..........	700,000	700,000	3,000,000
Totals......	$2,802,000	2,105,000	24,800,000
Grand total......................			$29,707,000

In commenting upon this statement, the "Locomotive Firemen's Magazine" says: "We presume the foregoing figures are largely guess work, mere approximations, and that there are those who would probably place sum totals much higher, and this could be done, we apprehend, while a strict regard for facts would be maintained. It will be admitted, we think, that the larger the sum total of losses occasioned by strikes, the more aggravating must be the causes which produce them. The trouble is that men contemplate the losses and lose sight of the wrongs which provoke them. The losses to such people obscure the wrongs. Fortunately there are those who, though the losses by strikes are enormous, maintain that the wrongs which produce strikes and occasion the losses demand first consideration, and they are right in their conclusions.

Take any of the industrial enterprises that have suffered losses by the recent strikes, and employers select the most expressive terms in speaking of their losses and to magnify the rectitude of their treatment of employes, as also the base ingratitude of those who struck. They are in positions to obtain the public ear—they have money and influence, and are the first to command audience. They never did say the employe was right—always wrong. The strikers come in later, and often after the verdict of the public has been rendered.

If the strike touches the transportation interests of the country, railroads or water transportation, or, if as in the case of the telegraph strike, it interferes with the transmission of intelligence, the strikers find at once that overwhelming opposition confronts them, for though the great public may not believe the strikers in the wrong, or may believe that their grievances are aggravating, still, as the method of redress involves the public in embarrassments and inconveniences, it demands that the strikers shall resume work or that others shall be employed in their places, regardless of the wrongs complained of, and as a consequence the wrongs which led to the strike are obscured. Take as an illustration the telegraph strike which occurred some years ago.

The real investment made by the owners of the telegraph lines amounted to about $40,000-000. The stock of the corporation had been watered until it swelled to $80,000,000. Now to declare dividends on $80,000,000, it became necessary to reduce the wages of employes. But when the employes struck it was difficult for them to get before the public the stupendous iniquity which provoked the wrong. The public demanded service without regard to wages, this demand strengthened the corporation, and as a consequence, when the strike ended, the wrong existed as when the strike began. The strikers suffered. The corporation came off with flying colors. Finally the great public condemned the corporation, but the condemnation resulted in no harm to the corporation nor benefit to the wronged employes.

It is not to be presumed that there will never be another telegraph strike. On the contrary, the probabilities are there will be another strike one of these days. Why? Simply because the flagrant wrong exists. It has not been removed. It has not been modified. Wrongs are like cancer. They eat their way to the surface. You must remove the roots or they will come again; hence, we observe, that the man who discusses the wrongs which produce strikes is a better statesman, a better citizen, and more of a philanthropist, than he who is eternally deploring the losses which strikes occasion, without giving a thought to their cause.

It is quite probable that men generally do not regard successful revolutions worth what they cost. Strikes are revolutions and rebellions combined. We read and speak of the American revolution— the British call it a rebellion. Rebellion or revolution, it was dear to England, because she provoked it and lost. It was costly and bloody to the colonies, but they won, and yet they were colonists who were opposed to the revolution. They did not believe that the tea tax and the stamp tax were of sufficient importance to warrant rebellion and revolution. It is not to be presumed that the colonies would have rebelled because of the amount of money involved in the taxation imposed, but the imposition of the tax brought into prominence the insufferable wrong of taxation without representation. It was taxation and chains, taxation and serfdom, and hence the colonies struck for freedom and independence, and had they been defeated in the war of '76 they would still have been striking for the recognition of their rights. It goes for nothing to say that strikes are always expensive. The fact is universally admitted, but it is not true that strikes ought not to occur because they are costly.

There is a way to prevent strikes, as there was a way in 1776 to have prevented the war of the revolution. Had England acted justly, there would have been no war, and if employers would act justly towards their employes there would be fewer strikes, or strikes would forever disappear from the industrial records of the country. Arbitration, compromise, reasoning together, should always precede a strike, but as certainly as rivers flow to the sea, when injustice is continued in spite of such things, strikes will come, and the more wide-spread the injustice the more terrible will be the consequences of strikes.

Manifestly, thinking men, who have the welfare of society at heart, are becoming profoundly interested in the labor problems of the day. They see distinctly that there must be less injustice or more strikes. If more strikes, then more turbulence, more losses, more mobs, more collisions, more blood, more demoralization. As a consequence, congress is discussing remedies, and the same is true of legislatures throughout the country; the supreme idea being to remove causes for strikes, enthrone justice and right and overcome wrong. We regard the signs of the times as cheering. We believe that strikes in the future will be less frequent, because we believe the working men will see that the great public heart is throbbing responsive to their demands for justice. The press of the country is evincing deep solicitude in the welfare of workingmen. The pulpit is taking a hand in the discussion, but above all, and better than all, workingmen themselves have resolved that they will master the problems, and by logic and law, and by the intelligent use of the ballot, remedy many of the evils of which they justly complain."

GENERAL MASTER WORKMAN POWDERLY ON STRIKES:

" The prospect for the future of the laboring man in America, is brighter to day than it ever was, notwithstanding the seemingly 'strained relations' at present existing between employer and employe.

"That we are passing through an epidemic of strikes, lockouts, and boycotts, is true, but the fact must not be lost sight of that were it not for the growing power of organization, we should have a great many more strikes to contend with than we have had.

"The growth of organization for the last ten years has been steady and healthy. It is only where organization is in its infancy, that serious troubles such as strikes and lockouts exist. The causes from which strikes and lockouts spring, are to be found in all parts of the country, but the methods of dealing with the troubles as they arise are different. In places where no organizations of labor exist, or where the seeds of organization have just been planted, disputing parties are apt to become involved in strikes. The reasons advanced in support of that proposition are as follows: Until recently very few workingmen dared to express their opinion in public on the subject of labor, for the reason that they were almost certain of an immediate dismissal from the service of the man or company they worked for, if it became known that they in any way favored the association of workingmen for mutual protection.

"With such a sentiment existing in the breasts of workingmen, they could not be expected to feel very kindly toward the employer, who so jealously watched their every movement, and who, by his actions, made them feel that they were regarded rather as serfs than freemen. While the real bone and sinew of the land remained in enforced silence, except where it could be heard through the medium of the press and rostrum, through chosen leaders, another class of men who seldom worked, would insist on 'representing labor,' and in making glowing speeches on the rights and wrongs of man, would urge the 'abolition of property' or the 'equal division of wealth;' such speakers very often suggesting that a good thing to do would be to 'hang capitalists to lamp-posts.'

"The employer of labor who listened to such speeches, felt that in suppressing organization among his workmen he was performing a laudable act. Yet he was, by that means, proving himself to be the most powerful ally the anarchist could wish for. He caused his employes to feel that he took no interest in them, other than to get as many hours of toil out of them for as few shillings as possible. The consequence was that the employer, who was himself responsible for the smothering of the honest expression of opinion on the part of labor, became possessed of the idea that the raw-head and bloody-bones curbstone orator was the real representative of labor, and determined to exercise more vigilance and precaution than ever in keeping his 'help' out of the labor society.

"The speaker who hinted at, or advocated, the destruction of property or the hanging of capitalists to lamp-posts, was shrewd enough to speak very kindly and in a knowing manner of labor associations, giving out the impression that he held membership in one or more of them. Workingmen, who were denied the right to organize, very frequently went to hear Mr. Scientific lecture on the best means of handling dynamite. And when the speaker portrayed the wrongs of labor, the thoughtful workman could readily trace a resemblance be-

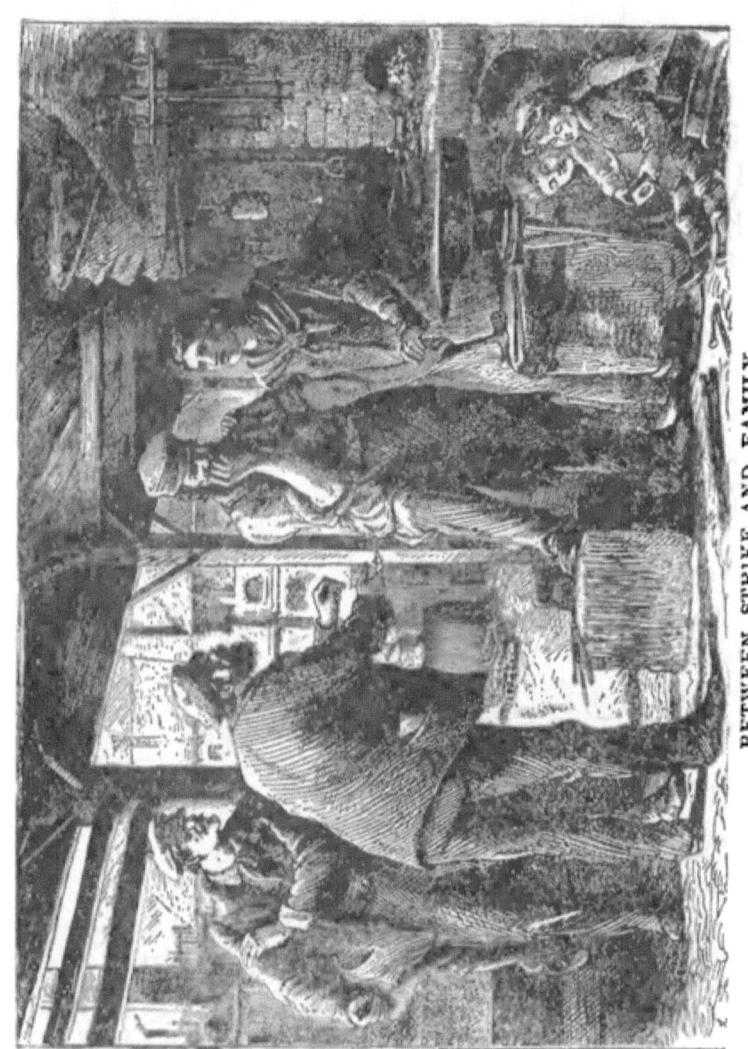

BETWEEN STRIKE AND FAMILY.

tween the employer painted by the lecturer and the man he himself worked for.

"Workmen employed by those who frowned on labor organizations became sullen and morose; they saw in every action of the superintendent another innovation on their rights, and they finally determined to throw off the yoke of oppression, organize, and assert their manhood. The actions of the superintendent, or boss, very often tended to widen the breach between employer and employe. When the organization did come, it found a very bitter feeling existing on both sides, and, before studying the laws of the society, they joined, or becoming conversant with its rules or regulations regarding the settlement of disputes or grievances, the workmen determined to wipe out of existence the whole system of petty tyrannies that had been practiced on them for years. Not being drilled in organization, and feeling that the employer would not treat with them, the only remedy suggesting itself was the strike. And, on the other hand, the employer, who felt that every move of his workmen in organization would be directed against his interests, determined to take time by the forelock and turn them all out on the street. Thus we find the organization in its infancy face to face with a strike or lockout.

"Absorbed in the task of getting large dividends, the employer seldom inquired of his superintendent how he managed the business intrusted to his keeping, or how he treated the employes. In thousands of places throughout the United States, many superintendents, foremen, or petty bosses, are interested in stores, corner groceries, or saloons. In many places the employe is told plainly that he must deal at the store, or get his liquor from the saloon in which his boss has an interest; in others, he is given to understand that he must deal in these stores or saloons, or forfeit his situation. Laws have been passed in some states against the keeping of company stores, but the stores are kept nevertheless, and workmen are made to feel that they must patronize them.

"In many cases, the owners of mills, factories or mines are not aware of the existence of such institutions as the 'pluck me'—the name applied to the company store—but they stand so far away from their employes that they cannot hear the murmur of complaint, and if a whisper of it ever does reach their ears it comes through the boss, who is not only interested in the store, but in keeping its existence a secret from his employer. The keeping of such stores is another source of injustice to workmen, for their existence tends to widen the breach between employer and employe. It may seem that I am dealing with insignificant things, but when the statement is made that seven out of every ten superintendents, or bosses, are interested in the management and derive profits from the operation of stores, which employes are forced to patronize, I make an assertion which can be proved.

"In a country where every man, however humble, is taught from his infancy that he stands the equal of all other men, it is but natural for a citizen who is given to understand that he must patronize a certain store, or that he cannot join a certain society, to feel restive, and, where so much is promised and so little obtained, men are apt to lose faith in a law-making system which obliges the workman himself to become complainant and prosecutor in cases where the laws are violated to his detriment. If he prosecutes he is discharged. If he does not prosecute for infractions of law, but simply complains, he is told to invoke the majesty of the law in his own behalf. In this way the law is disregarded; it becomes a dead letter; men lose hope in law and law-makers.

"The constant itching and irritation caused by the indifference of the employer to their welfare, and the injustice practiced on them by petty bosses, go on until the men feel that the only remedy is through the strike. In this way the men who belong to no organization are launched into strikes.

"Workingmen are not, as a rule, educated men. When the strike does come, while they feel that they have been wronged, yet they are lacking in the command of language necessary to state their case properly to the world, and hence set forth their claims in such a way as to arouse prejudices or create false impressions. The other side having the advantage of education, either personally or by right of purchase, can and does mold public opinion in a great many cases.

"I have pointed out one or two of the little things which cause a great deal of uneasiness and vexation to workingmen; others have pointed out the root of the evil. The workingman of the United States will soon realize that he possesses the power which kings once held—that he has the right to manage his own affairs. The power of the king has passed away. The power of wealth is passing away. The evening shadows are closing in upon the day when immense private fortunes can be acquired. The new power dawning upon the world is that of the workingman to rule his own destinies. That power can no longer be kept from him. How will he wield it?

"This question is of great concern not only to the workingman but to every citizen of the republic, and the hand of every citizen who loves his country should be extended to assist the new ruler. I have no fears because of the present apparently disturbed condition of the labor world; on the contrary, the signs are very hopeful. Wendell Phillips once said: 'Never look for an age when the people can be quiet and safe. At such times Despotism, like a shrouding mist, steals over the mirror of Freedom.'

"The people are not quiet to-day, but they are safe. It is the power of monopoly that is not safe. The men who pile up large fortunes must compensate for that privilege in the payment of a graduated income tax. The blessings which they derive from wealth must be shared by the nation from which they extract that wealth."

CHAPTER XV.

EIGHT HOURS.

EFFECT OF THE EIGHT HOUR AGITATION—NUMBER OF MEN IN THE MOVEMENT IN 1886 — THE BENEFITS CLAIMED—LABOR NOT A COMMODITY—A BIRDS-EYE VIEW OF THE WORKING WORLD — THE AGENTS OF CORPORATIONS—EXACTIONS ARE FETTERS—APPEALS AND MUTTERED DISCONTENT—A GREAT PLEA—THIRST FOR KNOWLEDGE SHOULD BE GRATIFIED—ROBERT G. INGERSOLL'S ELOQUENT WORDS ON THE SUBJECT—HOURS OF LABOR SHOULD BE SHORTENED.

The agitation for the reduction in the hours of labor was extremely active after the close of the war of the rebellion. Various conventions were held, demonstrations were made, and much discussion was had. Three classes of employers were created by the movement: Those who favored eight hours a day, and eight hours pay; Those who opposed reduction of either hours or pay, and those who were willing to concede ten hours pay for lessened time.

The men generally failed to secure what they sought.

The history of 1867 has been repeated in recent efforts in the same direction, yet considerable gain is reported at various points. It is calculated that about 450,000 men participated in the eight-hour demand in 1886, of whom 185,000 were granted shorter hours. Strikes continued during the months of May and June, with a total loss in wages of $2,802,000, and a stoppage in new business to the amount of the enormous sum of $24,800,000. Both employers and workmen find the eight-hour system to be impracticable in certain lines of business, while in others, it is a most gratifying success.

The chief benefits claimed for the eight-hour movement are: 1. Employment for all. 2. Steady employment. 3. Better wages. 4. Relief from anxiety and poverty. 5. Time for improvement, recreation, and home enjoyment.

"Labor is not a mere commodity or exclusive individual property," is the language of a reformer on this question. "It is human life and skill exerted to sustain human society through mutual exchange of works and services by means of money-wages. The application of physical forces in aid of human hands vastly increases production and the facilities of transportation, while the application of moral forces to the relations of employers and employes tends to distribute the beneficial results of civilized industries among the whole people through high wages, cheap goods and services. The national combination of working people's organizations enforces a rise in wages and a fall in profits, tending to equalize the standard of average living among the masses. The first cost of manufacture and transportation is getting minimized by the progress of discovery and invention, but the retail price paid for small distribution is yet very high, except in a few governmental services of water-works, post-offices, etc. The wasteful system of retail trade greatly enhances the cost of living and withdraws large numbers of able-bodied persons from productive labor.

"The average term of employment for all working people is not over nine months during the year, so that there is always a certain per centage of compulsory idleness. High wages for efficient work is comtemporaneous with cheap goods; a spinner on the hand wheel with one spindle can turn off three pounds of No. 10 cloth yarn in a week, a mule-spinner about three hundred pounds; a hand-loom weaver can weave fifty yards of common shirting a week, and the product of the power-looms which the weaver in a factory would attend to is 1,500 yards. Therefore, wages of the working people rise with the concentration of labor in great establishments, while the cost price of goods and services fall in proportion to the enlargement of organized labor in the processes of the manufacture. To enforce such general distribution of the benefits working in society, and by the best approved combinations of capital and labor, is the aim of organ-

LOCOMOTIVE WORKS.
Erecting Shop, with Average Number of Locomotives Under-way.

TUBE RIVETING IN THE BOILER SHOP.

FORCING THE DRIVING WHEELS ON THEIR AXLES.

ized labor in all the contentions throughout civilized communities.

"Fifty out of 500 trades and occupations are organized, and have established their own daily wages. Many trades have been under paid, while the aristocracy of organized skilled labor has succeeded in grabbing $3 to $5 a day by keeping competition down to a minimum by restricting the number of apprentices. Human working time is the measure of wages. Piece-work is usually paid at a rate which takes into account how much the worker should earn during the whole working day on a certain kind of work. By means of minute subdivision of labor, and the employment of so-called helpers—men, women, and children—the number of skilled mechanics and artisans has been minimized in the mammoth manufacturing establishments. This great mass of under paid working people is reinforced by a class of small farmers, and by large numbers of the middle class of business men, who are driven into bankruptcy by the competition of large farming enterprises, or by the cheapness of work in the great manufactories and large retail establishments.

"The old industrial system of a well-defined subdivision into about fifty standard trades and occupations, has entirely outlived its usefulness, and the working people are rising in their might to rearrange a mode of living wages for all. Labor is only a small proportion of the first cost of an article, and its wages are paid by the whole people as final consumers of goods, and therefore an attempt for a general rise of wages for common labor need not raise the retail price of goods and services to any appreciable extent. But interest, rent, profit, and unnecessary expenses will have to be curtailed and wasteful styles of business abolished. The newspapers which sold for five cents are being gradually supplanted by papers which sell for one and two cents, without any reduction in wages of compositors, reporters, editorial writers, or correspondents. When the trackmen, freight handlers, and other low-paid employes struck on Jay Gould's railroad system, all well paid employes were reduced to compulsory idleness, and the public suffered great losses as a penalty for allowing the system of starvation wages to exist.

Wages must be leveled up and profits, interest, rent, and taxes leveled down. High rents are paid out of the proceeds of overworked and under paid employes as, for instance, the rents paid for mammoth dry goods and certain clothing stores, where male and female employes are paid such small pittances that they depend upon their parents to make up the deficits in their standard of living. The owners of business blocks in central locations get these enormous rents owing to the competition of merchants, who bid against each other for the small area of the business center. Extortionate rents mean starvation wages for cashboys, cash-girls, salesladies, clerks, bookkeepers, and other help in wholesale and retail stores. In fact, the army of working people employed in distribution is outrageously overworked and under paid for the benefit of a comparatively small number of merchant princes and store keepers."

Between the men who pay the wages and the millions who receive them, there is not a proper recognition of the common ties of humanity. It is noticeable that when a man is placed in control of others, he soon learns to disregard their interests and personal feelings. We see in corporations extinction of sympathy for its employes, and the term "soulless corporation," is justly put. Through the superintendents, managers, presidents and directors, the workingman may appeal, but he never reaches any one but an agent. There is no one personally responsible to whom he may apply for the relief of a grievance.

Every man who acts as an agent feels it to be his duty to demand and exact strict service from those under him, but he is not at liberty to make concessions. It is not strange that workingmen are restive under this kind of supervision. They never come in contact with the power that can remedy their troubles, and show indulgence to their wants as men. An agent listens to their complaints with impatience, and often discharges them if they betray discontent.

The workingmen of to-day feel it their right to

have more time to themselves. The strict exactions of corporations and agents have become fetters which chafe and irritate. Appeals and muttered discontent have availed nothing, and the result has been a general demand and uprising for shorter hours.

The greatest plea the workingman has for more time away from the shop, factory and bench is, that he seeks mental culture. No one can deny that thirst for knowledge is a most laudable craving, and it is one which should be gratified whenever demanded. Ignorance never increased the product of a nation. As a matter of right he is entitled to education, if he creates the wealth of the nation.

"Why should labor," says Robert G. Ingersoll, "fill the world with wealth and live in want? Every labor-saving machine should help the whole world. Every one should tend to shorten the hours of labor. Reasonable labor is a source of joy. To work for wife and child, to toil for those you love is happiness, provided you can make them happy. But to work like a slave—to see your wife and children in rags—to sit at a table where food is coarse and scarce—rise at four in the morning—to work all day and throw your tired bones upon a miserable bed at night—to live without leisure, without rest, without making those you love comfortable and happy—this is not living—it is dying—a slow, lingering, crucifixion. The hours of labor should be shortened. With the vast and wonderful improvements of the nineteenth century there should be not only the necessaries of life for those who toil, but comforts and luxuries as well."

CHAPTER XVI.

ARBITRATION.

ARBITRATION NOT AN EXPERIMENT—THE JUSTINIAN LAW—ENGLISH AND ROMAN LAW—JUDICIAL BOARDS OF ARBITRATION—PRESIDENT CLEVELAND'S MESSAGE ON THE QUESTION — RICHARD GRIFFITHS, G. W. F., ON ARBITRATION—GEORGE RODGERS — FRENCH COURTS OF ARBITRATION — HOW THE GREAT BRICKLAYERS STRIKE IN CHICAGO WAS SETTLED—JUDGE TULEY'S DECISION—ARBITRATION JUST FOR EMPLOYER AND WORKINGMEN—THE SCALES OF JUSTICE A TRUE BALANCE.

There is nothing new or experimental in the idea of adjusting differences by arbitration. The old Justinian law contains a detailed system for this method of settling disputes, the chief idea of which is the promptness and certainty of the settlement. The general derangement and injury to business is always a great evil attendant upon strikes and similar troubles. All of the European nations have adopted the practice of the principles found in the eighth section of the IV Pandects, and even England over rides the common law in her preference for the Roman system.

Various propositions have been made to establish judicial Boards, or Courts of Arbitration, for the settlement of the differences which continually arise between employers and employes, some of which are feasible and some are vagaries of illusionists. President Cleveland, prompted by the pressure of the great question of the workingman's condition, sent the following message to congress:

"To THE SENATE AND HOUSE OF REPRESENTATIVES: The constitution imposes on the president the duty of recommending to the consideration of congress, from time to time, such measures as he shall judge necessary and expedient. I am so deeply impressed with the importance of immediately and thoughtfully meeting the problem which recent events and a present condition have thrust upon us, involving the settlement of disputes arising between our laboring men and their employers, that I am constrained to recommend to congress legislation upon this serious and pressing subject.

Under our form of government, the value of labor as an element of national prosperity should be distinctly recognized, and the welfare of the laboring man should be regarded as especially entitled to legislative care. In a country which offers to all its citizens the highest attainment of social and political distinction, its workingmen cannot justly or safely be considered as irrevocably consigned to the limits of a class, and entitled to no attention, and allowed no protest against neglect.

The laboring man, bearing in his hand an indispensable contribution to our growth and progress, may well insist, with manly courage and as a right, upon the same recognition from those who make our laws, as is accorded to any other citizen having a valuable interest in charge; and his reasonable demand should be met in such a spirit of appreciation and fairness, as to induce a contented and patriotic co-operation in the achievement of a grand national destiny.

While the real interests of labor are not promoted by a resort to threats and violent manifestations, and while those who, under the pretext of an advocacy of the claims of labor, wantonly attack the rights of capital, and for selfish purposes or the love of disorder sow seeds of violence and discontent, should neither be encouraged nor conciliated, all legislation on the subject should be calmly and deliberately undertaken with no purpose of satisfying unreasonable demands or gaining partisan advantage.

The present condition of the relations between labor and capital are far from satisfactory. The discontent of the employed is due in a large degree to the grasping and heedless exactions of employers and the alleged discriminations in favor of capital as an object of governmental attention. It must also be conceded that laboring men are not always careful to avoid causeless and unjustifiable disturbances. Though the importance of a better accord between these interests is apparent, it must be borne in mind that any effort in that direction by the federal government must be greatly limited by constitutional restrictions. There are many grievances which legislation by congress cannot redress and many conditions which cannot by such means be reformed.

I am satisfied, however, that something may be done under federal authority to prevent the disturbances which so often arise by disputes between employer and employed, and which at times seriously threaten the business interests of the country; and, in my opinion, the proper theory on which to proceed is that of voluntary arbitration as the means of settling these difficulties. But I suggest that, instead of arbitrators chosen in the heat of conflicting claims and after each dispute shall arise, there be created a commission of labor consisting of three members, who shall be regular officers of the government, charged, among other duties, with the consideration and settlement, when possible, of all controversies between labor and capital.

A commission thus organized would have the advantage of being a stable body, and its members, as they gained experience, would constantly improve in their ability to deal intelligently and usefully with questions which might be submitted to them. If arbitrators are chosen for temporary service as each case of dispute arises, experience and familiarity with much that is involved in the question will be lacking; extreme partisanship and bias will be the qualifications sought on either side, and frequent complaints of unfairness and partiality will be inevitable.

The imposition upon a federal court of a duty foreign to the judicial function, as the selection of an arbitrator in such cases, is at least of doubtful propriety. The establishment by federal authority of such a bureau would be a just and sensible recognition of the value of labor and of its right to be represented in the departments of the government. So far as its conciliatory offices shall have relation to disturbances which interfered with transit and commerce between the states, its existence would be justified under the provisions of the constitution which give to congress the power to regulate commerce with foreign nations and among the several states. And in the frequent disputes between the laboring men and their employers of less extent, and the consequences of which are confined within state limits, and threaten domestic violence, the interposition of such a commission might be tendered upon the application of the legislature or executive of a state, under the constitutional provision which requires the general government to protect each of the states against domestic violence.

If such a commission were fairly organized, the risk of a loss of popular support and sympathy resulting from a refusal to submit to so peaceful an instrumentality, would constrain both parties to such disputes to invoke its interference, and abide by its decisions. There would also be good reason to hope that the very existence of such an agency would invite application to it for advice and counsel, frequently resulting in the avoidance of contention and misunderstanding. If the usefulness of such a commission is doubtful, because it might lack power to enforce its decisions, much encouragement is derived from the conceded good that has been accomplished by the railroad commissions which have been organized in many of the states, which have little more than advisory power, have exerted a most salutary influence in the settlement of disputes between conflicting interests.

In July, 1884, by a law of congress, a bureau of labor was established and placed in charge of a commissioner of labor, who is required to collect information upon the subject of labor, its relations with capital, the hours of labor and the earnings of laboring men and women, and the means of promoting their material, social, intellectual, and moral prosperity. The commission which I suggest could easily be engrafted upon the bureau thus already organized by the addition of two more commissioners, and by supplementing the duties now imposed upon it by such other powers and functions as would permit the commissioners to act as arbitrators when necessary between labor and capital, under such limitations and upon such occasions as should be deemed proper and useful. Power should also be distinctly conferred upon this bureau to investigate the causes of all disputes as they occur, whether submitted for arbitration or not, so that information may always be at hand to aid legislation on the subject when necessary and desirable.

Grover Cleveland.

Executive Mansion, April 22, 1886.

Although there is much antagonism existing between the workingmen and their employers, both concede the advisability of mutually agreeing upon some just method for settlement. Voluntary arbitration is generally held to be a most useful and equitable course to pursue, but as cases constantly arise wherein there is much ill feeling, this method is beyond question, and recourse to a special tribunal seems the only way to reach a definite and binding settlement.

In reply to a letter of inquiry upon this topic, General Worthy Foreman Richard Griffiths, of the Knights of Labor, writes: "I am an advocate of and a firm believer in arbitration. Peace between capital and labor will be intermittent until the two are impelled, by self-interest, public sentiment, or public law, to meet each other in a spirit

BRICKLAYING.

of mutual respect and forbearance, and submit their disputes to the decision of impartial tribunals. The Knights of Labor are the evangels of this new gospel of good will. The twenty-second plank of their preamble and declaration of principles is as follows:

'To persuade employers to agree to arbitrate all differences which may arise between them and their employes, in order that the bonds of sympathy between them may be strengthened, and that strikes may be rendered unnecessary.'

"I can assure you that the practices of the Knights are in harmony with their theories. In proof of this I would call your attention to the fact that in the territory embraced in district assembly No. 30 —the manufacturing sections of Massachusetts— over one hundred disputes were settled by arbitration in the twelve months between January, 1885, and January, 1886. In not one instance that arbitration was resorted to did it prove abortive.

"At first, manufacturers objected strenuously to submitting to arbitration. Not a few resented the intimation that there was anything to arbitrate as an insolent and unwarranted interference with their prerogative. But the great majority of the employers in the old Bay state now admit, without reluctance, that their employes are entitled to opinions regarding their own wages and conditions of employment, and many of them eagerly avail themselves of the new and enlightened system of settling industrial disputes.

"The Knights of Labor favor the establishment of national and state courts of arbitration. Acting by authority of and under instructions from the general assembly, a committee composed of several of the brightest members of our order are now in Washington, laboring for the creation of such courts. I am advised that there are grounds for hoping that their efforts will prove successful. When the legislatures of the several states meet, this same matter will be pressed upon their attention.

"Arbitration, in my judgment, should be advocated by all thinking people; there is a crying need of it. But workingmen, especially, should bear in mind that, after all, arbitration is only the cap-stone of the edifice, that education and organization must precede, or least go hand in hand with it. Unless mechanics are thoroughly organized many employers might, as of old, decline to treat with them. While workingmen should always favor peace—should never strike until all other means of obtaining redress had failed — it is a duty which they owe to themselves to be prepared for emergencies.

"I am glad to observe that decent newspapers are taking an interest in this great question. The press can do more than any other single agency toward harmonizing the clashing claims of capital and labor. The day was when workingmen were set down as in the wrong in all disputes, and employers ever in the right—when reports were doctored, and editorial opinions made to order. But times are changing for the better, and I thank God for it.

"Please set me down as heartily in favor of arbitration."

Mr. George Rodgers expresses a similar opinion in the following words: "I consider arbitration to be one of the most important matters of the day. Thinking, being my forte, I usually leave the writing to others. However, I am a thorough believer in arbitration, and hold the same views on this method for the settlement of disputes in the industrial world that are held and practiced whenever possible by the entire organization of the Knights of Labor. The constitution and laws of the Knights of Labor expressly direct that all disputes shall be submitted to arbitration when the employer consents. Employes, who are Knights of Labor, are thus compelled to submit to arbitration; but there is at present no law to compel employers to do likewise. This is not so in other countries.

"Compulsory submission to arbitration is provided for in some parts of France. An examination of the consular reports made to the state department in 1884, will show that the law of arbitration is growing in the various countries of Europe, and that its growth there can be measured by the intelligence of the people.

"The fact that no courts of arbitration yet exist in

America, is no argument against them; for it is well known that all reforms are in advance of the law. Agitation always precedes remedial legislation. These courts will take labor disputes from antagonists to impartial juries.

"The people, in my judgment, understand that bullets and clubs are poor arguments—very much inferior to cool reasoning and reasonable conclusions. The proposal of arbitration made by the street-car strikers settled that very dangerous dispute. If arbitration were compulsory, the Lemont affair, wherein citizen-soldiers shot down workingmen, and used their bayonets on their wives, would not be something to recall with indignation. The aim of the Knights of Labor is to discourage strikes, to settle by arbitration, disputes, and to remedy wrongs, be they on the side of employer or employe."

In Europe the law has been found a satisfactory solvent for various phases of strikes and lockouts. A court of arbitration has long existed in France, and in 1859, Lord Brogham stated, that of 28,000 cases submitted to the Conseils des Prudhommes, 26,800 were settled without appeal. If such results have been secured in the crowded countries of Europe, there is no valid reason why the same ends cannot be accomplished in the United States.

The great bricklayers' strike in the summer of 1887, at Chicago, which caused a loss of over $2,-

000,000, was settled by Judge M. F. Tuley, who, as umpire, proposed the following scheme, which was accepted by both sides, and will undoubtedly prove efficacious in obviating future difficulties.

"That a standing committee, to be elected annually in the month of January, defining its powers and duties, we request shall be incorporated into the constitution of each association.

"This joint committee will be constituted of an arbitration committee of five members from each organization (the president of each being one of the five), and an umpire who is neither a working mechanic nor an employer of mechanics, to be chosen by the two committees. This joint committee is given power to hear and determine all grievances of the members of one organization against members of the other, and of one organization against the other; to determine and fix all working rules governing employers and employes, such as: (1) The minimum rate of wages per hour; (2) the number of hours of work per day; (3) uniform pay day; (4) the time of starting and quitting work; (5) the rate paid for night and Sunday work, and questions of like nature. And it is given power to determine what number of apprentices should be enrolled, so to afford all boys desiring to learn the trade an opportunity to do so, without overcrowding, so as not to cause the coming workman to be unskilled in his art, or the supply of labor to grossly exceed the demand therefor. It is also given exclusive power to determine all subjects in which trade organizations may be interested, and which may be brought before it by the action of either organization, or the president thereof."

CHAPTER XVII.

CO-OPERATION.

ALL GREAT ENTERPRISES DEPEND ON CO-OPERATION—A COMMON OBJECT IS COMMON ADVANTAGE—ORGANIZATION AND CO-OPERATION A GREAT POWER—THE WAGE SYSTEM OPPOSED TO CO-OPERATION—CO-OPERATION A SUCCESS—LECLAIRE'S GREAT ORGANIZATION—RAILROAD CO-OPERATION IN FRANCE—INDUSTRIAL PARTNERSHIP IN ENGLAND—ALFRED TAYLOR ON THE SUBJECT—D. S. CURTISS—DEVELOPMENT AND EXTENT OF CO-OPERATION IN THE UNITED STATES—COMPLETE REVIEW OF WHAT HAS BEEN DONE.

CIVILIZATION rests and advances, to a great extent, on the principles of co-operation. All of the enterprises and industries which produce vast and beneficial results depend, for development, on association. It is the channel by which discoveries in art and science are distributed, and thus inure to the benefit of the world.

The organization of individuals for a common object lends the strength and capacity of the strong and able to all, and the weakest and those of inferior capacity reaps the common advantage. When the principles of co-operation are fully understood, their adoption will be carried into effect by thousands of industries, and the injurious effects of incorporated concerns will be avoided. A country's wealth depends upon its production, and as organization and co-operation increases production, it naturally follows that the country adopting co-operation will enjoy an unbroken era of prosperity. The intelligent direction and application of labor has a direct tendency to enhance wages. A forcible illustration of this truth may be found in the production of wheat in Egypt, India, and America, which is sold in the English market. The laborer's day wages in Egypt is a small radish; in India, five cents, and in many of the United States, $2.00 a day, or forty times as much as the harvester in India. High wages are paid only from high production. The American, by improved machinery, cuts, threshes and sacks one hundred pounds of wheat at a cost of but a few cents.

The pages of history reveal the sad fact, that the want of the actual necessities of life has ever been the curse of labor. The cause of this distress lies in the fact that governments have legislated with the only thought to preserve the government instead of for the best interests of their producers. The immense armies of Europe are evidence of the truth of this statement. The declaration of principles in the constitution of the United States asserts that **every** American citizen has inalienable rights—

rights which secure him liberty, property, and the pursuit of happiness, even to the commanding the support of every citizen in the whole country. We need no standing armies to menace the people; and our time can be well directed to securing an abundance of the necessaries and comforts of life.

If the wage system were abolished and the equities of co-operation placed in its stead, the vast army of non-producers would vanish, and humanity would be in a better condition. Legislation would be directed towards the developing of the welfare of industries and to the creation of peace and plenty. To supersede the wage system by the introduction of the co-operative industrial system has always been the goal of the Knights of Labor, and the order has a supervising board which looks after its interests in that direction.

The practical application of co-operation is not an innovation. It is now in successful operation in hundreds of localities, and is everywhere meeting with the most gratifying results.

To directly interest the workingman in the profits of his labor is a sure means of avoiding strikes and lockouts, and to obviate all possibility of differences between the employer and the employed. Edme-Jean Leclaire, a house painter, the son of a poor village shoemaker in France, was the first to successfully introduce the principles of co-operative industry. In 1841 he put into execution his plan of surmounting the antagonism which existed between workman and master. He organized a number of house and decorative painters into a society, each member of which was to receive a proportionate amount of the profits of the year's work, over and above their wages. Considerable opposition was met with, and at every side he met with discouragement from masters. The press accused him of seeking to reduce wages; the police saw in his plans a cunning scheme for enticing workmen away from their employers, and did their best to thwart him by prohibiting meetings of his employes. However, on the 15th of February, 1842, Leclaire met his workmen, forty-four in number, and divided 11,886 francs between them.

All opposition vanished, and he was given unlimited confidence. In succeeding years larger sums were distributed. During the six years from 1842 to 1847 inclusive, about 20,000 francs were annually divided among an average of eighty persons. Leclaire's organization finally secured a legal status, and has never ceased to prosper.

There are at present over fifty industrial establishments in France, Alsace and Switzerland, working upon co-operative principles, all of them in a highly prosperous condition. The Paris and Orleans railway company have, since 1844, annually given their employes a share of the profits. Three other railroads in France, united with the Paris and Orleans road, give their operatives the same advantage.

KNIFE, FORK AND SPOON WORKERS.

Industrial partnership has, of late, been introduced in England with remarkable results. In 1864, the Whitwood collieries entered into an arrangement whereby their employes receive a share of the profits. The best results were obtained during the succeeding ten years, when, in 1874, a change in the trade necessitated a reduction of wages, the men struck, and the system was discontinued. Had the men intelligently investigated the situation, it is probable no strike would have occurred.

The success which has been achieved in England—and it has been a marked success—has been in co-operative distribution. Some of the societies do a vast business, and divide among those who are at once members and customers very handsome profits. Naturally enough, this has led to experiments by the same societies in co-operative production. This is a short and easy step. If the members are to divide the profits which would go, ordinarily, to the jobber, wholesaler, and retailer, why should they not also become manufacturers of some of the principal commodities, and so divide among themselves the manufacturers' profits as well? The principal experiments have been those of the "Wholesale Society" of Manchester and that of Glasgow, and the experiment in each case has been the manufacture of shoes. The Manchester society has two factories, employing 1,000 people and doing an annual business of over $1,000,000. Being able to sell their goods largely in their own stores and to their own members, the societies have had an advantage over ordinary manufacturers, and their new enterprises have been lucrative. The co-operative consumers—if we may so describe the members of the societies in their original capacity—are simply shareholders in the factories, those enterprises affording an opening for the investment of their surplus. The old force of competition—from which the new system of co-operation was to have effected deliverance—therefore comes in.

Wide application of co-operation offers a prospect of vivifying and purifying industry to an extent of which we have as yet but a faint conception, and the employers and consumers in America cannot do better than avail themselves of the profitable experience of those who have tested its merits. Capital is bitterly denounced on the one side, and the inefficiency and apathy of labor is execrated on the other. These extremes are one of the causes of strikes and increased depression during hard times.

"One of the prime causes of existing labor troubles," writes Alfred Taylor, "is to be found in the wage system itself. This system is erroneous to start with. While there is no doubt that the relations of employer and employe might be better than they are, it is still true that the system retains some of the spirit of master and slave. No man is at his best without the feeling of independence; the feeling that he is master of his own acts. Strive as he may, no man can take the same interest in the affairs of another that he takes in his own. It is not natural; it is a strained position and his trustworthiness will be in the ratio of his intellectual development. It is well known that wage slavery makes intellectual culture next to impossible, because of the want of time and means to obtain such culture. Hence, just in proportion that the employer is successful, just in the same proportion is the employe reduced to the mental and moral condition where his trustworthiness and interest in the welfare of his employer is at zero.

"The only true remedy for this is in co-operative industry. When each man can feel that he is a proprietor; when he can feel that he is working for himself and not for a master; when he can feel and know that his brain and muscle weighs equally in the scale with the dollar of his associates, and that the dividends on each shall be declared in the just ratio, then, and not till then, will labor stand upon its proper pedestal.

"The wage system places the laborer at the mercy of the employer, and the self-interest of the employer prompts him to get all the labor he can for the smallest price, while the self-interest of the employe prompts him to get the greatest price for the smallest amount of labor. This leads to antagonism where there should be harmony. The employer has the advantage in this antagonism in proportion to the amount of labor in the market. What difference is there under these circumstances between buying and selling men, and buying and selling the labor of men when there is but one party to the contract? And this is the case where the market is overcrowded, and where machinery enables capital to dispense with human labor. Capital is not to blame for taking advantage of these circumstances, nor is labor to blame for its dissatisfaction.

"It is the system that is wrong, and as soon as this can be made plain, there will be an universal effort to remedy it. Wherever co-operation has had a fair trial it has proved successful. And when capital can be convinced that co-operation will increase rather than diminish its gains, by creating a nobler incentive on the part of labor, it will fall readily into line and do its duty.

"Self-interest, after all, is the key to the situation. That is a chord in human nature that is always responsive. And while inordinate greed is reprehensible, a true self-interest is the parent of industry, economy and every material virtue. Guide this self-interest into the channel of co-operation, and capital and labor join hands upon one common ground of friendship and equality."

In a paper contributed to "The National View," Col. D. S. Curtiss says: "Co-operation is equally adapted to large or small enterprises—to very moderate or most extensive operations. It may be advantageously employed in constructing large bridges, mills, factories, in working large farms and even in digging canals and constructing railroads, and then in operating them, in any operation that requires more manual labor than the family can do, this mode will do. Under this system, in labor operations—such as building houses, carrying on shoe, cabinet, blacksmith or other shops, working farms, and running factories, according to mutual agreement—all the laborers or operatives will receive pay for the quantity and quality of work they perform, and an equal division of all the profits of the operation. So in trading and merchandising, all will be fairly paid by mutual understanding for the service performed, and all the parties in the co-operation will share the profits of the trade or store in the proportion which they buy or pay into it, while they who furnish any more capital than their purchases, will be paid a just interest for it, as shall be agreed upon. Thereby, on this principle, all of the customers, operatives and capitalists, justly share the profits and are fairly compensated, no class monopolizing an undue portion of the profits or gains of another's labor or efforts. But I need not dwell upon the mode of co-operation, as it is easy to understand; my chief object is to call attention to it as one of the lawful and inoffensive means of readily securing more adequate, even full reward, to laborers, and thus soon end the violent strifes now being waged between labor and incorporated capital, forced by the latter upon the former.

"Wealthy monopolies and chartered corporations have long and steadily combined to enhance their own interests, and to keep down the wages of all laborers, they have chartered privileges, not possessed by them individually, to aid their power of combination against labor, and those in government authority always aid the wealthy and monopolist, but strike down and coerce the laborer; therefore, laborers have a right to combine for their own welfare, they are justified in the most effective combinations they can make for their own protection and welfare. A further effect of this system will be to peacefully compel the more arrogant employers to act justly toward employes who do not happen to enlist in the self-employment of co-operation, as they will be rendered less dependent upon wealthy employers. Under this system there will be no motive or need for strikes, boycotts, lockouts, or other violent measures, to secure just pay and hours to the hard workers.

"When fairly and thoroughly organized in this manner, such a body of industrious, intelligent, and skillful workers would always and everywhere command the respect and confidence of the community; and should they at any time wish to enter upon more extensive enterprises than their personal means would enable them to carry out, they could find plenty of unemployed capital whose owners would be glad to invest it with them—to loan it to them at a reasonable low rate of interest. For instance, should a co-operative association, embracing many laborers, wish to enter into a contract to build a costly house or bridge, or mill, or manufactory, or to run a large grain and stock farm, but lacked the requisite means to start with, they would have no trouble in borrowing the money; it would be more difficult for money to find laborers than for labor to find money, when co-operation extensively prevailed, because most laborers would be better employed than working for capitalists; while large capitalists could not make large contracts for building, as they would be unable to hire much labor.

"Another effect that will result from the general establishment of co-operative organizations will be the more equitable apportionment of wages for services; under present customs a most flagrant disparity of salaries compared to the services performed, and the dangers assumed, obtains; in many positions and occupations extravagant salaries are paid where but little service is rendered, light accountability, with no hardship or danger incurred. As an instance, take the operating of railroads, superintendents, vice-presidents, and presidents receive variously five, ten, and even twenty-five thousand dollars' salary annually, with little responsibility for the safety of life and property, and none of the hardships and dangers of running the trains; but the trusty, skillful engineer or engine-driver, who stands at the open-mouth of danger and death, in night and day, light and dark, in storm and cold, holding in his hand, watchfully and secure, the safety of thousands of lives and millions of property—upon whose honest skill and care the lives of the passengers and the value of the entire train constantly depend for safety—this grandly skillful and highly responsible employe receives in salary scarcely more hundreds than those easy fellows, above named, receive thousands. It is a shameful injustice that those skillful, responsible, danger-beset men should be so meagerly paid, when those nabob officials are paid so much for no hardships, or risks, or dangers.

"The same fact holds true, to a large extent, to other train hands on railroads, and to some degree, in fact, among the operatives in express companies, large mills, and manufactories, telegraph companies, and some other avocations of the business world. Inadequate compensation to those who incur most toil, hardship, and exposure, and liable to greater dangers and responsibilities, but extravagant pay to those most exempt from danger and hardship is a shame and disgrace. This unjust and unreasonable disparity of wages will be mostly done away under the general adoption of co-operation. There is no just reason why a skillful compositor should not receive as much pay for setting up an article as the man gets for writing the same; it requires as many years for the printer to learn to set type, read manuscript, and punctuate correctly, as the writer spent in qualifying to write it. So in regard to a lawyer or doctor. There is no justice in paying them more for an hour or day's service than should be paid to a good carpenter, shipwright, or other skillful mechanic; it requires as long time and study to learn a trade well as to learn those so-called professions, while the latter has a more easy life.

"When this peaceful method of co-operation is generally adopted, and mechanics and other laborers unitedly vote for only their friends, observe economy, sobriety, study, and thoughtfulness, all workers will be better paid, happier, and more prosperous; then all branches will be fairly and equally paid."

A partial census of the co-operative undertakings in the United States, by investigators of the Economic Association, shows that there is much more co-operation in this country than is generally supposed. According to the New York correspondent of the Philadelphia "Press," reports have been received from New England, the middle Western states, and, with minute detail, from Minnesota. Both distributive and productive co-operation are included in the inquiry. In New England there are at least fifty-three establishments engaged in distributive co-operation. More familiarly these are known as co-operative stores. About one-half, or twenty-eight, are in Massachusetts; six in Connecticut, sixteen in Maine, two in New Hampshire, and one in Rhode Island. Most of these have been organized since 1870; one dates back to 1847, and another to 1850. These two early ones, and another founded in 1866, are the only survivals of the old union stores of forty years ago. At one time there were 106 of these. Somewhat similar are the Grange stores, which are patronized by the 25,000 or 30,000 members of this organization. These Grange stores in the East are confined to Maine, New Hampshire and Connecticut. They are the survival of the fittest, and have a successful basis.

Of the fifty-three stores, thirty-two report an aggregate capital of $137,000, the amount of each ranging from $1,000 to $40,000. In general, the par value of a share is $5. This is significant as indicating the possibility of investment by the poor man. The number of shareholders in fifty-two companies is 5,470, which indicates a rather wide interest. The trade reported by the thirty-three stores making full returns is $1,600,000. As many of the stores turned over their capital more than twelve times during the year, it may be safely stated that the entire business of distributive co-operation in New England was $2,000,000 during the past year.

In the West, the Grange store has not generally survived the misfortunes of its earlier days. In Illinois there were at one time co-operative stores in one-half of the counties of the state. These have been mostly failures. In Michigan there are three semi-successful stores; in Indiana and Ohio little remains of former prosperity. The idea has been better realized in Kansas, where at the present time

A HAPPY HOME.

there are twenty or thirty small stores. The oldest and most successful is at Olathe, which has increased its sales from $41,000 in 1876 to $210,000 in 1886.

The efforts of the Knights of Labor, or of other labor organizations, are too recent to justify much mention. In 1886, sentiment in this direction rapidly crystallized, and labor stores were established. It is here that interest in the future will be the greatest. A unique, though not, perhaps, strictly co-operative, institution is the Mormon undertaking, called the "Zion's Co-operative Mercantile Institution." The stock of the company is $1,000,000, and the sales between $4,000,000 and $5,000,000. It is more proper, however, to call this a joint stock corporation, although its results have been somewhat similar to those reached by the wholesale co-operative stores of New England.

Later in time there has been developed that form of co-operation known as productive. Of the twenty companies in New England, sixteen are in Massachusetts. There are eleven in Ohio, seven in Indiana, fourteen in Illinois, four in Michigan, nine in Missouri, and two in Kansas. Productive co-operation seems to have struck more deeply in the West than elsewhere.

Of more importance is the form of production which co-operation has taken. In New England there are seven co-operative shoe companies, three printing companies, and two furniture companies.

Five other companies have been just organized, and it is estimated that in this year there will be a business of more than a million dollars. The most successful, perhaps, is the stove company in Stoneham, Mass., which has an annual product of $150,000, with a capital of $20,000, divided among fifty-seven shareholders, twenty-five of whom are employed in the establishment. There are at least 1,100 shareholders in these twenty associations, and if we take into consideration those which have not reported, it is safe to say that ten thousand persons are interested in co-operation in New England.

In the West more kinds of industries are represented in co-operation. In 1886 there were at least seven co-operative mining companies in operation in Indiana, Illinois and Missouri. Three of them, with a combined capital of $55,000, are reported as prosperous; and in those cases where failure has occurred, it has been due to the hostile action of the railroads. These companies all originated either from strikes or disaffection with wages. The furniture-makers have enjoyed considerable success. Of their five undertakings, one dates back to 1878; three of them are situated in St. Louis. The greatest success has been achieved by the coopers in Minneapolis. The history of their work is of common report. Their one shop of 1874 has increased to 8.

Farmers have done little with productive co-operation. The few agricultural colonies are as yet experimental, but co-operative creameries are common in New England, New York and Ohio. It is estimated that about one-fourth of the dairying in some counties of the latter state is carried on in the co-operative form.

This completes the review of what has been done in co-operation thus far in the United States. In conclusion, it may be said, that this experience shows that the co-operative store can be made successful, but that as yet co-operation with dividends to labor is, except in Minneapolis, in such a tentative condition, that no definite judgment can be given. In addition to the forms of co-operation mentioned, there should be added, to make a complete inquiry, co-operative banks and building associations.

CHAPTER XVIII.

HOME THE PALLADIUM OF SOCIETY.[1]

MAN WITHOUT A HOME AN OUTCAST—THE STATE IS BUT THE INDIVIDUAL, THE INDIVIDUAL A MINIATURE STATE—HOME THE BULWARK OF VIRTUE—CICERO'S MAXIM—DEFECTS OF OUR SOCIAL SYSTEM—THE BURDEN OF INDIRECT TAXATION—HANDWRITING ON THE WALL—CO-OPERATION A BLESSING FOR THE PEOPLE—SUCCESS OF CORPORATIONS—"SWEET HOME" CAN BE MADE A REALITY—WISDOM FOR THE HOMELESS.

"Men who are housed like pigs can hardly pray like Christians; and where life is a long flight from starvation, it is not a flight that takes the fugitive towards heaven.

"I don't know whether it will shock you. She said that a home which a decent man can respect, has as much to do with holiness as have all the Seven Sacraments."

"THE OLD ORDER CHANGES."

WERE I asked, "What is the most important step to take, at once, in the interest of the whole people," I should say, without a moment's hesitation, place every head of a family in a home free from tax, rent and interest. Were the question then put, "How are we to do this," my answer would be, have

[1] By Albert Owen.

men and women, to incorporate themselves into companies, select and obtain lands suitable for town, farm and factory, and go to work upon a well matured plan to employ themselves, to build their houses, to grow their crops, to operate their factories, to exchange their services and to discipline their lives.

Home is the basis for every reform. Without homes people will be shiftless, nothing can be substantial, and the best effort, the kindest thought are but a mockery of what they might be were every one properly employed and comfortably housed. The homeless are the discontented, the diseased, the criminally inclined. The destructionists, the anarchists, the nihilists, only exist where there are homeless people. A man or a woman without a home is a waif. Society is ever and incessantly forcing him or her to move on. "The chattel slave had his or her cabin, but the modern tramp has not a place whereon to lay his or her head. A person without a home is a factor for revolution.

Evolution can be brought about only by those who have homes wherein they can study, think and plan. There is nothing certain connected with a homeless man or woman, except uncertainty. Justice can not be practiced, and equity is simply a name among a people who are but partly housed. Instructions in ethics, morals and science are worthless where people live along gutters, and sleep in houses and on lands owned by other people than themselves; and "reformers" may agitate about "the land's unearned increment," total abstinence, no distinction of sex in the political franchise, "salvation in Christ Jesus," eight hours for a day's work; and the trade unions may strike every day in the year, but until the producers incorporate to secure themselves agreeable, regular and remunerative employments, to handle and exchange their own products, and to place every head of a family in a beautiful home, free from tax, rent and interest, they will do nothing that is substantial to right the wrongs under which modern society is staggering, tottering towards its inevitable engulfment.

The great Plato maintained that "the state is but the individual on a larger scale, the individual is but a miniature state;" and the greater Aristotle, who was a pupil of Plato, based his philosophy on the principle of experience; that is to say, the principle that all our thinking should be founded on the observation of facts. Aristotle was the founder of the inductive school, and built not from theory but from established fact—from what had been actually done. Heraclitus was of the deductive school, and imagined a base, and then eloquently expounded a doctrine like our "land unearned increment" expounders do to-day. He began with "Fire is the substance of everything," "and everything flows;" and Pythagoras, likewise, took as the basis for his agitation and reform: "The numerical proportions are the real substance."

Well, what of it if they are? What has that to do with the employment and contentment of the people; how is that theory going to give employment to the 1,000,000[1] men and women, who are begging for work, lest they die, in these United States; why pass time—precious time— over nice theories when the census tells us that there are 500,000[2] young girls, in these United States, being prostituted, and that 100,000 of them are dying every year—dying disgraced, broken hearted and prematurely; and yet Pythagoras was in his day one of the great leading philosophers, and he roused the people up at town meetings and at cross roads then, just as our popular agitators do to-day, and with about as little result towards ameliorating the conditions of the people.

But it is claimed these agitators "make the people think." That is so, but of what—to think of things which entertains and diverts the producers from the real facts in the case, while the cunning tricksters, the lawyers, the brokers, the middle men and "the cannibals of Exchange Alley" put them more and more into debt, pile taxes upon them, increase their rates of interest; steal their highways, monopolize their exchanges, occupy their lands, buy up their inventions, and educate their children with false teachings. Aristotle, on the contrary, began all reforms from established facts,

---

[1] T. V. Powderly, July 22, 1887, at Wilkesbarre, Pa.
[2] The Prodigal Daughter, by Rachel Campbell.

and with lessons acknowledged after they had been practically applied; he took every step cautiously, methodically and in keeping with the logic of circumstances.

"It is, however, not so much by his philosophical system that Aristotle has wielded his enormous influence, especially as this begins only at present to be fully understood and justly appreciated, as by his logical inventions and his method of philosophy in general. He has, more than any other philosopher, set the world to thinking logically, to teaching science and art systematically, to banishing from the domain of science the rampant and arbitrary action of fantasy, to observing coolly before venturing to systematize, and to loving truth for its now sake."

Cicero, though a Roman, went to Greece, and studied in the inductive school of Plato and Aristotle. He said: "The first function of justice is that no one should do violence to another unless compelled by violence to himself. The second is, that no one should use public things otherwise than as public things; and should use private things only as his own." These are, to my mind, the greatest lessons ever expounded in any age or by any person. There never has been a nation which ever properly discriminated between public things and things private, and there never has been a nation which has ever succeeded in giving to its people diversified employments and beautiful homes; and, hence all nations in the past and present, have been held together by armed forces and by the intrenched influences of privileged classes.

The United States are no exception to the rule. What are the facts in the case. The institutions of the United States have had one hundred and eleven years of trial, under the most favorable circumstances, and they are a failure. They do not give to the citizen security for life, property or happiness. The inalienable right to life, to the use of property and to the pursuit of happiness, is thus far a myth. Those who are taxed do not necessarily have representation. Even the people who vote do not govern, and rarely a majority of them elect the candidates set up by privileged classes. A moneyed aristocracy has seized the nation. Incorporated and privileged classes own and control the exchanges, transportations, lands, waters, fuels, lights, powers, inventions and legislations.

The producers are slaves, without an hour to call their own: with bodies over-burdened, brains muddled, and without the right even to possess the things they make, the lands they improve, or the graves they are buried in. Even the children and women of the American laborer are driven, from necessity, and forced by hirelings, to toil from dawn till night, that others may luxuriate in over-abundance. The houses they shelter themselves in, the farms they cultivate, the factories they work in, the theatres they go to, the hotels they stop at, the cars they journey in, the wagons they haul in, the boats they steam in, are each made and operated by themselves, but they all belong to the privileged and incorporated classes.

The direct tax paid by labor, and every tax paid is paid by labor, whether it is land tax or interest on money, is unnecessary in every case; but it is infinitesmal in amount to the indirect tax—the interests, rentals, expressages, freightages, etc., which the producers are forced, by law, to pay for the use of their own credits, houses, highways, exchanges, transportations, etc.

Our agitators, however, are forever arousing public thought on the injustice of direct taxation; and never even whisper concerning the indirect taxation, which is really the question at issue. The facts, in a similar case, are that a great and incessant howl is made about free trade. This is a misnomer to begin with, for those who advocate "free trade" have no wish to see free home trade, but they advocate that foreign manufacturers who are kept up by English subsidies and pauper labor, shall be free to crush out our comparatively young industries at home. These brilliant reformers make all their noise about our "foreign trade," which amounts, at best, to but ten per cent of our commerce; and they ignore, as unworthy of their thought, the ninety per cent of internal, inter-state, or home trade.

Hence it is, that while our people's minds are at-

MIDNIGHT FIRES—BLAST FURNACES, PITTSBURG.

tracted by eloquence and sweet sounding phrases upon questions other than those at issue, that the population of the United States has only doubled, while the idiots, deaf and dumb patients, convicts, inebriates and those who are dependent upon the charities for protection, shelter and food, have increased eight-fold. What a picture for a republic to present after a little over one hundred years' of trial. Where did a despotism ever do worse in so short a time?

The hand-writing is on the wall. The decadence of our institutions is seen every day in the regattas, horse racing, prize fighting, burring matches, base ball gambling, and the ballet enacted for the depraved tastes of a class made luxuriously rich and indifferently selfish by the possession of privileged monopolies. The daily suicides, murders, robberies, crimes and filthy diseases of the homeless, overburdened and dissatisfied are the other side—are the shadows to the first picture. Well may our heathen friend, Wong Chin Foo, boast that among the four hundred millions of people in China, there are less murders in a year than there are in the single state of New York, within the same time.

The question is: What is to be done, and how, when and by whom? This is business. If the questions of our day are to be solved, they will be solved by business persons—others are not capable of looking into causes, or competent to mature a plan and perfect the details necessary to carry the same into execution. Induction teaches us that we must go from a part to the whole. In almost every community we see half a dozen or more business persons incorporate themselves into a company and obtain the privilege to receive money on deposit, to loan credit and to issue currency; and it does not take much watching to see that these persons get rich.

Again, some one or more of these bankers will associate with themselves four or more successful corner grocerymen, prosperous butchers, or well-to-do manufacturers, etc., and will incorporate and obtain the privilege to furnish gas; others to bring water into the town; others to buy, mortgage, improve and sell lands; others to build and operate street tramways; others to construct steam railroads; others to put up telegraphs and telephone lines; others to make toll roads and bridges; others to buy and control the oil production; others to operate steamships and sailing vessels; others to insure life; others to insure property; and others to build and lease hotels, theatres, flats, etc.; to buy, improve and monopolize inventions; to manufacture and control rubber goods; electric motors; to farm large tracts of land; to raise cattle; to publish papers, magazines and books, etc.

We see more and more companies incorporated every day, and we see the little companies being absorbed by the larger. Everywhere we see the individual business man associating with himself other business persons and taking out papers of corporation to do something too big for one man to execute. Everywhere we see concentration and combination and corporation limited. If we look close we will find that he or she who has had business forethought to get into two or more of these incorporated companies is richer than he or she who has only incorporated in one; we will see that the great wealth, in the United States particularly, has been made through investments in incorporated companies; and that there is scarcely a successful business person who is not in one or more ways connected with them.

Luxury and over-abundance of everything characterizes the surroundings of the incorporated individual; poverty, wretchedness and the absence of the common comforts of existence are the lot of the unincorporated individual.

Those who have incorporated, for a well-planned purpose, act independent of those they hire. Those who have not made a business alliance with others, and incorporated to carry their purpose into execution, are dependent upon those who have.

If these incorporated companies have been so uniformly successful in carrying out their plans and in making stockholders prosperous and influential, that they give their members more agreeable employments and better homes, and that the person who is in two is better off than the person who is in one, would it not be wise for a large number of men and women to take out papers of incorporation to establish a deposit and loan bank; to buy, lay out and improve a town sight and farm; to build houses, operate factories; to furnish gas. water, fuel, power, transportation, food, drink, clothes, etc.; to insure life and property: to secure inventions; to employ, educate, entertain, amuse, cremate, etc. If to incorporate and control any one of these has been found to be conducive to the good health, spirits, comfort and education, of those who have monopolized them, why should it not be better to pool all, or to consolidate a hundred or more, into one large incorporated company?

In doing this we will act in the strict line of the instruction given us by Cicero, "that no one should use public things, otherwise than as public things, and should use private things only as his own." The control of the land and its deposits, the highways, water ways, the atmosphere, exchanges, transportations, entertainments, amusements, instructions, sanitations, insurances, the ways and means of payment, etc., belong to the public; and society depends upon their equitable management for its safety and advancement.

To discriminate between what belongs to the public and that which belongs to the individual, has puzzled statesmen in all ages. Why is this not a good test. That which a man or woman can do unassisted is private, but all other things are public and should be made and controlled by the public. Equity does not admit of one person being employed by another in any way, time or place, but always in any way and in every place each individual should be assisted in the line of production he or she elects, by his or her own agent or the companies' director, and no two or more persons should be permitted to form a co-partnership or firm within the corporation. In this way every one is forced to be usefully occupied, to stand upon his or her merits, and to be paid for the quality and quantity of the work delivered to the agent elected to receive and to give credit for the same.

There is no equality, no communism, no license in this suggestion. It is a plain business proposition to combine into one company what has heretofore mostly been carried on by separate incorporated bodies. Men and women would enjoy more security, more privacy and more liberty in a community organized as suggested, than under any government ever yet proposed. Trustees of the association would simply conserve and utilize all public things for the use of the public, and assist the individual to be comfortable, useful and progressive. It does not permit a person or persons to get a special law passed, that he or they may take advantage of those who work, and hence, great individual fortunes would not be possible.

There is no necessity for a test to be made of the plan herein suggested. Everywhere, and for every purpose under heaven, we see incorporated companies in operation, and nine out of every ten are successful. The way for the laboring men and women to apply these suggestions to practice, at once, is plain, and may be made easy if method and discipline are conformed with.

In this way slowly, surely and in a strict business way, persons can be taken from farms, factories, shops, counting houses, etc., and placed in the occupations he or she selects, under their own management, upon their own lands, in their own homes, and where direct interests, taxes and rents need be unknown.

In such a community there need be no drones, every one can worship God after his or her own wish; and, while compensation between man and man should not be permitted, rivalry in all useful callings should be encouraged: the strong would be attracted to assist the weak, and the weak would be glad to co-operate to the best of their ability with the strong, because it would be the interest of each to do so: poverty being unknown, great individual riches would be impossible: and while the company would become wealthy and influential, the individual would receive full, prompt and cash payment for anything and everything he or she did, and would be protected in his and her labor, property and individuality: and housed, instructed, amused, transported and entertained better and at less cost, than has yet been dreamed of.

Such would be evolution not revolution: such would not interfere with any well-intentioned person on earth—such would be peace, prosperity and happiness to producers who organized to employ themselves, to exchange their own products, and to put every head of a family in a beautiful home free from tax, rent and interest. "Sweet Home" should and can be made a reality to every industrious man and woman.

The suggestion to producers is, act for yourself and be not satisfied with discussion and agitation: do not rest with organization, but incorporate—incorporate to employ yourself, to handle your own exchanges, to own the lands you improve, to grow your own crops, to own and occupy the houses you build. In this way you can each have a home.

CHAPTER XIX.

PRISON LABOR.

A GREAT QUESTION—HOW CONVICTS ARE EMPLOYED—OCCUPATIONS IN VARIOUS PRISONS — WORKING FOR THE STATE — THE CONTRACT SYSTEM — THE LEASE PLAN—E. C. WINES ON THE CONTRACT SYSTEM—ITS EFFECT—ABUSES—SHOULD BE ABOLISHED —LEASES AND FAULTS THEREOF—57,500 CONVICT WORKMEN PITTED AGAINST HONEST LABOR — DR. SEAMAN'S VIEWS — DEMANDS OF THE PUBLIC — CARROLL D. WRIGHT'S REPORT—PRISON LABOR MUST NOT CONFLICT WITH INTERESTS OF THE WORKINGMAN.

WHAT should be done with convicts industrially, has been a question ever since our present penitentiary systems were instituted. The distinction between penal, or hard labor and industrial labor, does not exist in the United States as in England. The sentence of "hard labor" here simply means industrial labor. This is an element of good policy and justice, because it is right that criminals should do something to reimburse the state for the expense they have incurred because of their crimes, and it is proper, because work is an essential condition of reform.

All kinds of productive labor is found in American prisons. In Texas, Alabama and North Carolina the convicts build railroads; they raise cotton in Mississippi, and in New York and Tennessee they work in mines; and in many states they do farm work and cultivate vegetables. Prison employments are mechanical except in the South, and deal with work in the metals, wood and leather, though a great deal of stone work is done where prisons are in course of construction. At Auburn, N. Y., agricultural tools are make in large quantities; at Philadelphia cell work is done in shoemaking, weaving, tailoring and light wood work; in Massachusetts, cabinet making, brush and shoemaking, and work on sewing machines; an important department of labor is making of carpenter's rules in Connecticut; in Maine, carriage manufacturing is carried on at a large scale; a great iron mine furnishes ore to the Northern New York prison, which is smelted, forged and wrought into nails; leather tanning is the chief product of the Michigan prison, chair making at the Detroit House of Correction, and in the Indiana prison (South) the convicts are mainly employed in building railway cars in all its branches.

Two prisons weave wire; bolts and hinges are

made in one; brushes in several; stoves in one; edge tools in one; car-wheels in one; iron work (bronzed) in one; cigars in five; machinery in one; axles in one; moulding in three; chairs in eight; weaving in three; cabinet making in six; farming implements in one, brooms in one; cooperage in nine; saddles and harness in several, and shoes in over a dozen; while tailoring, painting, carpentry and smithing in all.

At different prisons and times, convict labor has been employed in the following systems: 1. Working the prisoners for the state in the manufacture of crude material furnished by the state. 2. The contract system. 3. That of leasing the prison for a certain period; the lessee assuming entire control of both discipline and industries, and furnishing food, clothing, medicine, etc.

"The contract system," says E. C. Wines, in his 'State of Prisons, etc.,' "obtains in the major part of our prisons. In a few, perhaps a tenth or eighth of the whole number, the prison labor is managed by the prison administration; and this is especially the case when the building or enlarging of a prison is going on. There are many objections to the contract system of prison labor, but it has been found in general less expensive to the government than its management by the prison officers. This is, no doubt, due to the general instability of our prison administrations. Where party politics dominate these administrations, and where, owing to the fluctuation of parties, new and inexperienced men are so often put in charge of our prisons, it is not to be expected that so vast and complicated a machine as the industries of a large prison should be successfully managed by them. Even under our present system, the industries in prisons of moderate size, containing not more than three hundred or four hundred inmates, have been and are carried on by the authorities with fair success. Take the history of the state prison of Massachusetts as an example—a prison from which we have financial returns for a longer period than from any other in the country. During the sixty-two years covered by these returns, the prison has exhibited a profit above its expenses in twenty-three years, and a deficit in thirty-nine years. . . . . The first effect of the contract system is to place for the whole working day all the prisoners contracted for, to a great extent, under the control of men with no official responsibility—men who see in the convicts only so much machinery for making money: men whose only, or at any rate whose chief, recommendation to the positions they hold in the prison is that they were the highest bidders for the human beings hired by them. The second effect is to introduce among the convicts, as superintendents of their labor, strangers to the prison, who are employed by the contractors as agents, foremen, and in some instances even laborers—men entirely irresponsible—men selected with little regard to their moral character, and often without morals; men who do not hesitate to smuggle liquor into the prison and other contraband articles, and sell them to the convicts at an increditable advance on their true market value. A third effect of the system, is to set up in the prisons a power behind the throne greater than the throne; a power well-nigh omnipotent in its sphere; a power that coaxes, bribes and threatens in pursuit of its selfish ends; a power that makes and unmakes officers, imposes and remits fines through agents whom it has been able to bend to its will, and even stoops to mean devices to get the poor prisoner, who has incurred its wrath, into straits and difficulties, that its revenge may be gratified with the sight of his punishment."

In the lease system the whole control of the prison and its inmates is turned over to the lessee whose sole object is to make money. The general result of the plan is, that food and clothing are reduced to the minimum; the strength of the convict is tasked to the utmost limit of human endurance; the property of the state is neglected and injured; the prisoners are held as so many machines, and are valued upon the basis of the amount of work they can do; reformation is ignored and the higher ends of discipline are held for naught.

It was supposed when the various industries were introduced to prisons that the great problem of what to do with convict labor was successfully solved. Convicts who worked at an average of about fifty

HAY MAKING IN THE OLDEN TIMES.

cents a day produced certain articles which sold in the market at less prices than the same goods produced by free labor. The consequence is plain to be seen. Convict labor is pitted against honest labor to the detriment of the latter. The honest workingman must pay taxes, and the margin on prison made goods goes into the pockets of the contractors or prison lessees.

There are in the United States 57,500 convicts who are daily engaged in competing with free labor, and over one-half of them are skilled laborers. From this source the industry of the entire country is affected. Every prison is virtually an immense factory or workshop, with a daily output as against the honest workingman who is earning a bare subsistance.

It is universally held by legislators that this competition is the foe of free labor, and in many of the states the contract and leasing systems have been abolished, but an effectual remedy for the evil has not been put into actual practice. If labor is taxed for the support of penal institutions, the inmates should in some way be made to return the expenditure, and in a way so as not to interfere with free labor:

Dr. Seaman, late chief of staff of the Blackwell's Island hospital and penitentiary, spoke upon the problem of convict labor in a recent address before the Medico-Legal Society. He argues in favor of the English system of employing long sentence prisoners on great public works, such as harbor and fortification making. An effort is being made in another quarter to introduce transportation to Alaska. But there is a third alternative, suggested by some very common-place facts, here submitted for consideration.

Society is, perhaps unnecessarily, afflicted by having to bear two enormous burdens, costly, demoralizing and oppressive. These are (1) the maintenance of criminals, and (2) the maintenance of widows and orphans left destitute by "accidents." It is meant, here particularly, the families of miners killed by coalpit explosions, which occur so frequently. Now, the miner is probably the worthiest working citizen in the commonwealth. For our good he submits not only to tremendous toil, but to the sacrifice of sunlight and the pure air of heaven, and cheerfully faces the risk of being himself among the percentage of miners who every year get killed, something like one in thirty-eight. We owe more to the miner than we care to acknowledge.

On the other hand, the criminal forfeits ordinary sympathy. The worst class, criminals who have just (unfortunately) dodged the hangman, society pronounces unfit to associate again with the community for a long time, if ever; i. e., society says they are unfit to live in the world.

Yet we exalt these malefactors to the position of state pensioners, we give them palatial residences, a costly staff of liveried servants, with all the resources of medical and sanitary science to prolong their precious lives to the last possible gasp—all at the expense of the honest, law abiding, virtuous taxpayer. And the coal getter? Well, we condemn him to banishment into the bowels of the earth, with the tolerably sure and certain hope of an "accidental" explosion, with loss of life or limb, and the probable pauperization of widows and orphans to follow.

Suppose, by way of experimental reform, our all-wise legislature were to select the life sentence convicts of the most worthless and repulsive type, and single out also the most dangerous mines. Suppose they were to place the former in the latter, say, for ten years' daily labor. If, in the mysterious workings of Providence, an explosion were to bereave us of these our erring brethren, the calamity would not end the lives of our honest and industrious miners, who raise their families as good citizens. On the other hand, the saving in cost of prisons would go far to insure the safety of our worthy miners by providing better preventives of "accidents."

The public asks that prisons be made self-sustaining, and at the same time they must not interfere with free labor. As long as the industrial system is carried on in penitentiaries as at present, so long will their labor operate against the outside workingman, but there is a medium wherein reformation and productive labor may meet. There is no doubt but the "piece-price plan" is better than all others, as either the state or an individual may be in control. A convict at work is doing no more than he should do if free, and he certainly should be obliged to support himself during his incarceration.

If prison made goods are to be placed in the market, they should be sold at free labor prices, and the proceeds should be judiciously expended towards the accomplishment of the convict's reformation.

In the second annual report of the National Bureau of Labor Statistics, Carroll D. Wright, Commissioner, reports in favor of the state system, and favors what he calls the "hand-labor public account system." His conclusion is expressed as follows:

"Hand-labor under the public account system offers many advantages over any other that has been suggested to the bureau. It involves the carrying on of the industries of a prison for the benefit of the state, but without the use of power machinery, tools and hand machines only being allowed, the goods to be made to consist of such articles as boots and shoes, the coarse woolen and cotton cloths needed for the institution or for sale to other institutions, harnesses and saddlery, and many other goods now made by machinery or not now made at all in prisons."

Whatever policy may be pursued in the future,

it is well settled in the minds of the people, especially the workingmen, that convicts should be employed with the least possible expense for machinery, and that their product should be disposed of so as not to conflict with honest labor.

CHAPTER XX.

LIQUOR AND THE WORKINGMAN.

THE ENORMOUS AMOUNT OF MONEY EXPENDED FOR LIQUOR—MR. POWDERLY ARRAIGNS THE DRUNKARD—HIS POWERFUL SPEECH AT LYNN, MASS.—HOW LIQUOR PRODUCES POVERTY—FIFTEEN MILLION PEOPLE SPEND SEVEN HUNDRED MILLION DOLLARS ANNUALLY FOR LIQUOR—LIQUOR COSTS THE PEOPLE THREE TIMES AS MUCH AS CLOTHING—INTEMPERANCE A CURSE TO THE WORKINGMAN.

IN an article on prohibition of the sale and manufacture of liquor, a writer in a leading southern paper says, as a matter of dollars and cents, the question of a tariff for revenue or protection, the financial policy and all others combined, pale into utter insignificance compared with the amount of money that is annually expended for that which destroys the peace of thousands of happy homes, brings degradation and want, brings the unfortunate victims to premature graves, and consigns them to an endless hell—from the best statistical information obtainable about nine hundred millions annually for alcoholic drinks, all of which comes out of the pockets of the consumers. Estimating from all sources—federal, state and municipal—the revenue derivable from this source, on the sale only, amounts to about three hundred millions of dollars.

Mr. Powderly in a speech at Lynn, Mass., said: "Ten years ago I was hissed because I advised men to let strong drink alone. They threatened to rotten egg me. I have continued to advise men to be temperate, and though I have had no experience that would qualify me to render an opinion on the efficacy of a rotten egg as an ally of the rum drinker, yet I would prefer to have my exterior decorated from summit to base with the rankest kind of rotten eggs, rather than allow one drop of liquid villainy to pass my lips, or have the end of my nose illuminated by a blossom that follows a planting of the seeds of hatred, envy, malice and damnation, all of which are represented in a solitary glass of gin.

Ten years ago the cause of temperance was not so respectable as it is to-day, because there were not so many respectable men and women advocating it. It has gained ground; it is gaining ground, and all because men and women who believe in it could not be browbeaten or frightened. Neither the hissing of serpents nor the throwing of rotten eggs has stopped or even delayed the march of temperance among the workers.

Why do I so bitterly arraign the poor drunkard? For the reason that he is a drunkard, and because he has made himself poor through his love of drink. Did I or any other man, rob him of the money he has squandered in drink; did I make him poor, the vilest names that tongue can frame would be applied to me. Must I stand idly by and remain silent while he robs himself? Did he rob only himself it would not make so much difference. He robs parents, wife and children. He robs his aged father and mother through love of drink. He gives for rum what should go for their support. When they murmur he turns them from his door, and points his contaminating drunken finger toward the poorhouse. He next turns toward his wife and robs her of what should be devoted to the keeping of her home in comfort and plenty. He robs her of her wedding ring and pawns it for drink. He turns his daughter from his door in a fit of drunken anger and drives her to the house of prostitution, and then accepts from her hand the proceeds of her shame. To satisfy his love of drink he takes the price of his child's virtue and innocence from her sin stained, lust bejeweled fingers, and with it totters to the bar to pay it to the man who "does not deny the justice of my position." I don't arraign the man who drinks because he is poor, but because through being a slave to drink he has made himself and family poor. I do not hate the man who drinks, for I have carried drunken men to their homes on my back, rather than allow them to remain exposed to inclement weather. I do not hate the drunkard—he is what drink has effected, and while I do not hate the effect, I abhor and loathe the cause.

Take the list of labor societies of America, and the total sum paid into their treasuries from all sources from their organization to the present time will not exceed $5,000,000. The Knights of Labor is the largest and most influential of them all, and though so much has been said concerning the vast amount of money that has been collected from the members, yet the total sum levied and collected for all purposes—per capita tax, assistance fund, appeals, assessment, insurance and co-operation—up to the present time will not exceed more than $800,000.

The total sum collected for the first nine years of the existence of the general assembly was but $500,724.14. In nine years less than $600,000 were collected to uplift humanity to a higher plane, and to bring the workers to a realizing sense of their actual condition in life. It took less than $600,000 to teach the civilized world that workingmen could build up an organization that could shed such light upon the doings of landlords, bond-lords, monopolists and other trespassers of the domain of popular rights, that they were forced to halt for a time and stand up to explain. Less than $600,000 (not a dollar unaccounted for), and on the statute books of the nation will you find the impress of the workingman's hand. On the law book of every state can be traced the doing of labor's representatives. Less than $600,000 to create a revolution greater, further reaching in its consequences and more lasting in its benefits, than the revolution which caused the streets of the towns and cities of France to run red with human blood less than a century ago. Less than $600,000 to make men fear and believe that woman's work should equal that of the man. Less than $600,000 to educate men and women to believe that "moral worth and not wealth is the true standard of individual and national greatness." Less than $600,000 to cause every newspaper in the land to speak of the work being done by the Knights of Labor—some of them speaking in abusive terms, and others speaking words of praise, according to the interests represented by the papers or according as the work done harmonized with the principles of the order.

In one day an employer's association organizes and pledges itself to contribute $5,000,000 to fight labor. The next day the papers are almost silent on that point, but are filled to the brim with lurid accounts of the reckless autocratic manner in which the officers of the Knights of Labor levy a 25-cent assessment to keep over 1,000 locked out men and women from starvation. Putting two and two together, it is not hard to guess why papers that applauded the action of the employers in one col-

AMONG THE BOTTLE BLOWERS.

umn should in another column advise the workers not to pay the twenty-five cent assessment. $600,000 for sober men to use in education and self-improvement.

Now let us turn to the other side. In the city of New York alone it is estimated that not less than $250,000 a day are spent for drink, $1,500,000 in one week, $75,000,000 in one year. Who will dispute it when I say that one-half of the policemen of New York city are employed to watch the beings who squander $75,000,000 a year? Who will dispute it when I say the money spent in paying the salaries and expenses of one-half of the police of New York could be saved to the taxpayers if $75,000,000 were not devoted to making drunkards, thieves, prostitutes, and other subjects for the policeman's net to gather in? If $250,000 go over the counters of the rum-seller in one day in New York city alone, who will dare to assert that the workingmen to-day do not pay one-fifth, or $50,000, of that sum?

If workingmen in New York city spend $50,000 a day for drink, they spend $300,000 a week, leaving Sunday out. In one month they spend $1,200,000—over twice as much money as was paid into the general assembly of the Knights of Labor in nine years. In six weeks they spend $1,800,000—nearly three times as much money as that army of organized workers, the Knights of Labor, have spent from the day the general assembly was first called to order up to the present day; and in one year the workingmen of New York city will have spent for beer and rum $15,600,000, or enough to purchase and equip a first-class line of their own — $15,600,000, enough money to invest in such co-operation as would forever end the strike and lockout as a means of settling disputes in labor circles.

A single county in Pennsylvania, so I am informed, spent in one year $17,000,000 for drink. That county contains the largest industrial population, comparatively, of any in the state. $11,000,000 of the $17,000,000 come from the pockets of workingmen. New York city, in one year, contributes $15,600,000 to keep men and women in poverty, hunger and cold, while one county in Pennsylvania adds $11,000,000, making a total of $26,600,000.

I am not a fanatic—I do not damn the man who sells liquor. I have nothing against him. Many men who now sell liquor were once workingmen, and were victimized through a strike or lockout. I would not injure a hair of their heads, but I would so educate workingmen that they would never enter a saloon. Then the money saved from rum, and rum holes, would go to purchase necessaries, and such an increased stimulus would be given to trade that the rum-seller could return to an honest way of making a living.

I may be taken to task for being severe on the workingmen. It may be said that I slander them even. If to tell the truth is to be severe, then on this one question I hope some day to be severity itself: but I speak to workingmen, because it is in their welfare that I am interested. I have not been delegated to watch or guard the fortunes of millionaires, and in no way can I hope to accomplish anything until I state my policy freely and frankly to those I represent. We are seeking to reform existing evils. We must first reform ourselves."

In the report issued in July, 1887, by the Bureau of Statistics, at Washington, it is shown that the total annual expenditure for liquors at retail in the United States is SEVEN HUNDRED MILLLION DOLLARS, and that the drinking population is about FIFTEEN MILLION PERSONS. In 1880 (last census) the total product of our four great industries were, viz.:

    Clothing....................$241,553,254
    Cotton goods................ 210,950,383
    Woolen goods 100,606,721
    Iron and steel................ 296,557,685

By comparison we see that the amount of money spent for liquor was more than three times greater than that expended for ready made clothing: that it was in excess of the value of the total combined product of the cotton, woolen, and iron and steel industries, and not much less than the value of the product of all four of the industries named. Of the fifteen million people who wasted this vast sum, each man expended nearly one dollar a week in gratifying a base appetite. Every dollar of all this money was just as much wasted as if it had been dumped in the ocean. Indeed, such disposition of it would have been wise economy compared with that which was really made of it, for only the first cost of the rum appears in the sum of $700,000,000.

Probably the amount would be increased more than fifty per cent if we should ascertain the cost of the crime, pauperism, and insanity which always follow the product of the rum traffic. Now, suppose all this money, three times the value of the total iron product of the country, had been expended for things useful, comfortable, and necessary, does any man believe there would be complaint of overproduction? Would any laborer who wanted to work be forced into idleness? Is it not clear that there would be such a stimulus for business as would give to this country prosperity more than at any time in the past, with good wages for work. The great majority of these fifteen million people are workingmen.

CHAPTER XXI.

THE FARMER AND HIS INTERESTS.

CAPITAL DRIFTING AWAY FROM AGRICULTURE — THE LABOR QUESTION LINKED WITH THE FARMER — HON. W. F. SADLER BEFORE THE GRANGE — AN ABLE DISCOURSE — A STARTLING ARRAY OF FACTS AND FIGURES—THE AVARICE OF CAPITAL—MR. JOHN NORRIS ON RAILROAD MONOPOLY — CHARLES SEARS' MEASURES—A BALEFUL WARNING—MR. CHARLES SEARS' EXPOSITION OF TRUTHS — PUBLIC CARRIERS AND MONEY LOANERS ARE ABSORBING CAPITAL—A PEACEFUL MODE OF ADJUSTMENT—MEASURES AND REMEDIES—UNITED EFFORT BY REFORM PARTIES NECESSARY TO SUCCESS—LABOR ASCENDING THE THRONE OF POLITICS.

The gradual drifting of capital from agriculture to industrial centers, during the past fifty years, has produced its effect. Farming to-day is not the paying vocation it has been, and the true wealth of the nation is suffering from a great shrinkage on account of the farmer's inability to reap his due measure of products. Linked with the interests of our farmers are the interests of trade, manufacturing, commerce, and the welfare of the entire country.

Inseparably connected with the great question of labor, which has been forced to the surface of the stream of current affairs, is the depressed condition of agriculture.

Hon. W. F. Sadler, in speaking before the Grange inter-state exhibition, 1886, said: "While the pre-eminence of the importance of agriculture over that of any other art of man has always existed in fact, yet it will be conceded that it has been slow in securing deserved recognition and rightful appreciation: It will be also agreed by the intelligent and observant, that as its true relations to the other occupations is becoming thus more properly understood, the propriety, desirability and necessity that it should be thoroughly studied, wisely practiced, and it needs have due regard become the more apparent. It has not only long been, as it now is, the chief subsistence of the race, but its prosperity has had an intimate relation to the progression of the latter. Indeed, in the rudimentary tilling of the soil the individual could only produce bread for himself and family, and there was, therefore, no surplus human force to make development possible in other lines.

Men could only devote brain and energy and muscle to the other human pursuits which characterize our modern civilization, when less than the whole number could provide food for the whole.

It needs no demonstration to show that the fewer of the population required for the one purpose the more can be employed in others, and also that the more perfect system of agriculture the less number of persons will be needed to furnish the production necessary for supply

To-day the crops seem to be the business barometer of our nation. Trade halts until it learns what their condition is. The 'bulls' and 'bears' of our great commercial centres alike listen with bated breath, while the telegraph tells of the growing, gathering, garnering and yield of the harvest fields of the land. Upon them the railroad is dependent for freight, the banker for exchange, the country for exports, and the whole world for bread.

Their abundance, in short, is the harbinger of business prosperity, while their failure is the precursor of diminished trade, if not of pecuniary distress.

Besides, it claims special attention on account of the multitudes engaged in the cultivation of the soil. Of all those enlisted in occupations in the United States more than forty-four per cent are enumerated in our last census as being agriculturalists. So that, in addition to the relative import of this industry, there is the immediate dependence upon it of a much larger factor of our population than upon that of any other. It may be safely assumed, I think, that more than one-half of all our male population of an age fit to work are engaged in producing crops, and in the transportation and delivery of them to the consumer.

There has been too little of this in the past—there is not enough at the present. The Thomases, Piollets and Rhones of the Granger movement have done much to infuse a proper spirit in this respect into the farmer—but much remains to be accomplished. It is time that there was less of humility on part of those who cultivate the soil, and more pride. It has too long been considered degrading to dig. The tiller of the soil does the most beneficial work of man, and the regard of society for his labor should be proportionate in degree. It may also be observed that a proper estimate by the farmer of his own calling will tend to insure a juster one by others, and would be productive as well on his part of an assertiveness, justified by the position which should be accorded to, taken and maintained by those upon the skill and productivity of whose toil annually depends the chief food of all the people. The husbandman's boys would also more highly regard the father's occupation if he himself accorded to it due consideration, and there would thus likely be less anxiety on their part to seek other employments.

While press and forum and party platform properly vie in the attention given to the grievances, wants and rights of the employers of our great manufacturing, mining and mechanical industries, it were well to remember that the cultivators of the soil also have wrongs, and wants, and rights, entitled to a high and present regard—the laborers among them nearly equaling those in the departments alluded to. That while the nation's brain throbs with speculations and plans, as to how content may come to the hand at the factory and shop, and by what method of computation a fair distribution of the earnings of labor and capital may be allotted between employer and employe, it must not be forgotten that the husbandmen are a craft of workmen, not only more ancient in its institution, mightier in its proportions, and more essential to society's well being, as well as to existence of mankind, but also that problems, numerous, complicated and fraught with the highest importance to their welfare, demand consideration.

Some of these are even now invoking the concern and affecting the interests of the farmer, especially of the Eastern states—such as the rates at which these products shall be transported to market, while others, more serious, as how land shall be held and how let to the tenant, are eliciting not only the attention, but affecting the prosperity, disturbing the quiet and imperiling the peace of the most powerful as well as the wisest nation on the globe, and for which no method of solution has yet been found."

It is pertinent at all times to scrutinize our surroundings, and a glance backward over the road we have traveled never does harm. What progress we have made is a subject well worth examining. How has the farmer and wage-worker been affected by the absorption of railroads, by pools and by monopolies? A glance at results tells the tale. A dollar invested in one of the largest and most productive states (Pennsylvania) in 1880, yielded a smaller return than in any of the other states. Pennsylvania has thousands of miles of railroads.

Percentage of Farm Production to Farm Value in 1880.

NORTH ATLANTIC GROUP.

Maine,	.21	Connecticut,	.15
New Hampshire,	.17	New York,	.16 4-5
Vermont,	.20	New Jersey,	.15½
Massachusetts,	.16½	Pennsylvania,	.13 1-5
Rhode Island,	.14		

SOUTH ATLANTIC GROUP.

Delaware,	.17	North Carolina,	.38
Maryland,	.17	South Carolina,	.61
District of Columbia	.14	Georgia,	.59

NORTHERN CENTRAL GROUP.

Ohio,	.14	Iowa,	.24
Indiana,	.18	Missouri,	.25

NORTHERN CENTRAL GROUP—CONTINUED.

Illinois,	.20	Dakota,	.25
Michigan,	.18	Nebraska,	.29
Wisconsin,	.20	Kansas,	.22
Minnesota,	.25		

SOUTHERN CENTRAL GROUP.

Kentucky,	.21	Louisiana,	.71
Tennessee,	.30	Texas,	.38
Alabama,	.72	Arkansas,	.59
Mississippi,	.68		

WESTERN GROUP.

Montana,	.62	Nevada,	.52
Wyoming,	.44	Idaho,	.54
Colorado,	.20	Washington Ter.	.30
New Mexico,	.34	Oregon,	.23
Arizona,	.54	California,	.22
Utah,	.23		

Each combination of capital makes the workingman more dependent, and renders it the more difficult for the small manufacturer to conduct his business. By glancing over the census report of 1880, it is apparent that centralization of capital is crowding out the workingmen by reducing the number of establishments.

REDUCTION IN NUMBER OF MANUFACTURING ESTABLISHMENTS FROM 1870 to 1880.

STATE.	1870.	1880.	REDUCTION.
Pennsylvania,	37,300	31,232	5,968
Missouri,	11,871	8,502	3,279
Ohio,	22,773	20,699	2,074
Maine,	5,550	4,481	1,069
Louisiana,	2,557	1,553	1,004
Tennessee,	3,347	4,326	991
Indiana,	11,847	11,198	649
Connecticut,	5,128	4,488	640
Michigan,	9,455	8,873	582
Vermont,	3,270	2,874	396
Mississippi,	1,731	1,479	252
Georgia,	3,836	3,503	243
Florida,	659	426	233
Virginia,	5,933	5,710	223
New Hampshire,	3,342	3,181	161
Nevada,	330	184	146
Alabama,	2,188	2,070	118
West Virginia,	2,444	2,375	69
Kentucky,	5,300	5,328	62
Delaware,	800	746	54

"On every side we see," writes Mr. John Morris, of the "Philadelphia Daily Record," "that wealth and power are drifting into few hands. We find traces of this condition not only in railroad consolidations but in the coal combination, the coke syndicate, the Western Union Telegraph Company,

HON. JOHN SEITZ.

the Standard Oil Company, and the hundred other parasites of our railroads. We find combinations of capital against which the individual is helpless, creating classes that are fabulously rich and classes that are shockingly poor. We find deepening want with increasing wealth. Individual enterprise has given way to the corporations. The factory is superseding the mechanic, and the larger farm is absorbing the smaller farm.

"We find some few natural monopolies due to invention and to healthy business enterprise, and we find many artificial monopolies that are due to special and discriminating rates and to the evils that characterized our railroad policy. The harmony and symmetry of our development has been disturbed by these improper influences. A condition of affairs has been created which will soon become intolerable. In view of these appalling facts is there not a necessity for arousing the public conscience? Is there not a necessity for warning the people against these baleful tendencies of the times?"

Mr. Charles Sears, in an able essay on the causes of the financial and industrial depression of the times, says:

"Taxes are finally liquidated with products. There are no other means of payment. The accumulated wealth of cities, towns and country is surplus product. The rate of accumulation is estimated at about three per cent annually.

"From tables of statistics it appears that in the western states about three-fourths of the farms are mortgaged for one-third to three-fourths of their current value; and that this class of debt bears interest at seven to twelve per cent yearly; and that it is rapidly increasing, as it must do, for the rates of interest paid exceed the rate of property increase. The farmers, therefore, are contributing more than their surplus to the sum of wealth, they trench upon the capital, and consequently, are steadily passing out of the ranks of independent citizens into a class of tenant farmers, or that of wage-workers. Can this, in any sense, be deemed a safe state of affairs?

"Why do farmers have to borrow money? Because their produce will not pay the cost of production. Why are prices realized by farmers so low? A chief reason is the cost of transportation of products. The average cost of transportation is stated to be a fraction less than five mills per ton per mile. The prices exacted and paid range from three to six times that rate. It appears, therefore, that the transportation companies and money lenders are absorbing not only the surplus of production, but capital also; and that with the present rates of interest and freight, the production of grain, cattle, horses, wool, cotton, etc., are, economically considered, impossible industries.

"The government has delegated, by charter, the power to Banking Corporations to issue money and control the circulating volume and thereby determine the rate of interest; to railroad companies the power to tax the public 'what the traffic will bear.' Between these two the producer of raw material is confiscated, for with high rates of interest and high freight rates his property is confiscated, and this through chartered privilege. He might as well be out of the world as without property.

"This is an unsafe condition, an unjust relation of producer, middlemen and consumer. It is a condition which cannot endure, for in the end, property acquired without rendering a fair equivalent is an unsafe possession. An adjustment, in which the equities shall be considered, must come, either peacefully or through violence.

"When class rises against class in desperation, reason is in abeyance, passion rules. The steady drain of property from producer to the coffers of transportation companies and bankers is disintegrating society—dividing it into rich and poor, a state we are rapidly approaching—that of distinctly defined classes. This is the direct road to violent reclamations.

"A peaceful mode of adjustment would be for the government to acquire possession of the railroads at a fair valuation and manage them at cost. This would put railroads on the same footing as are country roads—both would be public property and both maintained at cost.

" Another measure tending toward a peaceful issue from dangerous wants would be the issue of money direct to the people on their own securities, repayable in five per cent yearly installments with yearly interest at three per cent, which would be part of the public revenue, divided equally to the treasuries of the counties, the state and the general government, and be so much in lieu of taxes.

"A still further measure tending in the same direction would be the organization of production and exchange in the interest of producer and consumer. These measures would save us from impending bankruptcy and perhaps a worse condition, for they leave to the producer the fruit of his labor and so remove the causes of discontent."

The stumbling block to reform movements heretofore, has been in a lack of united effort and the consolidation of different parties. Petty factions and egotistical opinions have served to prevent a national union of workingmen, and results have been of little value.

Labor is ascending the throne of politics, but until it fully comprehends the power of the ballot, and presents a united front at the polls, it will never grasp the sceptre.

CHAPTER XXII.

FOREIGNERS AND FOREIGNERS.

THE IMMIGRATION OF TO-DAY A GREAT EVIL—500,000 IMMIGRANTS IN 1887—OFFICIAL FIGURES—OVER 8,000,000 ALIENS IN THIS COUNTRY—A FLOOD OF PAUPERS AND CRIMINALS TAINTING THE NATION—H. H. BOYESEN ON UNRESTRICTED IMMIGRATION—THE EVIL OF ANARCHY AND COMMUNISM ONE OF THE CURSES OF THE FOUL STREAM—SUMMARY LEGISLATION A JUST DEMAND OF WORKINGMEN — AMERICAN LABOR MENACED BY FOREIGN IMMIGRATION — HOSTILE SENTIMENT THROUGHOUT THE LAND—A QUESTION OF THE DAY.

THE workingmen of the United States have awakened to the fact that a great evil lurks in the tide of immigration which has so long set in upon this country. Notwithstanding the extended limits of our domain there is a feeling that we are crowded, especially in large cities.

The huge ocean steamers daily land at their docks, and thousands of the substratum of European humanity swarm from their gangways. To this unrestricted immigration is justly attributed one of the disturbing elements which has much to do with the problem labor is endeavoring to solve. Since the Declaration of Independence was signed, over fourteen millions of immigrants have crossed the ocean and made their homes in the United States.

The increase in immigration in May, 1887, was 28,400 over the same month of the preceding year, and the increase in the eleven months ending with May, was 133,600. This means that over half a million foreigners have come to this country during the last fiscal year. The official reports do not give the number from Canada and Mexico across the border, and the number of such immigrants is known to be considerable. In 1884-5, the last year for which it was officially reported, this immigration was 38,614; with the general decline in immigration last year it may have fallen to 30,000, but with the general increase this year it has probably risen to 40,000 or more.

The most accurate computation for the increase of population during twenty years ending with 1880, proves to be that which allows 2 per cent yearly for increase by the excess of births over deaths, and then adds the immigration each year. At that rate the increase each year since July 1, 1880, would be as follows:

	Increase.	Immigration.
1880-1	1,003,115	669,431
1881-2	1,036,566	788,992
1882-3	1,073,077	603,322
1883-4	1,106,605	518,592
1884-5	1,139,109	395,346
1885-6	1,169,799	334,203
1886-7	1,199,878	500,000
Total	7,728,149	3,809,886

In the statement of immigration for the last and the current year the official figures are followed, embracing no allowance for immigrants from Canada or Mexico.

If 70,000 be added for these the aggregate population July 1, 1887, would be 61,763,818, unless the increase by excess of births over deaths has been smaller during the present than during the preceding decades.

Without any allowance for Canadian immigration the population July 1 would appear on this basis to be about 61,700,000. The fact that all treasury estimates give lower figures is in the main explained by their failure to make separate allowance for the immigration, which has been larger during the recent than in any previous decade. As the table shows, the addition by immigration alone, has exceeded 3,800,000 in seven years, and has been almost half the increase from all other sources.

Maintaining the same average increase of 1,650-000 for the remaining three years of the decade, the census of June, 1890, will find close on 66,000,-000 of inhabitants within the limits of the great republic.

In 1887 Great Britain and Ireland furnished the largest number. Of the arrivals in May, 29,277 were from the British Isles, 16,416 being from Ireland, while the German immigration was but 18,086 and the Scandinavian 13,139. Italy furnished the comparatively large number of 8,642. During March and April the British immigration greatly exceeded the Irish. There is a growing disinclination among the British mechanics who are not satisfied to live at home to go to the colonies. They prefer the United States. It is said that seventy-five per cent of those who go to Canada finally find their way here. The question whether this large European immigration is an unmixed blessing is engaging the serious attention of thoughtful Americans.

According to the last census, there were 6,677-360 aliens in the United States, and the succeeding years have swelled the number above eight millions. At present, the critical condition of military affairs in Europe and increased taxation has stimulated immigration anew, and public attention is called to the fact, that the quality of this influx of population is undesirable,

Stringent legislation is needed to divert the constant stream of pauperism and imbecility which is pouring into our fair land.

A recent editorial upon this subject, in the "Chicago Tribune," is as follows: "In Iowa for instance, the principal asylum has just been enlarged for the third time, and yet the improvement was hardly completed before more room was demanded, and this too, notwithstanding the fact that extensive hospitals for the insane had been established in other parts of the state. Much the same experience can be noted in all parts of the North and West where there is a large inflow of population from Europe, and yet by a singular inversion of logic the opinion is that overwork, nervous tension, or some other characteristic feature of American life has caused the remarkable increase in the percentage of insane persons. Dr. Gilman, a leading expert in insanity, says this is all a mistake; that the proportion of insane among the native-born population remains about the same, and the increase comes from the wholesale importation of lunatics from Central Europe. Along with the deported paupers and quasi-criminals coming to this country is a flood of wretched creatures on the verge of insanity and sure to become in a brief time tenants of our tax-supported asylums. Diseased blood is brought into this country, and capital and labor are taxed heavier every year to provide maintenance for the hordes of lunatics and paupers arriving from Europe.

"When General Master Workman Powderly, of the Knights of Labor, and President Depew, of the New York Central Railroad—men representing interests in wide contrast—are found equally urgent in **advocating a restriction of** immigration, it is clear that the **question** will soon **become one** of earnest agitation. Without wasting **any discussion on such a** matter as the importation of paupers, **lunatics, and criminals as still** carried on **under** the existing lax **laws, Powderly says** he is opposed to a great deal **of** immigration, pure and simple, and would allow no immigrant to land unless **provided** with means of support for **a year.** Depew **presents** something of the same thought when he **declares** that the exhaustion **of** the public **domain and the disappear- of** the unbought homestead **will soon put the** matter of immigration on **a new footing.** In fact, owing to the causes stated, the **character of the** immigration to **the United States** is changing already. The government reports show a **falling off of seventy** per **cent in the number** of farmers, mechanics, and trained **workers** entering the United States from Europe, and the substitution **of** unskilled laborers, **vagrants, paupers, and representatives of** all the **defective and dependent classes.**

"Such of these undesirable **newcomers** as do not become an immediate burden on **the** public, simply enter the overcrowded labor markets of the large cities, and 'throw their weight into the scale to depress **wages and promote labor** troubles and discon-

BESSEMER STEEL MANUFACTORY.

tent. Grandiloquent talk about the United States as an asylum for the oppressed of all nations was well enough when the government had an immense unappropriated domain, and by the offer of free homesteads was able to attract enterprising, thrifty home-seekers from Europe to the Western territories. These conditions are changing rapidly, and instead of attracting the old class of immigration the United States is becoming a dumping ground for the refuse of Central Europe. The evil is getting intolerable. The present restrictions on immigration are practically inoperative, and congress must provide some effective means to shut out, at least, the paupers, lunatics, and criminals voided on the United States from the jails, almshouses, and asylums of Central Europe."

Apart from the question of its necessity, according to Mr. H. H. Boyesen, there are indications on all hands that public opinion is ripe for legislation tending to restrict and regulate immigration. The congressman who shall initiate such legislation need have no fear of alienating the immigrant voters. The great majority of them, so far as I have been able to ascertain, would favor a law having such an end in view. The second biennial report of the Wisconsin Bureau of Labor and Industrial Statistics (1885-6) shows conclusively that public opinion in the West has been undergoing a great change on this question since the anarchists made their appearance, and labor troubles have led to disturbance and loss of property in many states. The report of the commissioner is of particular interest, because Wisconsin has a very large foreign population; and the overwhelming sentiment in favor of restriction may therefore be taken to indicate that the immigrants themselves would not object to having the gates shut against their own countrymen. The report particularly emphasizes the fact that 'a large percentage even of those demanding total prohibition for longer or shorter periods are foreign born, and some mention this circumstance as a reason why they know better than others the necessity of taking the question thoroughly in hand.' Out of a total number of about 40,000 employes interrogated, 14,561 returned no answer, 5,728 declared themselves in favor of 'unqualified restriction,' 4,059 favored 'total prohibition,' 6,316 wished to exclude socialists and anarchists, 2,928 paupers and criminals, 1,998 wanted a property qualification, 220 an educational test, and 1,320 thought all should be excluded except those of 'good character.' Among the employers, too, a similar sentiment in favor of restriction and even exclusion was proved to exist; and I do not doubt that, if the commissioners of labor statistics in other states should extend their inquiries so as to include this question, they would arrive at similar results.

That something must be done before very long is obvious. Merely to extend the term required for naturalization, as the Wisconsin legislature has recently done, is of no avail. It is not the privileges of American citizenship which entice the immigrant away from his old home; it is the prospect of earning an easier living. The sentiment hostile to immigration, which from time to time has swept over the country, has usually found expression in some such law; as when congress, in 1798, required a residence of fourteen years before citizenship could be acquired. This law was, however, repealed in 1802. Restriction, if it is to be effective, must prohibit entrance to certain specified classes of people; and no immigrant should be permitted to land unless he can exhibit a certificate, signed by the American consul at the port from which he has sailed, showing that he possesses the qualifications, whatever they may be, which the law shall require. Such a requisition would, of course, greatly increase the labor and responsibility of the consuls, and might necessitate an increase in the numbers of these officials. But as a consulate, in all but the principal commercial cities, is at present almost a sinecure, this objection can scarcely be regarded as a serious one.

The unexpended surplus now in the labor market is steadily increased by immigration, and the fact is patent that our republican institutions are menaced. The alarming outbreaks of socialistic and communistic conspiracies unerringly show the character of the material which is pouring into the great industrial centers, and the evil annually increases. Effective restriction of immigration is imperatively demanded by American workingmen.

CHAPTER XXIII.

THOUGHTS OF TO-DAY.

Hon. John Seitz—Labor entitled to first consideration—Opinions of R. F. Rowell—Hon. George L. Wellington—Hon. Jesse Harper — Hon. O. W. Barnard —H. E. Baldwin—Hon. Alf. Taylor—N. M. Lovin— O. B. Fenton—C. T. Parker—Rev. Dr. Thomas — G. W. Phillippo — O. J. Sutton—W. H. Robb—J. D. Hardy—W. W. Jones—Com. Miners and Mine Laborers—W. H. Davidson—R. C. McBeath—D. W. Smith—N. B. Stack—Hon. William Baker—James Mitchell—Hon. A. J. Streetor—The notorious Hazard Circular — A. A. Beaton.

While "issues" may change from time to time as a result of changed conditions, the objects of government should ever be the same—to protect all men and all classes of society in the enjoyment of "life, liberty, and the pursuit of happiness." Give all occupations equal legal opportunities for self-support and self-improvement, and protect the weak against the cunning of the unscrupulous, and the rapacity of the strong.

"With Lincoln, I believe that 'Labor being prior to and the creator of capital, is entitled to the first consideration.' That not the laborer only, but all classes of society are interested in the elevation and prosperity of the productive labor of the country. The peace and safety of society and the stability of good government demand encouragement and respect for honest industry. Hence a broad and wise statesmanship will aim at the upbuilding of the laboring people so that every willing worker shall be able to acquire a home of his own, the dearest spot on earth, which he can improve and beautify without fear of losing; where he can rear his little ones like a true American freeman. Thus will contented labor become the sheet anchor of law and order at home, and the right arm of the state against foreign foes.

"With Daniel Webster, I believe that a concentration of the country's wealth in few hands fastens aristocracy upon us, no matter what the form of our government. The colossal fortunes made in a few years through corporate privileges should alarm every lover of justice and republican government. Natural resources, the machinery of production and distribution, and the government itself have fallen into the hands of organized greed. Hence poverty and destitution in the midst of plenty, and the blasphemous cry goes out, 'Over-production is the cause.' There can be no over-production till every industrious person shall enjoy a comfortable share of the good things of life. The prime cause of labor's hardships may be found in the inadequate and costly machinery for distributing the products of labor.

"When congress shall resume its constitutional power 'to coin money and regulate its value,' and render it stable by supplying an ample and uniform volume, and drive the 'money changers from the temple' by making all money of equal legal tender; when it operates telegraphs and railways at cost, when it drives foreign and domestic landlords and nabobs into the sea by a 'graduated tax;' when these things are done, 'labor strikes' because of 'hard times' will be remembered only as an ugly vision of the past. There are other questions, but these be the main timbers in the new republic which enlightened organized labor will secure in the near future, by taking control of the government the rightful prerogative of the majority."

JOHN SEITZ,
Union Labor Candidate for Governor of Ohio.

"What is now needed is to abolish the necessity for the unnatural use for money, by the abolition of the debt and credit system."

R. F. ROWELL, L. A., 4616, K. OF L.

"Labor is the great force by which civilization has been evolved from savagery and barbarism. Labor is the power which has created wealth. Labor is the giant which has sent the world forward and upward in its course. All history gives proof of this. As we look backward over the past and view the ruins of the nations that have been and are no more, and as we turn and look upon the grandeur, magnificence and wealth of the nations which are in existence now, and then ask the chronicler of the world's annals, 'by what power and force came all this?' the answer shall be, 'by labor, the great creative power which is God's greatest attribute, and which, when exercised by man, makes him akin to God.' While this has been demonstrated among all nations, its grandest exemplifications has been given in our own land. Four centuries of time have backward rolled since Columbus first saw the shores of the 'New World.' When its discovery was made known the adventurous spirit of the European nations sent men forth to search the Western hemisphere for new houses and better fortunes. Almost a century was consumed in gaining a foothold upon the soil on the Northern portion of the continent. At last, however, the indomitable spirit of the English, French, German and Dutch settlers founded colonies, which lived and prospered, and in an apparently unlimited wilderness."

Hon. George L. Wellington.

MINING IN COLORADO.

"The object of the noble order of the Knights of Labor is to educate a man to his own best interest, and by the association of ideas and proper comparison of things and events, and by bringing familiar subjects under debate, that it will set a man thinking for himself, and bring his latent faculties into play, and in a very short time surprise himself."

A True Knight.

" There are two great evils that are afflicting humanity to-day as it has not been plagued in all the ages bygone. One is a false money system (and its correlatives), a system which, in its operation, is a crime against the right of man. The other is a legalized liquor traffic. These two giants in wickedness, monsters in iniquity, are endangering, as it never has been before, the Christian civilization of the nineteenth century.

"The substitution of full legal tender paper money, in volume sufficient for all purposes—is the remedy so far as the money question is concerned.

"We have over one hundred and twenty-five thousand miles of railroad, costing about two thousand million dollars.

"The monopolies of transportation have also a land gift, munificent as an empire—as large as nine states like Ohio.

"The telegraph, costing twenty million dollars, is watered up to eighty million dollars.

Ninety bushels of wheat and one hundred and sixty-five bushels of corn, per capita, to each wage-worker; fifteen per cent above an average of potatoes, and eighteen per cent above an average hay crop; the best wool crop in ten years, less sickness than in any year for twenty—and at the end of it two million workers out of employment and destitute to a degree unprecedented in the past.

America! the ægis of liberty: the beacon light of hope. Land of the free church; land of the free school; land of the free man. The divinely guided Magi came from the East to worship in the manger, the Omniarch of the world. His star moved west until it bathed in the silver waters of the ocean of setting sun. Then its burning corruscations shone back upon the track where man had taken his weary march, and the glory of that double shining made brighter than halo—America.

Hon. Jesse Harper.

The ennobling pursuit of agriculture, forming as it does the very basis of our national prosperity, should have every fostering care thrown around it, lying legitimately within the domain of legislation.

Toward the railroad and manufacturing corporations, as such, I have no feeling of hostility, but believe that the states, and national government, if necessary, should place wholsome checks upon their power, to the end, that the producing classes may not be burdened and oppressed, and that the law should be enforced against such corporations the same as against individuals.

"I believe we should maintain the dignity of labor, by giving it its just reward, and inasmuch as the wealth and capital of the world are the creatures of labor, the latter should receive the higher consideration at our hands, and the laborer be permitted to enjoy fully the fruits of his labor."

Hon. O. W. Barnard.

"That labor demands is such legislation as will conform strictly to the principles laid down in the Declaration of Independence. Make it possible for the industrially inclined to decently exist, educate their children and reduce crime to a minimum."

H. E. Baldwin.

"Wealth and labor bear the same relation to each other that exists between the mill-wheel and the water in the dam; the stream in the boiler and the engine. They are the complements of each other and wealth has no right to treat labor with contempt."

Alfred Taylor, Ed. Alabama Sentinel.

"Labor demands but one reform—Emancipation."

W. C. Owen, L. A., 8133, K. of L.

"The bonded indebtedness of the nation, the national banking system, the convict labor, Chinese and foreign pauper labor, transportation—both of freight and news—and the great land question, are among the many questions now before the people."

N. M. LAVIN, M.W., L. A., 4001, K. OF L.

"One of the measures required is a change in our mode of taxation, to the end that the burdens be taken off of labor, and that capital pay its just share."

C. B. BENTON, L. A., 1917, K. OF L.

"As long as there is one living being on the face of the globe to be benefited through use or consumption of natural or artificial products, resources, or elements, there can be no over-production."

C. T. PARKER, L. A., 2514, K. OF L.

"The strikes cannot last long, and the radical question of labor is yet to be settled. It will be settled by the principles of right and justice. There is no monopoly in truth and love."

REV. DR. THOMAS.

"The stars and stripes will afford all the protection we may need, and is the only flag that should be allowed on American soil. Under it let labor assemble and march on to victory. There are hundreds of thousands of people who are in sympathy with legitimately organized labor, and if we will keep radicals in the rear, our success will soon be assured. Everywhere organized labor, free from red flags and radicals, makes a stand for their rights as against oppression and monopoly, wonderful progress has been made.

"There is but one way to deal with men who march through the streets of any city in this country with any other than the American flag, that is to shoot them on the spot. If the stars and stripes are not good enough for them to march under, they are not good enough to be tolerated in America.

"Our fight is not for a class, but for all. The small business man, the farmer, the mechanic and small capitalist, is equally interested with us."

GEORGE W. PHILLIPPO,
L. A., 10,459, K. OF L.

"The only way for the great body of producers to secure laws favorable to themselves, is to send their own men to the law making bodies, who will not be bound by party obligations that are antagonistic to their interests."

O. J. SUTTON, L. A., 5531, K. OF L.

"As the wrongs of which the laboring man complains have come through legislation, the remedy must also come through legislation. Organization is doing a great work in educating the working classes in the principles of political economy.

"Prison labor should not be brought in conflict with free labor. The present system is a pernicious one, because it brings the labor of our convicts in competition with the honest artisan, and has a tendency to lower his wages. In my opinion, the convicts should be placed at work on our roads under the supervision of the state. And magnificent highways, something after the manner of the celebrated Appian Way, should be constructed by this labor. In this manner the convict can be kept at work without interfering with honest labor."

W. H. ROBB, L. A., 2127, K. OF L.

"Those who have been intrusted with the power to enact the laws, as well as those who have been intrusted with the execution of these laws, have pandered to the influence of money and power, instead of the will of the people, until they have gone beyond the danger line.

"Arbitration is the best method for the adjustment of all differences between capital and labor, or between individuals."

J. D. HARDY, L. A., 9306, K. OF L.

"Money performs precisely the same duty to a nation that the blood does to the human body. To have a healthy body there must be the necessary amount of blood, and it must be good and must circulate to the extremities of the body. If this be not the case, the body cannot be in good health; but if all of the blood flows to the head, apoplexy and death ensue."

W. W. JONES, L. A., 9189, K. OF L.

"The history and experience of the past make it apparent to every intelligent and thoughtful mind that strikes and lockouts are false agencies and brutal resorts for the adjustment of the disputes and controversies arising between employing capital and employed labor. They have become evils of the gravest magnitude, not only to those immediately concerned in them but also to general society, being fruitful sources of public disturbances, riot, and bloodshed. Sad illustrations of this truth are now being witnessed in certain of our large cities, and in several of the mining and manufacturing centers of the country. These industrial conflicts generally involve waste of capital on the one hand and impoverishment of labor on the other. They endanger bitter feelings of prejudice and enmity, and enkindle the destructive passions of hate and revenge, bearing in their train the curses of widespread misery and wretchedness. They are contrary to the true spirit of American institutions, and violate every principle of human justice and of Christian charity.

"Apart and in conflict capital and labor become agents of evil, while united they create blessings of plenty and prosperity, and enable a man to utilize and enjoy the bounteous resources of nature intended for his use and happiness by the Almighty.

"Capital represents the accumulated savings of past labor, while 'labor is the most sacred part of capital.' Each has its representative duties and obligations toward the other. Capital is entitled to fair and just remuneration for its risks and its use, and must have security and protection, while labor on the other hand, is as fully and as justly entitled to reward for its toil and its sacrifices. Each is entitled to its equitable share, and there is no law, either human or divine, to justify the one impoverishing and crushing the other."

COMMITTEE OF MINERS AND OPERATORS,
National Federation of Miners and Mine Laborers.

"Labor is the honorable thing anong men. There is not a neatly graded lawn, a pretty garden or a well trained tree that does not tell of it. It builds magnificent cities, navies, bridges, rivers, lays the railroad track, and drives the flying locomotive; whenever a steamer plows the waves or a canal bears the nation's inland wealth; wherever the corn, cotton or wheat fields wave and the mill wheel turns, there labor is the conqueror and the king. The newspaper, wherever it spreads its wings, bears the impress of toiling hands.

" Should not the laborer be well housed? Should he not have the best wife, and the prettiest children in the world? Should not the man who produces all we eat and clothes the nation be honest? To us there is more true poetry about the laborer's life and lot than in any other condition under heaven. It matters not in what calling a man labors, or toils, if he toils manfully, honestly and contentedly. The little tin pail is a badge of nobility."

WILLIAM H. DAVIDSON.

"The present monetary system of the United States is a stupendous obstacle in the way of educational advancement; the most potent engine of demoralization, and fruitful source of evil, now extant; doing more to destroy patriotism and veneration for law, than all other influences combined; leading to peculation, speculation and extortion upon the one hand, and degradation and brutalization upon the other."

R. C. McBeath.

"As long as individuals are allowed to monopolize the industries of this nation, so long the people must live in poverty. They will render it impossible for the remainder of the people to prosper. If the remainder of the people work harder and increase more, the monopolists will increase their demands.

"The monopolists have it in their power to regulate the amount the people may retain, and all they will allow them to retain, whether they produce much or little, will be just enough to live on and keep producing, and under such circumstances it is idle for the people to think of bettering their condition. We must legislate monopolists out of existence as we have legislated them into existence."

D. W. Smith, L. A., 3215, K. of L.

"The tramp, convict, anarchist and such characters are legitimate productions of society. If we would eliminate them, we must first purge society of these abnormal conditions giving birth to them, by adopting what the doctors call a constitutional treatment; purifying the blood and whole system, for these characters have had little to do with their own formation. When we locate the cause of these abnormal productions, we find it to be what the phrenologist calls acquisitiveness, or the love of property, abnormally developed."

J. J. Woodall, Agricultural Wheel.

"If the laboring masses would conform strictly to the preamble and declaration of principles of the Knights of Labor, and use every effort to have them carried out to the letter, their God given rights would be restored to a suffering people with the grandest government on earth to protect them."

N. B. Stack, L. A., 5009. K. of L.

"The eight-hour law should not be overlooked. The nation, by enactment, says it's right. Why do not states follow the decree? Men are not slaves, vassals, or menials, crouching under a kingly power, but freeman who dare assert their rights. This world's a stage and we its actors, and in its daily battle, eight hours for rest, eight hours for work, and eight hours for recreation and improvement."

Hon. William Baker.

"Organization, agitation, co-operation and education are the four mighty auxiliaries for raising the moral, mental and material status of the toiling millions."

JAMES MITCHELL,
Ed. Fort Wayne Dispatch.

"The farmers want protection—government protection from the cormorants that are eating up their substance. And while they need protection badly, they will not get it without some kind of revolution shall first obtain among them. Farmers should remember that our government has, in a measure, ceased to be a government of the people, and in lieu of it we have a government of aristocratic wealth. This aristocracy is now the governing power in both state and nation. Aristocracy says, 'Money makes the mare go,' and with it they manipulate elections, legislatures and the administration of the laws.

"Yes, the farmers want relief from the government, but they will not get it. No, never, unless they shall organize purposely to accomplish it."

HON. A. J. STREETER.

"When at last, through the devotion of the 'boys in blue,' and their fidelity to the principles of eternal justice, the Great God of Battles crowned them victors, peace returned to our beautiful land, these sad and terrible scenes ceased, and we, as a nation, commenced to build up what cruel war had laid desolate.

"Since that time, monopolies of every kind and in every conceivable shape, have been arising on every hand, until we find the practical 'land of the free and the home of the brave,' practically monopoly ridden. We have land monopolies, railroad monopolies, telegraph monopolies, telephone monopolies, coal monopolies, iron monopolies, oil monopolies, and so on, ad infinitum.

"In the organization of the Knights of Labor, the wage-workers of this country are organizing for the common defense. Our homes, our liberties, our very lives are jeopardized under the present industrial system. Mammon sits enthroned to-day in the temple, where the common people thought the goddess of Liberty was reigning queen. He rules with an iron rod. At his beck our judges, created by his power, decide momentous questions, but always in accordance with his wish; legislatures fawn and cringe before him, enacting only such laws as he approves; juries frame their verdicts with an eye for business principles, and are but the tools of this almighty power.

"The 'Chicago Express' makes a startling disclosure by the publication of a confidential circular sent by the celebrated English capitalist, Mr. Hazard, to his American attorneys in 1862, from which I extract the following:

"'Slavery is likely to be abolished by the new power, and chattel slavery be destroyed. This, I and my European friends are in favor of, for slavery is but the owning of labor, and carries with it a duty to care for the laborer: while the European plan led on by England is CAPITAL CONTROL OF LABOR by controlling wages and the price of property. This can be done by controlling the money. The great debt that capitalists will see to it is made out of the war must be used as the means to control the volume of the money. To accomplish this the bonds must be used as the banking basis. We are now waiting to get the secretary of the treasury to make this recommendation to congress. It will not do to let the greenback, as it is called, circulate as money any length of time, for we cannot control them. But we can control the bonds, and through them the bank issues.'

"While one kind of monopoly was being crushed in the South, its twin brother in the North, taking advantage of the helplessness of the government, dictated its financial policy. The grip which it secured on the government at that time, has never been released. If the transactions of the bankers of this country with those whom the people believed had the interests of the people at heart could be unveiled, what an educating revelation that would be. Were that revelation made, we might, at least, measure the patriotism of the vampires who control the industries of the nation to-day."

A. A. BEATON, S. M. W., D. A., 86, K. OF L.

CHAPTER XXIV.

SIGNS OF THE TIMES.

VIEWS OF DAVID ROSS—THE MAGNITUDE OF THE LABOR PROBLEM—OUT OF AGITATION COME MANY BENEFITS—EDUCATION IS REQUIRED FOR ADVANCEMENT—THE MASSES ARE THINKING—REFORM PARTIES—UNION LABOR PARTY IN THE VAN—ORGANIZATION THE WATCHWORD—HON. J. W. BREIDENTHAL—BRIGHT PROSPECTS WEST, NORTH, SOUTH AND EAST—LABOR IN POLITICS—WITH ORGANIZATION AND COMMON PURPOSE SUCCESS IS CERTAIN—A PLATFORM BROAD ENOUGH FOR ALL IS NEEDED—HON. HENRY SMITH—FUTURE OF THE WORKINGMAN—CONCLUSION.

The signs of the times indicate that labor is gathering its vast strength to take a long step of advancement. The position and demands of the workingman is the giant with which coming statesmen must grapple and make terms of peace. "One is justified in asserting," says David Ross, "that no question of late years has monopolized a larger share of public thought and attention than that covered by the term 'labor.' Nor can the magnitude of the task of adjusting equitably the unnatural relations existing between capital and labor be exaggerated, and it deservedly stands at the front demanding above all others, a peaceable and speedy solution.

"A question of such vast interest, involving the welfare of this republic, affecting directly the interests of those upon whom all forms of prosperity depend, is worthy of being first considered by that large and increasing class, who with brain and brawn toil ceaselessly, with but one benevolent object in view, the amelioration of industrial conditions. Out of this universal agitation of a great theme has come many benefits to the workers. Disagreeable in some respects, as the present order of affairs is to many of us, we can value the importance of the progress made, by comparison with past systems and past methods.

"The gloomy pictures drawn in the perverted imagination of pessimistic writers cannot affect the conclusions of the candid mind, that the condition of the working people, with many of their plans frustrated, many objects unattained, and many grievances of which they complain, is tending to still greater improvement, with present prospects indicative of continued betterment.

"We are not surprised at the terrible struggle that, in the past, has taken place between capital and labor, when the causes are considered that produced it. Capital, ever greedy to add to its gains, in many instances every opportunity seized to express its contempt for the laborer, denying the sacred right of the workmen to combine for their own protection. Capital ever powerful, and having every advantage, has been unscrupulously employed in making manhood merchantable, by offering tempting sums that men, elected to make laws and administer justice, might become blind to the diabolical nature of their designs, to still further rob and oppress those at their mercy. It is no wonder that men at times have been goaded to desperation, and when living under a burning sense of their merciless treatment, were prompted in the commission of acts, which only the circumstances of the time could suggest and justify.

"The demands of the working people have not been of themselves so unjust as their often unfair and impractical methods of securing them. Many painful conflicts of the past, between capital on the one side and labor on the other, have had their origin in a stupid misunderstanding of the differences existing between them. In the absence of a proper knowledge of the best methods of treating such points of difference, when they did present themselves, and in almost absolute ignorance of each other's real position, all these and other causes combined to disarrange the relations, intensify the hatred, and widen the breach between their respective interests.

"The great lessons learned at a prodigious cost of suffering and unprofitable experience, has wrought a marvelous change in the positions of these interests towards one another. Reason permits us to indulge the hope, that one portion of a common brotherhood will not forever be pitted against the other. The light of experience enables us to realize the folly of continuing an antagonism, the effect of which is to stifle the progressive spirit, and result more or less injuriously to interests which a just economic system would consider mutual and dependent upon each other.

"One of the most gratifying signs of the times is the reasonable hope of an early removal of many of the prolific sources of division, through the rapid increase of intelligence among the industrial classes, which of itself, while it may not mean absolute harmony in all things between the consolidated forces of labor and capital, points unmistakably to a clearer and fuller recognition of the rights of those whose lot it is to toil, by those whose fortune it is to furnish employment. This is certainly a great stride in the direction of future triumphs. That the minds of working people are being educated and disciplined by the discussion of this question, none who are familiar with them will deny. No one with ordinary powers of observation, who mingles with working people, irrespective of the occupation in which they are engaged, can fail to be impressed with the wonderful awakening of intelligence, which recent agitations in the sphere of labor have produced.

"The masses are beginning to think, study and reflect for themselves. They cannot longer remain satisfied with the concessions won for them through the exertions of their predecessors. They feel the duty of the hour is to think, act, and give the world the benefit of their thought and action, and thus accelerate their evolution from a degrading stage of mere wage slavery to one of profit-sharing, in which all are recognized as equals, or better still, to a universal system of co-operative production."

The constant discussion of such subjects as labor, finance, transportation, etc., has awakened universal interest. There is no mistaking the object and aims of the thousands of organizations throughout the land, nor can it be said that the men at the heads of the various reform political parties are afflicted with delusions.

The most conservative elements of the reform movement are represented by the Typographical Union, Trades Unions, Grange, Patrons of Husbandry, Knights of Labor, National Greenback Labor party, Prohibition party, Anti-Monopoly party, Knights of Industry, Grand Agricultural Wheel, National Homesteaders of America, Progressive party, Industrial League, Plow, Commoners, American Society to Promote Justice, Woman's Christian Temperance Union, Woman Suffrage Association,

THE VOICE OF LABOR.

The Industrial Union, American General Reform party, United Labor party, Union Labor party, Order of American Patriots and Anti-Poverty Society.

Of these, the Union Labor party is rapidly gaining strength, and leads the van. A liberal platform was adopted at a general convention held at Cincinnati, February 22, 1887, which has been favorably received by nearly all of the other parties. The principal planks of their platform are a graduated land and income tax, governmental control of transportation and means of communication, payment of the national debt, the non-issue of bonds, senators to be elective by a direct vote of the people, and universal suffrage.

Hon. J. W. Breidenthal, in commenting upon the future of the labor movement in the West, writes that "The prospects are flattering. The people are reading for themselves; they are reading labor papers; they are doing more quiet thinking than for many years; and as a result, the Labor party is having a wonderful growth. County tickets are being placed in the field this year, and in many localities, even this early in the campaign, the prospects for success are good. By 1888, the party will be well organized throughout the West, and will undoubtedly have a full ticket in the field. The men who are joining our ranks know why they do so, and can generally give well defined reasons in support of their views."

Organization is the watchword throughout the middle and western states, and there is a great effort being made to consolidate the outlying factions into a party of national strength. In New England and the Eastern states, the political phase of labor is attracting the attention of statesmen and politicians, and has already been recognized as a powerful element, which will have much to do with future politics. As in the West, the labor movement is rapidly organizing, and has made great progress in undermining the old political parties, despite of considerable internal dissension.

The campaign at hand will present, undoubtedly, a national labor ticket, and its strength at the polls will be the fruit of organization. Mr. Powderly, who is in a position to know, asserts that the prospects of the workingman were never better, and confidently predicts an era of political prosperity for labor. The signs of the times unmistakably point to the fact, that organization upon a thoughtful and intelligent basis is gaining ground. Education upon the living issues of the day, will enable the cause of the workingman to be presented as a solid phalanx, and with the ballot, from which there is no appeal, legislate all grievances into oblivion.

"The agitation now so prevalent," writes G. R. Williams, "strongly indicates the formation of the great people's party, which is labor's only salvation. The laboring man must be true to himself, and see that the now impending struggle does not waste itself in dust. Labor must unite with other organizations, as the Wheels, Greenbackers, Farmers' Alliance, Grangers, etc., all of whose interests are identical, and carry their common grievances to the ballot box, America's point of final settlement, where relief to their depressed condition can alone be found. Those who are laboring for the uplifting of the workingman's condition see this necessity, and are urging labor and producers to cast minor issues into the back ground, and to arise in a united mass to speak at the polls, which is the only true American mode of settling American questions. Such a consolidation is shadowed in the daily prints."

The officers and leaders of the Knights of Labor, the representative organization of the workingman, have persistently urged moderation and have sought to quell violent measures. They condemn the virulent features of anarchy and rabid socialism, and counsel the more effective forces of education and intelligent organization. In these forces exist the true sources of future success.

The decisive action of their convention at Minneapolis, October, 1887, in declaring against anarchists and the extremists of socialism, shows a determined effort in the right direction, which has met with general approval.

Beyond question, the intelligent workingman sees labor's best condition obtainable through the medium of the ballot, and the tendency of his course has turned to that path. Hon. Henry Smith writes on this truth as follows: "A careful look over the field of organized labor, reveals the fact that with the Knights of Labor all workers whether professional, mechanical, agricultural, or the laborer who swings the pick or shovel, can and do meet on one common level for the advancement of humanity, by mutual education on all questions affecting the emancipation of the wealth producers from the monopolist, speculator and usurer.

"The organization of skilled mechanics, or crafts, in unions, does not fully meet the requirements of the present time, because their field of operation is limited. The farmer and laborer cannot become a member of the Brotherhood of Locomotive Engineers, or Amalgamated Iron and Steel Workers, and the result is, the great majority of the wealth producers cannot aid them or have much sympathy for them, in any contest in which the several craft unions may be engaged. If labor is ever to enjoy the fruits of its efforts, it must throw aside the I-am-better-than-thou system, and come together in one fold on a platform of principles broad enough to take all. At present, the best offered is the platform of the Knights of Labor, which is in harmony with the American system of government and justice.

"Strikes as now carried on, are but a feeble and momentary make-shift of no lasting benefit to those engaged in them. There is only one way of inaugurating a strike, the benefits of which, with no drawback, will accrue to all labor, and that is at the ballot box. Experience has shown that a strike entered into at the polls by the wealth producers, has always sent consternation and confusion into the ranks of the labor oppressors. It cuts deep, awakens the guilty consciences and causes gnashing of teeth. Therefore, let labor lay aside all differences, join heart and hand, enter into a strike at the ballot box for justice and humanity, and let that strike never be declared off."

Many have predicted the downfall of the vigorous plea that labor has advanced for a better condition, as expressed in the varied forms of its organization, but the future will tell a different story. What the coming years have in store for the workingman is yet to be known, yet the signs of to-day do not augur ill. In reply to a query as to what the future of the workingman will be, G. W. Johnson[1] writes:

"The future is a mirror, and to forecast events is to but criticise its reflections. It is continually before us, opaque, but beaming with what past experiences have hinted is in store for us, and revealing in the present only reflections of sad experience—this is the continued round of all time.

"The idea of considering, then, what may be expected as a future for the workingman, carries with it a long train of past events and present

---

[1] L. A., 7020, K. of L.

conduct, from which reasonably safe conclusions may be drawn.

"The problem is not a new one; neither is it confined to the present or succeeding generations merely, but bears important relations to all future progress. It is in fact the great corner stone of all civilization and being. Nothing is produced without labor, and nothing labors save it prey upon production. No station is without labor, neither exists any labor without station. Thus woven so distinctly and finely in all things, the most subtle and refined distinctions become necessary to define its position and just relations. This is the problem as it lays before the people.

"Great men have arisen at different times who have discussed well and, in many instances, properly, this question; but none, to the present, but the scientific mind seemed scarcely even temporarily concerned about it. The accumulated force, however, of these thoughts and discussions seem to have broken into a storm—a hurricane for to-day. As a mighty vessel kept in its proper course by a master mind through the storm, cleared of rocks, bars and troughs of the sea, so are the workingmen of to-day. They have the master minds of ages; the storm is raging, they themselves are the vessel and with what degree of safety they will reach their desired haven depends upon their conduct. Time alone best can tell. Demosthenes, Cicero, Savonarola, Pitt, Fox, Sheridan, Chatham, Washington, Webster,

Lincoln, Jefferson, Jackson, Clay, Calhoun and a host of other orators and political economists of all time, from Bible times inclusive, to the present, have never ceased to warn the nation against oppression of labor. There have been under these teachings, at various times, spasmodic attempts to right labor's wrongs. But, unfortunately, the participating working people have been too ignorant, too filled with prejudice, too overcome with unnatural awe at accumulation, to maintain themselves in their justice.

"To-day a vastly different aspect greets even the casual observer. Trades unions and councils with their fraternity and mutual assistance among their fellow tradesmen have sprung rapidly up, and for their time filled a great need. But all the relief they could ever expect seemed to be nearly altogether of a temporary nature. They were, and are now, too circumscribed in action. They stood well as abutments to a bridge which is to cross the chasm. They served well for their time. What was needed when the trades union idea first sprang up was unity and fraternity—just what is needed to-day, only needed on a broader scale than trades unionism admits. They seemed to be well calculated to open the gate which led into a broader field. Uriah Stephens came in at the proper time to complete the work started, by teaching his lesson that not only should men of a certain trade join a certain organization which kept the harmony of that trade to the exclusion of all other trades, but that all should join together and be united as one. This met a greater exigency, and as the fruit of it we have the noble order of the Knights of Labor.

"In this connection strikes should be mentioned. Like chaff they show which way the wind is blowing. Destructive and as liable to abuse as they are, still they are not without their uses. As the bloodiest and most warlike times have marked the times of greatest progress in civilization, so the strikes of to-day are simply marking the remarkable progress toward industrial liberty and social equality. The Knights of Labor, however, by their education of members on the subject, are making rapid strides toward the obliteration of the strike as a barbarism of the past. Political economy in general, through them, is fast becoming a part of every workingman. Their papers and assembly discussions are doing much toward popularizing that study among them. In fact, the whole aim of their organization is in that direction.

"There are present in this, as in all other similar movements, those whose hot-headed ideas produce much trouble, and in a movement composed so entirely of working people, uneducated and ignorant, I wonder that there is not more of them. Even they are not without use. The strong, conservative men who lead in any movement would be powerless indeed were there not hotheads and 'anarchists' enough to stimulate strife, and force general agitation on their subjects. Their presence seem to be necessary to prove the presence of gold. They are required to give a certain strength otherwise unattainable. Ideas, like sailors, would amount to but little encountered they no storms. But too much storm swamps all. Hence too much can scarcely be done to keep the power of hotheads limited.

"In short, the situation reveals every prerequisite necessary for a change; all tends to show that great principles are bound to be settled; great wrongs to the working people must be righted. Wise men are at the helm. The sturdy sons of toil are fast educating themselves to the justice of their demands.

"They are beginning to see, and vast numbers are every day awakening to the fact that the land, the government, and the people are fast drifting into the hands of the few. The enterprise, the industry, the resources, the government, all passing rapidly into the hands of avaricious and all-grasping monopolists, who would soon be able to bind the father in the workshop or mine, the mother in the home, the child in the cradle, to eternal ignorance and ceaseless toil.

"In these facts lie the primal elements of a successful revolution. It is already on its wings, and as the old saw runs, 'revolutions never turn backward.'

"Hope, patience and perseverance will certainly find their reward."

CHAPTER XXV.

THE FARMERS' ALLIANCE.

EARLY STRUGGLES OF THE FARMERS' ALLIANCE — ITS RULES — ITS PROGRESS — ADVANTAGES OF CO-OPERATION — THE TEXAS CHARTER — THE NATIONAL ALLIANCE — PREAMBLE — EDUCATION FUNDAMENTAL TO GOOD GOVERNMENT — BUSINESS MATTERS — POLITICAL MATTERS — GENERAL REMARKS — WOMEN OF THE ALLIANCE.

SUPPLY is always regulated by the demand, and it is a fact that in the history of ages long past, when tyranny and oppression prevailed and honest men were groaning beneath the yoke and earnestly desiring a better state of affairs for the general welfare of humanity, that commensurate with the necessities and needs has come the redress for those wrongs arising out of the evil itself.

The first settlers in Texas had endured much at the hands of the wealthy cattle kings who were opposed to the settlement of the country, and acts of outrage had often been perpetrated upon those early settlers; their cattle had often been driven off by the minions of those wealthy rangers, and other stock taken from them without remuneration, and as the direct result of these outrages came the Farmers' Alliance, which was organized in 1875, in the county of Lampasas, Texas. These outrages compelled the common farmers of moderate means to unite and confer with each other as to some course to be adopted for self-protection; and as the result of this conference came the Farmers' Alliance, which organized, as it were, by magic. Its growth was as wonderful and surprising as its origin. In three years, with very little effort, it had permeated the four contiguous outlying counties. But like other new organizations, it was destined to receive a blow, as circumstances and conflicting interests conspired to merge this alliance into politics which became partisan in its interests, causing divisions; and, as a "house divided against itself cannot stand," so this organization was brought to naught. But in the year 1879, one W. Baggett, reorganized an Alliance in Texas, at Poolville in Parker County, upon the foundation stone of the old by-laws and constitution.

Some of the names of these brave and undaunted men, whose frontier life had eminently fitted them to engage in so noble a work, were J. N. Sullivan, Jeff. Womack, J. N. Montgomery, G. W. McKibbins, I. T. Reeves, and many other self-sacrificing men, who, inspired by right and proper principles, having the prosperity of the producing classes uppermost in their minds, and a sincere desire to benefit the world in general, have by their unwearied exertions rendered a valuable service to all who were willing to avail themselves of the advantages accruing from the Alliance.

For many years past the more systematic and advanced of the farming communities have sought to establish an agricultural society of their own, and maintain it upon a scientific principle and basis. They had failed, however, in consequence of a lack of enterprise, and the ignorance, superstition and prejudice still remaining in the minds of the more illiterate portion of the yeomanry of the country whose frontier life was largely responsible for their opposition to any innovation upon the process established and adhered to by the fossilized representatives of the old and nearly obsolete customs of a dogmatic theory.

But under the control and guidance of self-sacrificing and generous individuals who dare do anything that may become a man, who dared even to do right regardless of the frowns of large and influential monopolies, this Alliance organized at Poolville, July 29, 1879, which was destined — like the stone cut from the mountain by power divine — because of its principles of right embodied, to roll on and fill the earth. It was at once constituted in its incipiency a non-political and non-partisan brotherhood, whose object was the greatest good to the horny-handed sons of toil who had borne the burden and heat of the day.

Twelve branch or sub-alliances were soon established in various places during 1879, and being established upon such a principle as love and charity for all, with malice or enmity to none, its founders confidently looked forward to ultimate prosperity and success; and to-day in this "bounteous birth-land of the free," the songster and the philosopher laud, in sermon and in song, the virtues of these untiring and noble men.

The principles of right which inspired the founders of this National Alliance to earnest and persevering endeavor, should be graven upon the tablets of enduring memory, and like seed scattered upon good ground, find a lodgment, and bring forth fruit one hundred fold in every honest heart.

We embody the following rules of this organization, which must stand approved by every lover of humanity:

1. To labor for the education of the agricultural classes, in the science of economical government, in a strictly non-partisan spirit.

2. To indorse the motto, "in things essential, unity; and in all things, charity.

3. To develop a better state, mentally, morally, socially, and financially.

4. To create a better understanding for sustaining civil officers in maintaining law and order.

5. To constantly strive to secure entire harmony

C. W. MACUNE,
President National Farmers' Alliance.

and good-will among all mankind, and brotherly love among ourselves.

6. To suppress personal, local, sectional and national prejudices; all unhealthful rivalry, and all selfish ambition.

7. The brightest jewels which it garners are the tears of widows and orphans, and its imperative commands are to visit the homes where lacerated hearts are bleeding; to assuage the sufferings of a brother, or a sister; bury the dead; care for the widows, and educate the orphans; to exercise charity toward offenders; to construe words and deeds in their most favorable light, granting honesty of purpose, and good intentions to others; and to protect the principles of the Alliance unto death.

Its laws are reason and equity, its cardinal doctrines inspire purity of thought and life, and its intentions are "Peace on earth and good will to men."

The Farmers' Alliance built upon this sure foundation stone of equal rights to all, embraces all the grand fundamental principles of honest government, without which no honest government can exist. The close relationship of families and the fraternal clasping of hands, as a bond of friendship; the tribal relations of aboriginal inhabitants, were organizations for self-protection; the various orthodox religious denominations associate for mutual benefit, both socially and financially.

Judging from the success of the organizations to which we have referred, the Farmers' Alliance entrenched behind the impregnable palisade and adamantine bulwarks of eternal right and truth, it needed no prophet's ken, while looking through the horoscope of her future as a National Alliance, to predict a prosperous and brilliant career in its "work of faith and labor of love," which "suffereth long and is kind." From our little Alliance organized at Poolville, it now, in less than ten years, numbers hundreds of thousands; and in its ramifications has penetrated and permeated the entire land from the Atlantic to the Pacific, and from the ice-bound lakes of the north, to the flower-embossed banks of the streams of the sun-kissed waters of the tropics.

In its incipiency it was said of this Alliance: "Oh! the farmers can do nothing, as the issue is between capital and labor." We do not wish to be understood as ignoring capital—it is a necessity, as also is labor. They are contingent one upon the other. Capital is the result of labor and economy. Capital and labor are brothers, and therefore there should exist between them friendly relations.

The Alliance is not antagonistic to the interests of any class of honest men, either socially or financially. The sentiment emulates the true spirit of order which underlies the cardinal principles of justice and law, both human and divine. Does the purity of human nature find pre-eminence in the present age outside of the true spirit of progress in organization and advancement? Usefulness is still trammeled by passion, which is the outgrowth of ignorance and selfishness, prejudice and bigotry, superstition and ignorance, which injure society and impede progress by introducing discordant elements. And under the mild rule of the present high order of American civilization, we still have a morbid condition in society, which, if not as vicious, is as odious as that which has characterized the annals of the past century.

To-day the intelligent progressive class recognize, and begin to realize, the advantages of hearty co-operation. Some have their boards of exchange; farmers have their Alliance; dairymen their unions; and trade and labor unions meet to discuss and adopt measures intended for their mutual protection and prosperity. We bid a hearty God-speed to any organization intended to diffuse general knowledge, enlightening the ignorant, dispelling the gaunt shadows of superstition, and taking one more step toward the inauguration of that period when on those peace-crowned heights men shall beat their swords into plow-shares, and their spears into pruning hooks, and learn war no more.

The higher mankind rises in the scale of moral being, the less will they be inclined to oppress, wrong or injure each other.

Opposition and difficulties to the progress of the Alliance proved to be blessings in disguise. The storm and persecution it received at the hands of its enemies had only the effect to cause its founders to dig deep and lay their foundation upon a rock. Like the storm-bent oak, its contact with the disturbing element only caused it to send its roots deeper into the soil, until in the majesty of maturity it may now bid defiance to every storm, firmly anchored in the hearts of the people of America. They who went forth weeping over the wrongs perpetrated upon the innocent, "bearing precious seed," have now come with rejoicing, bringing their sheaves with them, fully confident of success; and knowing the justice of their cause, came to the front and took a bold stand. A meeting was convened at the court-house in Weatherford, Parker County, Texas, July 7, 1881, in response to the following call:

PUBLIC MEETING.

"The undersigned members of the Farmers' Alliance desire a meeting of the business men of Weathersford, and citizens of the town generally, at the court-house in this city at two o'clock p. m. to-day, in order to fully investigate the charges of lawlessness and other outrages preferred against the order. We deny the assertions made by the Weatherford 'Times,' charging our order with improper motives; and as citizens we ask the co-operation of all good people in a public investigation of this matter. We respectfully ask the attendance of the sheriff, county attorney and other officers of Parker County."

The call was signed by B. G. Gilliland, J. N. Frazier, O. G. Peterson, C. M. Wilcox, T. B. Gilliland, J. W. Caldwell, W. L. Garvin, K. A. Patterson, T. C. Ensey, W. T. Culwell, T. N. Niblett, E. J. Ensey, J. H. Dover, Andrew Dunlap, and S. O. Daws.

B. G. Gilliland called the meeting to order, W. L. Garvin occupying the chair. Andrew Dunlap, by request of the members, stated the purpose for which the meeting had been convened, stating briefly that it was for the purpose of vindicating the justice of their cause; also to show the injustice of the attack and the malicious falsehood contained in the charge through the columns of the Weatherford "Times." The following resolution was then submitted:

"Resolved, That we the officers and representative members of the Farmers' Alliance do allege that the statements made in the Weatherford 'Times' of June 25, 1881, with regard to the Farmers' Alliance, are false and malicious. We do most emphatically deny that the Alliance as a body recognizes mob law, or any thing else that is not in strict accordance with the laws of our state, from which we as a body hold a legal charter, and that the order of the Farmers' Alliance has never sanctioned or authorized any individual or body of individuals to violate the laws of the state at any time or place. And if the editor of the 'Times,' or any other person, will apprise the Farmers' Alliance of the fact that any individual member has been guilty of any violation of the laws of the land, we will pledge ourselves to the expulsion of all or any such members from our order."

The above resolution was unanimously passed by the Grand State Alliance, and was adopted by the mass meeting.

Dr. O. G. Peterson then submitted for the consideration of the meeting the following:

"WHEREAS, the editor of the Weatherford 'Times' has made repeated attacks upon the Farmers' Alliance, as a body, through the columns of his paper, and sent to the world the false impression that a reign of terror exists in the counties of Parker, Wise and Jack, on account of mob law carried out by the said Farmers' Alliance;

"We the members of the Alliance and citizens of Parker County, Texas, in mass meeting assembled at the court-house, in the city of Weatherford, do most emphatically deny that any such state of affairs, as named and charged by said editor, exists; and we do hereby challenge said editor to produce proof of the statements made by him through the columns of his paper."

It was evident that the Alliance had scored one and made a favorable impression upon the audience who were willing to know the truth. Indeed, Judge Richards arose and in scathing and well-chosen words, uttered his supreme contempt for a man so void of principle or honor, who would attempt to tarnish the reputation of men engaged in so commendable a work.

TEXAS CHARTER.

THE STATE OF TEXAS, COUNTY OF PARKER:

Know all men by these presents that we, L. S. Tackitt, J. H. Dover, and G. M. Plumlee, citizens of the state and county aforesaid, and such others as they may hereafter associate with them, have heretofore — to wit: on the 12th day of August, 1880—formed themselves, with J. N. Montgomery, J. C. Gilliland, J. S. Welch, William Thompson and others, into an association and organization under the name of "Farmers' Alliance," said association being formed for the purpose of encouraging agriculture, horticulture, and to suppress personal, local, sectional and national prejudices, and all unhealthy rivalry and selfish ambition. The business of said corporation is to be transacted in the city of Weatherford, county and state aforesaid. The term of existence of this association is fixed at twenty-five years from August 12, 1880.

THE TRUSTEES, TO-WIT:—J. H. Dover, W. T. Baggett, and L. S. Tackitt, residents of Parker County, were duly elected for the first year ending August 12, 1881.

"Said society has no capital stock, and the estimated value of the goods, chattels, lands, rights and credit, owned by said association, is fifty dollars."

The following persons were elected officers for twelve months: President, J. N. Montgomery; vice-president, W. T. Baggett; secretary, J. H. Dover; assistant secretary, J. C. Gilliland; lecturer, L. G. Oxford; assistant lecturer, A. Dunlap; treasurer, J. W. Sullivan; doorkeeper, J. S. Welch; assistant doorkeeper, Wm. Thompson.

In witness whereof, we, as citizens of the state of Texas, have on this 6th day of October, 1880, subscribed our names.

[Signed.]
L. S. Tackitt.
J. H. Dover.
G. M. Plumlee.

The State of Texas, County of Parker:

Before me, J. M. Richards, judge of the county court of Parker County, State of Texas.

This day personally appeared L. S. Tackitt, J. H. Dover and G. M. Plumlee, citizens of Texas, to me personally known, and acknowledged that they signed the above and foregoing instrument of writing after the contents of the same had been fully made known to them, and that they voluntarily signed the same for the purposes and associations therein expressed.

In witness whereof I have hereto signed my

name and set my seal of office this 6th day of October, 1880.

[Signed.] J. M. Richards,
County Judge, Parker Co., Texas.

The State of Texas, Department of State.

I hereby certify that the foregoing is a true copy of the original charter of the Farmers' Alliance of Parker County, with the indorsement thereon, now on file in this department.

Witness my official signature and the seal of state, at the city of Austin, the 9th day of October, A. D., 1880.

[Seal of State.] T. H. Bowman.
Acting Secretary of State.

ORGANIZING THE NATIONAL ALLIANCE AT SHREVEPORT, AND THE DECLARATION OF PURPOSES OF THE FARMERS' ALLIANCE AND CO-OPERATIVE UNION OF AMERICA.

PREAMBLE.

Whereas, the wealth, strength and permanency of a government depends mainly on the prosperity and success of its agriculture and labor, and in these being kept in a healthy state, lies the vigorous germ of all true patriotism, and that pure and elevated moral sentiment, necessary to vitalize and keep in active operation the principles and teachings that alone can preserve and perpetuate republican institutions, and the blessings of human liberty; and,

WHEREAS, one of the prime objects of good government, should be to promote the intelligence, loyalty and conservatism of its citizens, and afford them the highest possible facilities for securing and enjoying the full measure of liberty, prosperity and happiness; and,

WHEREAS, viewing with alarm the tendency in this government to reverse these cardinal conditions — a republican form of government and a free and prosperous people — by the concentration of its wealth and power in the hands of a few, to the impoverishment and bondage of the many, and the rapid growth of centralization and aristocracy; and,

WHEREAS, believing further, that the overthrow and certain destruction of the growing and menacing dangers to the institutions of the country and the liberties of the people depend on agitation, education and co-operation, carried on by the means of thorough organization of the masses, and especially of the agricultural and laboring classes, established upon just and correct principles, non-partisan and non-sectarian in character, with clear and well defined objects and purposes.

THEREFORE, we, the Farmers' Alliance, and Co-operative Union of America, in national convention assembled; in order better to protect our organization and meet the necessities of our class and a public want, adopt these resolutions; and,

WHEREAS, believing that if these baneful influences and tendencies are not checked and overcome, they will subvert the government, destroy its form and spirit, and in the end utterly impoverish and enslave the people.

We therefore publish and adopt the following declaration of purposes:

EDUCATION.

Regarding the education of the people as fundamental to good government, in sustaining its institutions and multiplying its blessings, as well as an essential qualification for accomplishing our purposes, we shall at all times advance and encourage it in the highest possible degree among farmers and laborers, and their children, by every means in our power. Through the means of investigation and discussion in our Alliance meetings, our press and public speakers; we propose to examine the various methods and systems of education in use, with the view to determine the best adapted to the wants and conditions of the agricultural and laboring classes; believing the correct theory, when established, will enhance the moral, physical and industrial, as well as the mental culture of our children in every grade of schools; that this system will strengthen the attachment of these classes to their profession instead of alienating them from it, as the prevailing methods have a tendency to do; that it will better qualify them for success and happiness in life; will render the farm and shop more attractive and remunerative; give the means and time for more general thought and useful study; increase the opportunity and inclination to adorn the home and practice the social virtues, broaden the sphere of their knowledge and usefulness and give character and influence to husbandry and labor; and for these reasons we are especially friendly to industrial education, and shall labor to advance and build up the agricultural and mechanical schools of the country, by extending to them every possible encouragement and support in our power.

BUSINESS MATTERS.

In business matters we believe the prevailing system is in many particulars wrong, and that between the producer and consumer, the buyer and seller, the methods should be changed, the process shortened and expenses reduced. Plans should be adopted that will more justly and satisfactorily distribute profits, and give to labor a fair share of its earnings. We believe that in co-operation, a remedy may be found for most of the evils and inequalities growing out of the methods now in use; that in co-operation exists, as we believe, fairness and equity; that when well understood, and closely observed, its principles, by intelligent and honest management, may be successfully applied to most, if not all, the business pursuits and enterprises of the country; that it possesses the elementary forces for solving the vexed question of capital and labor, and for breaking the power of monopoly; and, hence, we shall urge the study and practice of co-operation in the Alliance, as a mighty lever that will lift the burdens and weight from labor and the productive industries of the country that lie with such crushing force upon them, and by which the possibilities of the Alliance for carrying out its good work may be increased and strengthened.

POLITICAL MATTERS.

Without disturbing political party lines or party affiliations, or provoking partisan feelings or strife, we shall boldly enter into the discussion and investigation of all laws, public measures, and governmental policies that have a direct or remote bearing on the productive industries of the country, and its welfare in general; approving the good and condemning the bad, and offering through the ballot and other means in our reach, such remedies for existing evils and threatening dangers as we believe the public interest demands. We shall teach unfalteringly hostility to all class legislation, the tyranny and oppression of monopoly, excessive taxation, the lavish expenditures of public money, and to every species of wrong and abuses practiced in government affairs. We shall denounce and expose fraud and corruption in official places whenever discovered, no matter from what source they may emanate. We shall encourage and strive to increase the facilities among ourselves for a closer study and better understanding of the organisms, powers and purposes of government; more attention to the laws of the country, both local and general, the better to understand their scope and meaning, their influence on society and the public good; and thus educate ourselves in the science of economical government, elevate the standard of citizenship, and qualify ourselves, without bias, to judge correctly of the merits of candidates for office and their efficiency after elected. Then we shall co-operate with them in the execution of the law, that it may be respected, order maintained and society improved.

IN GENERAL.

We shall discourage law-suits and litigation between members of the order, and shall teach and insist that all differences and misunderstandings should be settled and adjusted by arbitration in the Alliance. In general, we shall strive to cement our brotherhood in the closest bonds of a common interest, and perpetuate our order by frequently meeting together on all matters that relate to our mental, moral, social and financial interest; and to educate, train and discipline ourselves to work together in carrying out the laudable objects of our order.

We shall teach and strive to induce our member-

From a photograph of the largest Orange Tree in Florida. Measures 8 feet 6 inches at base, is 37 feet high, and has a crop of over 9,000 sweet Oranges hanging on its boughs. The fruit from this tree brings from $150 to $175 every year. Situated near Waldo, on the Transit R. R.

ship to act upon the important truth, that no great undertaking and reform like the Alliance movement can be successful without a clear understanding of its principles, purposes and plans, and an earnest and intelligent devotion to the cause; that harmony of feeling and action, coupled with a persistent effort, based upon the great central thought or fundamental idea, that in things essential there should be unity, and in all things charity and brotherly kindness to one another, and good will to all mankind, are necessary to insure strength, influence and final triumph to our cause; that the evils of which we complain and the condition we would improve are the growth of many years, aided largely by class legislation, and that it will require bold efforts and long and continuous struggles to change and better them; that it must be accomplished largely through a change of public sentiment produced by agitation, that will arouse and enlighten the masses; and that we shall constantly strive to suppress personal, local, sectional and national prejudices: all unhealthful rivalry and all selfish ambition, and teach that, as citizens of one government, we should feel a common interest in its affairs; and that our patriotism and good will for one another should not be measured by sections or geographical lines, to suit the purposes of politicians.

By our frequent meetings we confidently believe we shall be able to break up the isolated habits of farmers, improve their social condition, increase their social pleasures, and strengthen their confidence in and friendships for each other.

We propose to make the study and improvement of practical agriculture in all its branches a part of the mission of the Alliance, that its standard may be elevated, its profits increased, and its followers made more prosperous and contented.

We shall encourage more diversity of farming; the production of less cotton, and more grain and meat; selling less raw material, and more in manufactured articles.

In our meetings and through our press we shall discuss and examine into the best and most approved methods of farming; the preparation of the soil; planting, cultivation, harvesting, handling and marketing of crops, farm and agricultural products generally. Also the raising of stock, dairying, fruit-growing, gardening; and, in short, every branch of agriculture that goes to make up a full line of farming, and render it pleasant and profitable.

Through our Alliance, we shall endeavor to furnish facilities for, and shall encourage the study of the laws of business and trade, the best methods for buying and selling, and the transaction of all kinds of business it may be found desirable for farmers and laborers to engage in; and under all circumstances we shall discourage the credit system.

We propose to attend to our own business affairs in our own way, and make no fight against any legitimate business; but we shall oppose methods found to be contrary to justice and equity.

Believing that a strict observance and practice of these teachings, principles and purposes will insure our success, we submit our cause to a fair and impartial public, invoking the blessing of Heaven upon our undertaking.

WOMEN OF THE ALLIANCE.

The grand secret of unprecedented success of the Farmers' Alliance has been the subject of much comment, and finally it has been conceded that one of the most efficient and prime factors in building up this institution is the admission of women to full membership, making them eligible to fill any office in connection with the Alliance. And why should it not be so? When God placed man in his Eden, he saw it was not good for man to be alone, and the first man's happiness was incomplete until woman was admitted as a member of that first family circle, and since then she has ever held her place in the most responsible relations in life. Could man expect to prosper in any kind of enterprise, society or Alliance who would advocate the exclusion of the wife of his bosom, and the mother of his children, from any association or Alliance which has for its object the happiness, prosperity and general good of our common humanity founded upon right and proper principles?

It is an evidence of semi-barbarism, or a low

state of civilization that does not accord to woman her right, in placing her on an equal with man. Many, and most of the correct and honorable, as well as the most successful business transactions a man ever engaged in are those in which he has been guided by the advice of his wife. And with woman as an ally, what wonder if prosperity and success unprecedented has attended the Farmers' Alliance.

That voice which first fell in bird-like melody upon the ear of man, sounds equally as sweet when raised in denouncing the evils of monopoly and oppression. The refining and purifying influences received from the society of pure and noble womanhood are more potent for good than the pulpit or the press. The gentle hand that soothes by its magic touch the fevered brow of stricken humanity can wield the pen mightier than the sword. For the "hand that rocks the cradle sways the world."

United effort and hearty co-operation now is all that is necessary for the Farmers' Alliance in order that her banner may proudly wave till the victor's wreath shall crown their noble and united efforts; till from the ranks of intelligent toilers in agricultural pursuits shall come noble men to take their place in the senate-chamber and legislative halls of Congress and raise their voice against oppression and injustice.

We urge our brethren of the Alliance to united and untiring efforts, regardless of any form of party politics, stand side by side in the rank of the noble men of our Alliance until monopoly shall hide in shame its cruel head, and victory be inscribed upon our banners, remembering that "eternal vigilance is the price of liberty."

www.ingramcontent.com/pod-product-compliance
Lightning Source LLC
Chambersburg PA
CBHW022121290426
44112CB00008B/766